D0359611

RICHARD POSNER

RICHARD POSNER

WILLIAM DOMNARSKI

OXFORD
UNIVERSITY PRESS

OXFORD
UNIVERSITY PRESS

Oxford University Press is a department of the University of Oxford. It furthers
the University's objective of excellence in research, scholarship, and education
by publishing worldwide. Oxford is a registered trade mark of Oxford University
Press in the UK and certain other countries.

Published in the United States of America by Oxford University Press
198 Madison Avenue, New York, NY 10016, United States of America.

Library of Congress Cataloging-in-Publication Data
Names: Domnarski, William, 1953– author.
Title: Richard Posner / William Domnarski.
Description: New York : Oxford University Press, 2016.
Identifiers: LCCN 2016000686 | ISBN 9780199332311 (hardback) |
ISBN 9780199332335 (e-book)
Subjects: LCSH: Posner, Richard A. | Judges—United States—Biography. |
BISAC: LAW / Legal Profession. | LAW / Courts. | LAW / Legal History.
Classification: LCC KF373.P595 D66 2016 | DDC 347.73/2434—dc23
LC record available at http://lccn.loc.gov/2016000686

1 3 5 7 9 8 6 4 2
Printed by Sheridan Books, Inc., United States of America

For Kathleen, Colleen, and Erin

CONTENTS

—————◦◦◦◦————

Introduction   1

1. The First Thirty Years (1939–1969)   9
    Manhattan (1939–48)   9
    Scarsdale and the Edgemont School (1948–55)   14
    Yale College (1955–59)   19
    Harvard Law School and the *Harvard Law Review* (1959–62)   29
    Clerkship with Justice Brennan (1962–63)   39
    Philip Elman and the Federal Trade Commission (1963–65)   44
    Office of the Solicitor General (1965–67)   48
    President's Task Force on Communication Policy   51
    Stanford Law School (1968–69)   53

2. University of Chicago Law School Professor (1969–1981)   59
    Economic Analysis of Law   66
        Journal of Legal Studies   69
        Foundations to the Theory   70
        Economic Analysis of Law   72
    Strategies   76
        Articles   77
        More and Somewhat Different Economic Analysis   82
        Books   84

        Antitrust Law: An Economic Perspective 85
        The Economics of Justice 86
     Proselytizing in Person 88
  Consulting/Practice 89
  Lexecon 90
  Nomination 94

3. Making His Judicial Mark and Challenging Others (1982–1989) 96
  Starting In 97
  Henry Friendly 99
  Posner's Style and Approach to Law as Expressed in His Opinions 101
     Interpretation 112
  Push for Economic Analysis 114
     The Hand Formula 115
     Constitutional Torts 116
     Resistance 119
  Supreme Court Review 123
  Evaluations 126
  Books 127
     The Federal Courts: Crisis and Reform (1985) 127
     Judges and Lawyers 130
       Economic Structure of Tort Law (1987) 133
       Law and Literature (1988) 134
  Federal Courts Study Committee 137
  Supreme Court Consideration 138

4. Law Assaulted and Pragmatism Asserted (1990–1999) 140
  Personality Revisited 143
  Judicial Greatness Judged 148
  On the Bench 152
     Bar 152
     District Judges 154
     Hand Formula 154
  Chief Judge 157
     Resistance 158
     Supreme Court Review 160
     Evaluations 164

      Cited 166

      Clerks 167

      Articles on Influence and Citations 170

   Books and Articles 171

      Major Social Issues 171

         Overcoming Law 175

         The Problematics of Moral and Legal Theory (1999) 176

         Law and Legal Theory in the UK and USA 178

      A Major Political Issue 179

5. Public Intellectual (2000–2009) 183

   Microsoft Mediator 184

   Ronald Dworkin 186

      Breaking the Deadlock (2001) 188

   New Yorker Profile 190

   Public Intellectuals 190

   Everywhere 195

   National Security and Terrorism 197

   Economic Crisis 199

   Honored 201

   The Economic Structure of Intellectual Property Law 202

   Essay Collections 203

   Other Books 205

   On the Bench 206

      Economic Analysis Applied or Encouraged 206

      Resistance 208

      Supreme Court Review 209

      Cited by Name 212

      Evaluations 214

      Law Clerks 215

      Writing about Judging 216

6. Push for Change and Measurement Taking (2010–2014) 219

   Supreme Court Review 222

   A Critic Takes Action 226

      Supreme Court 226

      Scalia Alone 228

Championing Patent Law Reform   232
Campaign against the Brazen   234
A Push to Go outside the Record and Meeting Resistance   239
Oral Arguments   241
Taking Measurements   243

Conclusion   246

Acknowledgments   257
Notes   259
Index   291

Introduction

THERE WAS NO INDICATION early in Richard Posner's life that he was heading toward a career in law. There were certainly no indications that he would come to dominate American law and become with his more than three thousand opinions the most respected and most influential (and the most cited) appellate judge of his generation, à la Learned Hand and Henry Friendly in their respective generations. Nor was there any indication that he would go on to dominate law as an academic with more than fifty books, five hundred articles, and more in citations than anyone to his academic work. Law was the default career selection he made coming out of college at Yale, where he had been a dazzlingly successful English major. If anything, he seemed destined for a literary life. The core of his life as it has unfolded has been such a literary life, even within a career in the law, so that he has always been a writer first and a lawyer second.

Groomed in the humanities at college, he showed great intellectual gifts—gifts that were edged with a fierce belief in himself and the correctness of his opinions. Moving on to Harvard Law School, he became a remarkable student, thriving on the Socratic method and making his mark with his sophisticated and mature engagement with the law. Law school success led to government jobs in Washington as a law clerk to a Supreme Court Justice, assistant at the Federal Trade Commission, assistant to the solicitor general, and general counsel to a presidential commission while on loan from the Office of the Solicitor General. Working with and learning from others, he found an intellectual attraction to economics as it applied to law and, despite having no particular conviction for it, began a legal academic career.

His interest in economics got the greatest cultivation imaginable, first at Stanford in the tutelage of renowned economist Aaron Director. He then moved the next year to the University of Chicago, the hotbed of law and economics, with giants such as Ronald Coase and George Stigler. There he set out to convince the intellectual world that economic analysis of law made the most sense and that it should be learned and applied. Of his strategies to support his proselytization push, the most important was his dazzling *Economics Analysis of Law*, published in 1973 and written when he was only thirty-three years old. Its main theme was that the doctrines undergirding judge-made law, otherwise known as the common law, advance economic efficiency, even if the judges are not aware that their opinions push this economic agenda. Its undergirding philosophical belief found expression in his phrase "wealth maximization," which meant that society should move toward results that produce the most wealth for the greatest number of people.

The law and economics movement, with its antiregulatory core (which Posner trumpeted as one of his strategies to push law and economics), dovetailed with the developing antiregulatory political environment of the Reagan administration and helped Posner's serendipitous ascent to the federal appellate bench on the US Court of Appeals for the Seventh Circuit in 1981, at the age of forty-two. From the beginning he saw his appointment in the context of economic analysis and as an opportunity for both it and him. The appointment, he wrote to Aaron Director a few months before taking the bench, would give him "a chance to measure himself against Learned Hand and Henry Friendly, better lawyers both, but without as much economics."[1] Once on the Seventh Circuit, he insistently sought to bring economic analysis into the way judges approached their cases, with an emphasis on applying the cost-benefit negligence analysis approach of Learned Hand—the famous Hand Formula—in ways that Learned Hand would likely never have contemplated. The law does not take easily to innovation, though, and Posner met resistance from his colleagues on the Seventh Circuit. His pushes to innovate were met by colleagues keen to push back, limiting the overall effect of his economic analyses within the Seventh Circuit.

In an against-the-grain approach, Posner from the beginning wrote opinions the likes of which no one had ever seen before. That at least was what the great Henry Friendly wrote to Posner as part of a friendship that developed between them in the last four years of Friendly's life. Like Friendly, Posner from the beginning saw writing opinions as a judge's work and joined him as the only judges not using law clerks as ghostwriters. But unlike the more traditionally inclined Friendly, Posner has bent the genre of the judicial opinion to his will. He doesn't even consider precedent, at least the first time through. He's told us, remarkably, that the way he approaches a case "is first to ask myself what would be a reasonable, sensible result, as a lay person would understand it, and then, having answered that question, to ask whether the result is blocked by clear constitutional or statutory text, governing precedent, or any other conventional limitation on judicial discretion."[2] That he would cite his own cases first as authority (without identifying himself) helps make the point that it is law as Posner sees it—or wants it to be—that matters most. And since his thinking process sometimes detours a bit to consider issues near the center line, we get instances of Posner spinning away from the reasoning supporting a case's conclusion—its holding—to language known as dicta that relates to and perhaps even supplements or supports a case's holding but is not essential to it. These detours resemble stream-of-consciousness writing and help make clear that Posner's opinions are all about his engagement with the law. Perhaps not surprisingly, Posner's boldness in making the opinion about his thinking process is matched by the boldness of his unprecedented prose style, which above all reflects his personality. It is a prose style that in its elements features casual language, allusions, epigrams, and an insistence that the jargon of the law be avoided and scorned in the process.

However unprecedented or even radical Posner's opinions might be in their approach and style, they are opinions that have sold well in the marketplace of circuit court judges outside Posner's Seventh Circuit. These judges have cited Posner by name more often by far than any other judge. These references come in one of two forms, as in "Judge Posner" or as in "(Posner, J.)," as part of a tip-of-the-hat case citation practice. His numbers have so far outstripped those of his closest competitors that he has become the Wayne Gretzky of appellate judging. Ironically, though, the marketplace has not shown any particular interest in Posner's economic analysis approach and has instead used him for his views and analyses on pretty much everything else. Nor has the Supreme Court, as a different marketplace, been much impressed with Posner's use of economic analysis when it has reviewed his opinions. Nor has his brand of statutory interpretation, which looks primarily to a statute's purpose, much impressed the Supreme Court.

Posner's contrary spirit and generally inquisitive mind led him in 1985, when new to the bench, to deliver an academic book intent on reshaping the federal judiciary. A caustic critique, it criticized the federal judiciary for not working hard enough and for not being sufficiently interested in science and statistics. But that was only the beginning. He continued with his complaints about judicial performance in his opinions through all his years of judging and most recently has in books and articles become even more pointed in his criticisms, including the Justices of the Supreme Court. These complaints have merged with his complaints that lawyers underperform and do not make themselves useful with either their briefs or their oral arguments. We see in going through the years and decades of his opinions that poor judging and poor lawyering are central to what might be called his structural jurisprudence.

His academic work continued in the against-the-grain vein following his critique of the federal judiciary. With a 1988 book he took on the law and literature movement and its wellspring in legal education, which he argued had gone astray and was more interested in "law and ..." subjects than in producing the kind of doctrinal scholarship of benefit to the bench and bar. This attack on legal education was the first of many waves of attack on law professors, especially those working in the fuzzy areas of legal and moral philosophy. He then applied, again in an against-the-grain fashion, economic analysis in the 1990s to social issues—old age, sex, and AIDS—taking his cue from Nobel Prize–winning economist Gary Becker's application of economic analysis to the family. He returned to law later in the decade in his books and provocatively argued that legal theory is not what it should be. Law, he argued, could no longer think of itself as autonomous and self-sufficient. It could not continue with applying customary legal analysis based on precedent to all legal problems. This approach, known as formalism, might work well enough for most cases because they are straightforward, but for the minority of difficult cases something more—pragmatism—was needed. As applied, pragmatism looked to both the case at hand and the broader social interests to fashion a result not cabined by precedent that made the most sense for the various interests at issue. Its roots were in realism, in the social sciences, and in recognizing the judges are not observers but policymakers guided by interpretations of what legislators intended with their legislative handiwork. Pragmatism was what he had been practicing on the bench, and he wanted to see more of it from others. It was really the only way to respond to our increasingly complex modern world. In the same way—a declaration delivered with remarkable nerve and verve—he argued that moral and legal philosophers have nothing to offer law and that moral and legal philosophy should not be thought of as alternatives to pragmatism. More than just bristling at their denunciation, the moral and legal philosophers responded with a fury. This was happening at a time when Posner in his academic writing was backing away from the sharp edge of the wealth maximization principle driving economic analysis. But for the moral and legal philosophers, what they thought they had gained when Posner softened on wealth maximization they lost when he argued for pragmatism and saw them as its enemy.

The push for pragmatism defined Posner on and off the bench. His work on the bench showed pragmatism in action, and in books and articles he pushed pragmatism by showing that it was better suited than other approaches to solve problems. He did this first with a book on the Clinton impeachment crisis and then with a book on the 2000 election mess. These books revealed Posner emerging as a public intellectual interested in reaching beyond an academic audience to the general reading public. True to form, though, he took to this new role in an against-the-grain fashion. He attacked public intellectuals for inadequacy and underperformance, both in his books on the impeachment and on the election and in a 2002 book devoted solely to the subject. As a way of showing how public intellectuals should do their jobs, he began to work within areas of his competence and provide near contemporaneous analyses and assessments rooted in clear exposition of the most important problems facing the country. He took on national security and terrorism first and then later in the decade took on the economic crisis. His contributions as a public intellectual appeared not just in books but in articles, blogs, book reviews, debates, and interviews. In the first decade of the new century (and millennium) he was everywhere. He wrote—including his work on the bench—as though he was the nation's critic at large.

His take on these pressing national problems was, not surprisingly, contrarian. He thought the government was getting it all wrong in its response to national security and terrorism. It was taking the wrong approaches in reforming various institutions, and it was underestimating the imminent danger facing the country. He argued that recognition of the dangers in our new age of terrorism required a new way of thinking about civil liberties. Our core beliefs in freedom and privacy needed to be balanced against an acknowledgment that the threats we faced required compromise to give government more tools—as in acquiring more electronic information—to combat terrorism. All of this followed from the application of a cost-benefit analysis. Costs in compromising on civil liberties had to be balanced against the extraordinary harm promised by the terrorist threat. His contrary approach to the economic crisis came in the way he rethought fundamental economic principles. He concluded—the horror, the horror—that Keynes had been right about government's needed response to a depression and that free market enthusiasts were wrong to oppose governmental cash infusions and other attempts to increase consumer spending.

Posner's pragmatism, however, has not found much support on either the political or judicial fronts. The pragmatism he pitched to better solve the political crises of the Clinton impeachment and the disputed 2000 presidential election was provocative but not influential. This was especially true for his critique of the Supreme Court's handling of the election crisis, in which politics and law were both in play. The Supreme Court has given no indications that it has been much affected by Posner's call for judicial pragmatism. It in fact more often seems to rebuff, in cases of his that it has reviewed, both his pragmatism and its companion purpose-oriented brand of statutory construction. Justice Scalia's brand of statutory interpretation—which he calls textualism but which is but a variant of its predecessors, strict constructionism and originalism— seems to have carried the day and can be found in the opinions of even a liberal such as Justice Sotomayor. Nor have circuit court judges in any significant way embraced pragmatism, leaving Posner on the outside looking for followers, even though he is the most-cited judge by far.

His reaction, now that he is on the other side of seventy five, is to show increased irritation at the work of the Supreme Court and to both act, and act out, in commentary off the bench and in his work on the bench to draw attention to pragmatism. The result is a concerted effort to sketch a path to reforming the law and the judicial process. He has continued in his academic work to criticize the judiciary, and to this he has added general audience commentary criticizing, if not attacking, the Supreme Court. He has gone after the Justices as a group, but he has also singled out Chief Justice Roberts and especially Justice Scalia for scathing commentary. The flavor of his commentary is given by his criticisms that the Justices do not work hard enough and that they ask too many questions as part of the clown show known as oral argument. As a commentator he has also asserted in a variety of magazines and news outlets that the American patent system is broken and needs to be reformed to meet the demands of our technological age, in which far fewer patents are needed to achieve economic efficiency. This campaign followed his widely reported handling as a trial judge of the patent dispute between Apple and Motorola (really Google) in which he dismissed the case after finding that neither side could prove damages to his satisfaction. The Federal Circuit in reviewing the case concluded differently and in a near rebuke pointed out that Posner had gotten both the facts and the law wrong. In his opinions, he has in recent years shown little patience, if not irritation, at litigants making brazen arguments not supported by facts or even theory.

In rather dramatic moves on the bench that seem to bring his entire career into focus, Posner has taken to the offensive to assert how he thinks law should work. In the first move, Posner has in recent years often gone beyond the appellate record and beyond the briefs of the parties to conduct his own Internet research. He is quite open about this research and has defended his practice in the face of critical commentary. He went even further in one recent case and conducted an experiment, decried by some of his colleagues, to test the facts asserted by the parties. As his colleagues pointed out, to go outside the record in this way is to breach a fundamental rule of appellate procedure. In the second, we see his anguish in not being heeded in occasional over-the-top performances at oral argument in which he pummels not just the lawyers but the system itself for not choosing what he considers optimal performance. These are likely exaggerated expressions of his urge to reform (he has long had a fondness for stage acting), but they are of a piece with a recent comment in which he said, remarkably, that he would like "to see the adversary system taken down a peg." These oral arguments represent the collision between the lawyerly approach of the adversary system on the one hand and Posner's pragmatic approach on the other hand. His is the urge to tear back formalism and substitute pragmatism. Seemingly not content with lawyers escaping confrontations with the best result by hiding behind the interests of their clients, we see Posner breaking down a fourth wall, so to speak, forcing lawyers out of their role as advocates to answer questions as to what they rather than their clients think about a particular issue. With this move the client is suddenly without a lawyer, and Posner has an open field.

Looming over our look at Posner's unfolding careers as an academic, judge, and public intellectual is the fact Posner has never thought of himself as a good fit for the law. He has described himself in an interview as not being fully socialized into the law, and we know from his personal correspondence that he has had great doubts about the ability to lead a great and rewarding professional life in the law. There is too much about law that cuts against the interests of a literary-minded person of the sort that he is. Consider that ten years into his time on the bench he wrote to a colleague that he thought of judging as his day job, in the Hollywood way,[3] and what this suggests about the extent of Posner's somewhat awkward fit with the law. Then there are useful nuggets from his archive correspondence we should keep in mind as Posner's life unfolds herein— not enough of them upon which to build an argument but enough that affect judgment of him when considered as background. Consider that, when asked whether he thought he had any affinities with Shakespeare's characters, he responded that he saw a good deal of Hamlet in himself, to go along with a little Macbeth and a fair amount of Coriolanus.[4] It's enough to want to bring a psychiatrist into the mix to look at him. Finally, consider that Posner at age fifty-three wrote to a colleague that part of him wants to be a conservative establishment figure, while part of him "wants to be a Promethean intellectual hero" (followed by "that is as close as I get to confession"). These admissions may say it all, or at least put us on the right path to sorting him out.[5]

I

The First Thirty Years (1939–1969)

Manhattan (1939–48)

Given the name Allen but called Dick from the beginning, Posner was born on January 11, 1939, in New York City, an only child, to Blanche (who usually went by her maiden name of Hofrichter) and Max Posner.[1] His mother was born in Austria in 1900 and came to the United States with her family at the age of five, speaking German and no English. His father was born in Rumania in 1901 and immigrated with his family at the age of just three months. They married July 1, 1925. The name "Posner" comes from the German city of Posen, formerly a part of Prussia but now a part of Poland and called Poznán. The surname "Posner" was the result of an economic transaction. Posner's great-grandfather, living in Rumania in the nineteenth century, bought the name from a man who had completed his military service in the Rumanian army, a common draft dodge of the time.

The world of his parents as Eastern European Jews starting out in New York City at the turn of the twentieth century was the world of Irving Howe's magisterial *World of Our Fathers* (1977). For these new immigrants it was marked by hardship, conflicted loyalties, assimilation, ambition, and success.

Posner's parents had had eventful lives by the time he was born. His father had grown up in poverty in the Lower East Side of New York. Politically he was a radical and a member of the Communist Party, something that got in the way when he was a student at City College

9

of New York. The college had made ROTC compulsory for male students after the Russian Revolution and the seizing of power by the Bolsheviks. Posner's father refused to participate and was forced out of the college. He then worked for a time in the jewelry business, where he had some relatives, and he also taught English to foreigners. After a few years of what might be called "bouncing around," he went to New York University Law School at night and became a lawyer in 1926. He started as a criminal lawyer with the help of a cousin who was a prominent criminal lawyer in the city and was successful at it. Dissatisfaction with the nature of his clientele, though, led him into business, lending second-mortgage money on commercial property in New York, a move that pleased Posner's mother. By 1948, when the family moved to the suburb of Scarsdale, New York, the Posners were well off financially.

Posner's mother also grew up in genuine poverty in the Lower East Side (her family used toilet paper, while Posner's father's family used newspaper) and graduated from Hunter College. She took up high school teaching, insisting, in the face of contrary school board employment rules, on using her maiden name of Hofrichter. She was active in the teachers' unions. In a heated dispute with the city in 1934 over pay reductions and payless furloughs, she was chairman of the union's classroom teachers' groups and was quoted in the *New York Times* on several occasions on this and other labor clashes with the city. By 1941 she was chairman of the editorial board of the union's organ, the *New York Teacher*. In a 1941 *New York Times* article about the influence of the Communist Party on the union, she was described as the actual editor of the magazine, though not listed as such on the masthead.[2] Somewhat ambiguously, she never admitted to being a Communist, but she did tell Posner that she had been forced out of her teaching job because of the Feinberg Law of 1948. That law stated not just that current membership in a subversive political organization such as the Communist Party was enough for employment termination but that past membership by itself acted as presumptive proof of current membership absent full disassociation. Her Communist association came up again later when she joined the feminist Women Strike for Peace organization, which engaged in "militant political action in the name of motherhood," such as massing together in 1962 across the nation and demanding that President Kennedy "End the Arms Race—Not the

Human Race." She was called before Congress in 1962 as the first witness in the House Un-American Activities Committee hearing "relating to the Communist Party's united front tactics of infiltrating peace organizations, with particular reference to Women Strike for Peace and its Metropolitan New York, New Jersey, and Connecticut section." In a scene of high drama, as recounted in Amy Swerdlow's *Women Strike for Peace*,[3] the large contingent of Women Strike for Peace members rose as one when Blanche Posner was called and proceeded to become a hero to her fellow members. She paid no attention to interruptions from the committee members and lectured them on their foolishness. When the questions turned to the asserted organizational connections between the feminist movement and the Communist Party, she refused to answer about her organization's structure or personnel, invoking the Fifth Amendment privilege against self-incrimination forty-four times, not because, as she explained years later to Swerdlow, she was a member of the Communist Party—she wasn't—but because she believed that if she answered any questions about the organization she would be pressed to divulge details of others in the organization, something she refused to do.

The Posners lived in a rented apartment on 104th Street and Central Park West with a view of Central Park. The Posners' was a secular household. His parents wanted to be Americans and did not want anything to do with European Jewishness. There was no religiosity in the household and no participation in traditional Jewish events, such as a bar mitzvah. Later, when he was asked by a writer preparing an entry on him in a compendium of Jewish intellectuals about what was Jewish about him, he answered that "aside from my circumcision, nothing."[4] Posner never went into a synagogue as a youth. One stereotypical Jewish trait did apply to his mother, however. She doted on him in the classic fashion. "A very Jewish thing," he put it. "Too much so, they're too protective. They make people nervous." With his mother working, Posner first had a German refugee as a nurse while an infant. She was followed by a series of black women who worked in the house as maids but did not live there.

Posner's mother's radicalism was matched by her outsized, almost theatrical personality. She was flamboyant and had a streak of anti-Semitism in her that had its roots in her communist beliefs. She also had a flamboyant sister who spent time with the family and impressed Posner. His mother was a fun person. His father, on the other hand, was rather taciturn, "pleasant but taciturn." She was "always more stridently radical than my father," Posner explained to a correspondent.[5] Two weeks later, in a letter to the same correspondent, he added, "Whether either or both of my parents were actually members of the Communist Party I do not know."[6]

Posner's mother took the lead in his early education. She read the *Odyssey* to him when he was two years old or so. She went further and smoothed his experience with the book by ripping from the edition she was using a picture of the Cyclops that was terrifying the young Posner. She read him Shakespeare and took him when he was five years old to see Lawrence Olivier in *Henry V.* He loved the film's striking volleys of arrows scene and remembered it all his life. That first reading experience with the *Odyssey* sparked in Posner a lifelong interest in the tale. Posner wrote of his mother reading him the *Odyssey* in a letter about the books that had made the biggest impression on him, mentioning that as an adult he had learned ancient Greek (though not particularly well, he hastens to add) so that he could read the book in the original. He goes on to note that he had "reread it most recently in Robert Fagles' magnificent translation." "I don't know why," he volunteers, "the *Odyssey* has preoccupied me so, but my guess is that it's because it embodies a conception of the career or life trajectory of the individual that I find strongly appealing."[7] In a letter to University of Chicago Law School colleague Martha Nussbaum, Posner added that "in my childhood and teens I was drawn to the grandiose— Homer, Dante, Milton—and to the adventure books—Bulwer-Lytton, Haggard, etc."[8]

Posner's formal education began with a series of private schools in Manhattan. He first went to Walden School at Central Park West and Eighty-Eighth Street, known for its progressive educational approach, for what was likely preschool when he was two years and eight months old. Prekindergarten was at Columbia Grammar School on West Ninety-Third Street. In a striking student assessment delightful for its details and important because of the relationship between its insights and what we see in Posner throughout his life, Posner's teacher there reported for the period ending May 5, 1943, that "Dickie has matured so rapidly that he himself seems to stand a little in awe of his own capacities. He is timid about trying his new wings, possibly for fear of failure, but is always shyly delighted when he finds a new success. He is meticulously self-sufficient and this trait may be the cue for a suitable method of unfolding him. More and more may gradually be expected of him in the way of mature behavior and achievement, but should be casually approved to avoid embarrassing him. He enjoys approval but is able to detect over enthusiasm."

Grammar school grades 1–4 were at Ethical Culture, located at 33 Central Park West. Posner provided a critique of the education he experienced there nearly fifty years later when he wrote to Beryl Levy, a noted Benjamin Cardozo scholar, in response to having read Levy's account of the school in a letter to the *New York Times*. He wrote, "Your letter about Ethical Culture was fascinating. As a student there—first through fourth grades, 1944–1948—I hadn't the faintest idea what 'ethical culture' signified. I recall no tincture of ethical instruction; if there was any, it made no impression whatever, at least on me. It was quite a dull school, focusing on the basics—reading ('The Weekly Reader,' which I still recall with horror), writing, arithmetic. I had, however, a very nice male teacher in fourth grade, where the focus shifted to New York state and city history, which was a lot of fun. I didn't much enjoy the school overall; nor was I a successful student—I was shy, dreamy, and abstracted. I blossomed both scholastically and socially when we moved to Scarsdale in 1948 and I was put into a public school, which had a much more cheerful atmosphere and where the kids were friendlier and more fun."[9]

In his personal correspondence archived at the University of Chicago Posner sets straight the facts relating to his parents giving his model train set to the Rosenberg children, as had been reported in the *New York Times*. The newspaper account erred in saying that his parents had forced him to give up his train set. What actually happened was that his parents asked him if he minded if they gave the train set to the Rosenberg children. He said that of course they could, since he had outgrown the trains. He was, after all, thirteen at the time. Moving to a bigger point with the same correspondent, he knew from about the age of nine until he went away to college at the age of sixteen that his parents, as he put it, held "unconventional political views of a distinctly leftist hue." For them the Soviet Union was almost always right in what it did, and stories of Soviet concentration camps were fictions spun by the American press. As he puts it, "In other words, they swallowed the Communist line."

He writes also in his correspondence that his parents did not try to shape his political views to match theirs. "They did not try to mold me as a revolutionary," he explains, though until he went away to college first and then to law school and was exposed to different ideas and influences his own political beliefs had been "an uncritical copy of my parents." His parents, to be sure, were not revolutionaries, when put to the commitment. They were, he explains, "limousine radicals." They had political beliefs but were not prepared to act upon them. Once away from home, his views drifted from theirs. Between the two parents, his father never cared much about political issues, while his mother would argue about political matters with him. She continued this way until the late 1970s, or until he was almost forty years old. Posner's father's interest was with Posner's career, not politics. When the same correspondent asked Posner if he had turned out to be much different as a father than his father had been, he pointed out that he had become a father while in his early twenties while his father had become one at a much older age, thirty-eight, and that the age difference between Posner and his father led to "a certain remoteness" on his father's part. He also had been an only child. One aspect of his father's relationship with him that he did consciously imitate was not pushing his two sons to achieve. That had been his mother's role for him when he was growing up.

Scarsdale and the Edgemont School (1948–55)

The family moved to the affluent New York City suburb of Scarsdale in 1948. There they built a modern ranch-style house on a lot that abutted a nature preserve and proved to be a popular place for friends to visit. The friends report that it was a large, comfortable, and upscale house with lots of books.[10] "We are all happy here," Posner had written about the move to Scarsdale in a four-hundred-word essay composed when he was ten. He certainly seemed happy, judging from the description of his pets (a dog and a canary) and his stamp-collecting and toy soldier hobbies. Even being housebound with a bout of pneumonia did not get him down. He liked the attention he got and did not seem to miss school and his classmates: "Altogether I didn't mind pneumonia at all."

The Edgemont School was Scarsdale's junior high school and ranged from grades 1 through 10. There were forty-seven students in Posner's 1954 graduating class, twenty-three girls and twenty-four boys. The class produced, aside from Posner, a career CIA officer in Tom Whipple, a parliamentarian of Congress for twenty years in Charles Johnson, and a bestselling author in Alexandra Penney. Following graduation, many of the students stayed in touch and had frequent reunions.

Posner indeed thrived in Scarsdale. At Edgemont he was a straight-A student each year, with the exception of lower grades in Industrial Arts and Physical Education and one grade of 85 in science in seventh grade. He was the top-ranked student upon graduation in 1954. This seems to have been a time before grade inflation. On his report card we find the warning that a passing grade is a D and that "pupils planning to study beyond high school should have all grades C or better." Posner in the tenth grade had an A in his final examination in English and grades of either 98 or 100 in math, science, Latin, and French.

He is listed in the yearbook as Richard Allen Hofrichter Posner. The yearbook reveals that his nickname was "The Brain" and that he was active in school clubs and activities. He was the business manager of the yearbook itself, called *Respectus*, and was the student adviser to the school newspaper, the *Ink Spots*. He was president of the Science Club in tenth grade, was in the tenth-grade play, and was a member of the Projectionist Club. He was described as "the Absent-minded Geometry teacher" and was commonly known as "Professor." In the Class Will, he left "teaching Geometry" to a student in the class behind his. His listed song for Class In Song is "The Creep." In the Class Poll he was the "Brainiest" of the boys. For the Class Future segment of the yearbook, in which the conceit imagined a gathering of all the graduates years in the future at a dinner club, he is among a group of the well-suntanned back from a stay at a famous resort run by a classmate. He had been there "resting up after revising Einstein's theory of relativity." He was one of two students to represent the school in a local high school radio quiz that was taped in New York City. The teams of boys and girls played for various charitable causes. In Edgemont's case it was to raise money for a teacher who was struggling with an illness and medical bills.

Like nearly everyone else in his class, he took dancing lessons at one of the two dance studios in town, though the lessons were encouraged but not strictly mandated by the school. He shot rifles at a local shooting range with friends and also played tennis with them. Fellow students report that his mother arranged what were described as play dates with different girls. One play-dater, Alexandra Penney again, explained that Posner's mother contacted her mother to set up the date and that she and her mother visited Posner's house on various afternoons. The mothers talked in one room and she and Posner in another. Male friends report going to Posner's house for various kinds of fun. One tells of making a movie behind Posner's house, with Posner directing. Another tells of one or two friends going to the house to play in the woods with Posner. They would make up a variety of mysteries as they went along. Posner was also a founding member of a gang of youthful desperadoes and aspiring marauders known as the Mule Skinners, who hid themselves among a rock outcropping near the school grounds, only to descend and mock-terrorize students walking home. The victims of choice were girls. Posner led the group, made up of a half-dozen or so friends, and organized it along military principles of rank, giving out citations to especially successful raiders.

His parents sent him when he was twelve to Buck Rock's summer camp in New Milford, Connecticut, where he joined other campers in not knowing that it was a Communist camp—and a well-known one at that. It had been started in 1942 by the Austrian educators Dr. Ernest Bulova and Ilse Bulova, both of whom had studied under Maria Montessori. That the camp offered programs designed for the creative and the artistic did not matter as much to Posner as the camp's real attraction, a farm and its animals. Posner loved the camp because of the farm.

He took an extra year of Latin in high school. Outside of school Posner took piano lessons and otherwise applied himself as a serious reader. At the age of twelve he taught himself to type. He had written in longhand two very long papers for school (eighty and one hundred pages) and thought it would be more efficient if he could type rather than write in the future.

Members of Posner's 1954 graduating class all had the same memory of Posner's intelligence and how he got along with others. The students recognized from the beginning that he was brighter by far than anyone else and that in a real sense he was not like anyone else. By the same token, all reported that Posner did not have airs about him and that he never, as one fellow student put it, lorded his intelligence over anyone. He was so well liked and respected by his fellow students that he could make jokes about his intelligence and poke a bit of fun at himself. He coined the phrase "the Poze knows" and signed some yearbooks with the amusing "The mighty one salutes you, and welcomes you as a High Priest of Posner Worship." He was mild-mannered in his intelligence, not aggressive, fellow students reported.

The story most frequently told was about how Posner was asked by the principal to teach the geometry class Posner was enrolled in when the teacher took ill for a couple of weeks. Each person who brought up the story noted that the most interesting part of the experience, and the part that most reflected on Posner, wasn't that he knew the material and taught well but that the students did not take advantage of his status as fellow student to act up. They accepted him and treated him as though he were a credentialed teacher. One student explained that Posner had something that even an excellent, experienced teacher might lack. Another classmate said, "You will get better stories from others, I suspect, about how he performed as our substitute geometry teacher. My own experience was that, while I expected him to present the course material accurately and intelligently, I found him to be aware of, and responsive to the learning readiness of the individual students. I was a very troubled teenager and was surprised to find that he was sensitive to me as a nervous, awkward kid. He had a sensitivity that I would expect from a much older, degreed teacher."

This same former troubled teenager from the geometry class also took study hall with Posner and reports that there were limitations to Posner's patience with the antics of fellow students. "At a study hall," he writes, "I squirted him repeatedly with a hidden squirt gun as a kind of joke. He didn't like it, of course, and warned me to stop. I didn't take his warnings seriously; until he reported me to the study hall teacher, who confiscated my squirt gun."

Posner attended the fortieth anniversary reunion of his 1954 graduating class. He was a member of the planning committee and is listed jokingly in committee materials as serving as the committee's legal counsel. Classmates who attended the reunion made the same general comments that Posner had not changed and that he seemed mild-mannered and humble. They were aware of his standing in the academic and judicial worlds.

For his part, Posner in a letter to a friend wrote that "the reunion was fun. It was *extremely* odd to see a group of people whom one once knew very well for the first time in 40 years—to peer at them and finally see, as Proust said one would, the young person imprisoned in the old—but it was remarkably easy to pick up the threads, and by the end of the day we were all best friends again, albeit superficially, despite the large differences in life experiences and even social class (it was a public school, after all, and in the less affluent part of Scarsdale). It is remarkable how great an impression the school made, so that the reunion was like a reunion of wartime comrades—the shared memories overcoming all normal differences."[11]

He was presented with an award and gave a brief talk that describes the importance of his Edgemont experience to his development.

I can speak only for myself. The six years that I attended Edgemont, 1948 to 1954, fifth through tenth grades, are etched with extraordinary clarity in my memory. This is partly because of the contrast between New York City, where I'd lived until then, and Scarsdale, which to me had the excitement of country; and between the rather grim and austere private schooling that I had had in Manhattan and the much more cheerful and relaxed, yet also academically richer and more stimulating, experience of Edgemont. And it is partly because I had only one more year of high school before going off to college, so that Edgemont was my dominant experience of high school.

Not everyone thinks fondly of his high-school days, especially when he or she is in high school. But after forty years, almost everything is seen through a haze of nostalgia. And yet I do think that we were privileged, and that this is not just an impression distorted by time. Growing up in Scarsdale in the post–World War II period, a period that in retrospect was an oasis of social peace, simplicity, order, and pride in country between turbulent decades before and after, and attending a wonderful public school of a kind that has become rare in this country, a school not wracked by controversy over prayer or multi-culturalism or political correctness, or torn apart by drugs or gangs, was a privilege that relatively few Americans have had or will have. Edgemont gave us a sense of place and home. We are entitled to revel in the memory of it.

Two months after the reunion Posner wrote to the reunion's chief organizer and again indicated the significance of the Edgemont experience to him. "I was very moved to receive the award for the classmate who had conferred the most credit on the class and was likely to continue doing so," he wrote. "I don't think it was deserved but it was very nice anyway. I have received other awards and hope to continue doing so but this is the one that I shall prize the most."

Yale College (1955–59)

Scarsdale in 1954 was in the process of building a high school. In the meantime it sent its juniors and seniors to the high schools of two neighboring towns, Bronxville and New Rochelle. About half the Edgemont School students went to each, Posner among those who attended Bronxville High School. Some of his fellow students report that after that junior year at Bronxville Posner seemed to have disappeared, giving no word to anyone. Posner's father had learned that Yale was one of a few colleges and universities in the country which accepted students after their third year of high school and without a diploma. Harvard was another. Posner followed his father's encouragement and applied to Yale and Harvard and was accepted at Yale. Because he had started school a year early and now had jumped past twelfth grade, he was two years younger, at sixteen, than most of his fellow freshmen.

Posner as a freshman was offered a place, open to approximately 10 percent of the class, in Yale's Directed Studies Program.[12] The program had been started about a decade earlier in response to arguments that students needed a unified and coherent set of courses in their first two years rather than the miscellany that so many students took. The goals were to provide a core educational experience—with courses stressing art history, philosophy, and literature—and a core student experience among the forty to fifty students selected for the experience. Posner recalled that "they were seminar-size courses taught by all regular faculty. I never had a graduate student teacher. These teachers were terrific." There were three prescribed courses for each of the first two years. In the first year History of Art I, Philosophy I, and Literature I were two-semester courses. In the second year History I, Philosophy II, and Studies in Society I were also two-semester courses. It was in Studies in Society I that Posner had his first exposure to economics. He described it in his essay "An Accidental Lawyer" for a Yale twenty-fifth anniversary publication as "a sliver, devoted to elementary economics." In his third year, Posner took two yearlong English courses and one one-semester course. Yale's Department of English at the time was perhaps the finest in the country and with some of the biggest names, such as Maynard Mack, Robert Penn Warren, Louis Martz, W. K. Wimsatt, Aubrey Williams, Cleanth Brooks, and Harold Bloom, who was just starting out. He had a second year of German, two one-semester courses in the History of Art and two one-semester courses in philosophy. The titles of some of the papers Posner wrote at Yale—"Ascham's Prose Style," "The Question of the Renaissance Attitude," "The Interview between Volumnia and Coriolanus Act V, sc. 3," "The Apocalyptic Vision: Book XII, *Aeneid*"—sketch the shape of his education there.

Posner did well at Yale. His first-year average was 91, his second 89, his third 92, and his fourth 94. For seven of his eight semesters he ranked in the ninety-ninth percentile. In the eighth it was the ninety-eighth percentile. He was Phi Beta Kappa in his junior year and graduated summa cum laude and Honors with Exceptional Distinction in the Scholar of the House. The college did not assess a final ranking of the students. A classmate who went on to maintain a friendship with Cleanth Brooks reports that Brooks told him that Posner was perhaps the brightest student he had ever taught.

Posner wrote with assurance, perhaps too much so. An example of his assured writing style is the opening sentence of his paper "Marvell's Garden—The Stable Vision," where we find "Marvell's unique poetic genius consists, I think, of being able to achieve a dispassionate intensity." The instructor's response to his paper on Ascham's prose style was twofold. The paper, on the one hand, received a 90. On the other hand, the instructor began his comments this way: "I wish, as a matter of strategy, you would get the 'pontified' element out of your own writing. I don't believe I have noticed it in your other papers, but it is present here. You give the impression of being so right. Even if you are, you should be careful not to convey that precise impression." But the criticism of his prose style continues in the spirit of good teaching. "Perhaps it might be a good idea to show this paper to Mr. Williams. I would like to know whether he agrees with me on the question of tone. If you weren't so promising a student, I wouldn't bother making this criticism. But sometimes we create impressions of which we are not wholly conscious."

Assurance and what was perceived as a stubborn unwillingness to grow intellectually got Posner into trouble with his Philosophy II instructor. The paper was "The Place of Ethics" and sought to bring "a cold scalpel and an extensive reworking" to the body of ethical writings to show that it "is a very different thing from what its modern theorists and bibliographers suppose" and that it is "encumbered by an obsolete vocabulary and a provincial righteousness." The instructor gave the paper an 83 (marked down to 80 because of lateness) and commented: "You write well and the paper is well organized, but its substance is exactly what it would have been nine months ago. I can only suggest that you owe it to yourself to go back to Plato, Aristotle, Kant and Locke, Hegel, Kierkegaard—or many of a host of others—with a humility and genuine desire to understand what they are talking about." "This late in the game," he continued, "further argument would be useless. Until you understand the problems, you will never understand the solutions offered. You still accept description as though it explained and as though it did not raise more questions than it answered. You still operate on unexamined principles—which could not survive examination very long."

Posner responded to the grade and the comments with an extraordinary seventeen-hundred-word rejoinder. It begins by challenging the motivation of the three-point grade reduction for lateness, since it does not act as a deterrent for students like him who are not shirkers and only rarely hand in papers late. It then proceeds to implicitly claim unfairness by contrasting both the style and the content of the paper with other papers of his that had been graded in the nineties earlier in the term. What has changed to warrant the low grade? he asks. The meat of the response calls the grade into question on the ground that the instructor simply did not agree with his take on ethics, which is followed by a remarkably assured and sophisticated conclusion. He writes: "Perhaps I have been tactless in failing to disguise my

disparagement of traditional moral philosophy, with its puritan righteousness, its antiquated vocabulary, its theological predilections, its
flavor of impossible alienation from life, art, and the world. These are
personal prejudices, no more, and I can well understand your annoy-
ance at them, since, were they justified, they would destroy your rai-
son d'etre as a moral philosopher. No one likes his life's work called
trivial. But there is an underlying vein of truth, if not truth, of valid
argument. I deny your easy assumption of ethics' worth. I think a case
can be made for the frivolity of much of traditional moral philosophy. Your failure to grant this, the simple impossibility that your field
may be grounded in shifting sands, is as much prejudice as anything
I assert. Perhaps my ethical attitudes require revaluation. But equably
perhaps your attitude toward them requires similar revaluation." Years
later Posner would describe himself as rebellious and as "a disrespectful
brat at Yale College in the 1950s."[13]

Posner had two freshman-year roommates, chosen by lot. Both
remember that Posner arrived at school with a notebook he had put
together in high school. One roommate remembers it as a three-inch,
soft-bound notebook summary of various philosophers. The roommates say that Posner kept to himself and that he was patient, low-key,
did not talk down to others, and was not arrogant around other smart
people. He wanted to be "under the radar," as one of the roommates
put it. It came out, the roommate explained, that Posner did not have
a good relationship with his mother. Posner complained that she would
not allow him to play sports in high school for fear of head injuries, and
on one occasion at Yale in which far too much Ron Rico rum was drunk
and Posner ended up in the shower as an antidote to drunkenness, he
in anguish let out his feeling about his mother and the resentment he
felt toward her. One of the roommates, who saw Posner and his mother
interact at a dinner, reported that Posner's mother doted upon him,
to the point where, when Posner wanted the butter dish, he looked to
his mother and, with a plaintive "Mother," had her direct the butter
to him, so accustomed was he to her assistance. When a care package
from home arrived containing cans of tuna fish, Posner revealed that
he did not know how to use a can opener. A later roommate explained
that Posner "was arrogant, yes, but he was sort of friendly in a way. He
did not have a great deal of patience with people of lesser intelligence,

which was what we all were." He described Posner as a very positive person "with somewhat dominant, not domineering, ways."

A student who lived across the hall from Posner freshman year reported that there was little to know about him. He was always totally absorbed in a book but was always polite when speaking. He had an impressive collection of classical music records, and music could frequently be heard coming from his room. He was not particularly sociable. On football weekends, he did not attend the parties held across the hall and would at best pop in only to politely say hello. Another student who lived nearby that freshman year remembers "wandering across the hall to see Richard busily typing a paper of some sort with several reference books laid out next to his typewriter. He was typing and grabbing reference books. I was impressed with his speed." Robert Prentiss Walton, a student from the floor above, was similarly impressed and reported in the Yale twenty-fifth-anniversary supplement, "Another problem I had was that I had not previously known that individuals with the intellect of some of my classmates even existed. One such individual, Richard Posner, lived in a room on the floor below. While I was spending hours in the library researching and then hand-writing a paper, he would simply sit down at his typewriter, perhaps with a book or two at his side, and in a half-hour his paper was done."

Posner was active in student clubs and activities. He was a member of the Elizabethan Club, but not the Manuscript Club, which was by invitation. He was active in the Political Union, as a Liberal Party member. One of his second-year roommates described Posner as a Marxist but at the same time thought of him as too questioning a person to be a satisfactory Marxist. He engaged in debates as part of the Political Union, which this same roommate described as having a strong Marxist tinge. On the debated issue of a United Nations proposal that the United States support the Hungarian Revolution, Posner voted for the proposal and learned later that the vote made its way into an FBI file. He was active in the drama group Saybrook Players and served as its president. He acted in several productions and helped write a parody of *My Fair Lady*. Senior year he played the minor character Renfield in *Dracula*. It was directed by Dick Cavett, then a student at the Drama School. He was also on the board of the undergraduate literary magazine, *Yale Lit*.

He was often out and about with friends and roommates. One of his first-year roommates was old enough to rent a car, and the two of them drove to Vassar for a double date with students there. Later Posner had his own car. A roommate recalled that Posner's mother wanted him to have his car on campus. He was described by roommates who rode along in the car, which gave Posner de facto status as the leader of the group, as the linchpin of whatever combination of friends or students were involved.

Posner sometimes did not make a good impression on fellow students. One of his fellow Scholars of the House reports that Posner was a loner and that he did not have "great personal skills." Another reported that Posner did not suffer fools gladly. Richard Rhodes, who went on to write the definitive history of the development of the atomic bomb, among many notable books, reports that in a Political Union debate Posner revealed an ugly side to his personality by taking a bit of personal information about Rhodes that he had given Posner while chatting before the debate and using it against him as if it were a dagger. Several fellow students reported that Posner was considered a phenomenon on campus. There was a rumor in his senior year that he had written the thesis of his roommate, who was also a Scholar of the House.

As judged by issues of the *Yale Daily News*, Posner in his junior and senior years had acquired a reputation as an iconoclast and radical. From his letters to the editor and from his contribution to a student literary magazine called *Criterion* it was clear that he had, to go with his iconoclasm and radicalism, a powerful prose style and a willingness to assault enemies with invective, usually delivered from a platform of smugness and condescension. He was one of six members of the group known as the George Orwell Forum, which joined in with a campus protest supporting an invitation to have the Russian writer Boris Pasternak come to Yale to speak. The group's participation in the campus rally led to a letter to the editor attacking Yale students for not being vigilant enough in condemning instances of politically motivated encroachment on intellectual freedom. The group argued in the letter for the principle of "nonconformity without retaliation"—apparently to deaf ears, based on the yawning and dismissive responsive letters in the paper.[14] He was also a member of the National Student Council for a Sane Nuclear Policy and was one of six students who put his name to a full-page appeal that ran in the *News* calling on students to sign a petition in which they joined dignitaries such as Albert Schweitzer and Eleanor Roosevelt in demanding that at an upcoming Geneva meeting the representatives consider a pledge to end the testing of nuclear weapons.

An alleged exposé by the campus paper of dull teaching in the Department of Political Science prompted Posner in his junior year to lash out at the paper and its chairman, Robert Semple (who went on to become an editorial page editor for the *New York Times*), also a junior. Semple had written editorials based on the reports of bad teaching in political science, which Posner mocked as a crusade for an "Academically Better Yale." The problem, Posner argued, was not with the political science department, though he could not resist a query as to whether it was an intelligent undergraduate major to pursue, given that it is so closely derivative of history "that one wonders whether the average Yale man possesses, after two years, a good enough historical background to pursue it profitably."[15] To go the way of Semple, to make political science courses bouncier and more fun, would be to cater to intellectual mediocrity. All that matters is that the political science instructors have scholarly ability and write books in their field, he argued, since for him "the core of education lies, anyway, in books and not in lectures." "But as long as responsible scholars write the books and give the lectures, an industrious student should be able to extract a rich education."[16] Semple, an editor without an "incentive to disciplined thought," should have known better. This is charged writing. Posner refers to Semple as officious and intellectually incompetent and derides his editorials as "bumptious," "arrogant," and "pontifical," to say nothing of his "murky syntax and pretentious vocabulary (enlivened occasionally, I should add, by resounding journalistic cliches)." The result is "turgid bombast."[17]

Posner contributed a two-thousand-word vituperative essay on the nature of Yale itself titled "Yale, a Confusion of Values" in the student literary magazine, *Criterion*. He challenged Yale's philosophy of education, which he argued was tied to the school's approach to its alumni. Alumni wanted Yale to continue to mirror their world of privilege, which led to lower admission standards for their children, gut courses for them to take, and a quota on Jewish admission. The world of privilege found expression in fraternities and especially in Yale's famous secret societies. The school was dumbed down because that was the version of Yale that the alumni identified with, all of which made life harder for the serious students, who were also the brighter students. "The bright student," he writes, "often feels isolated by the hostility of a mass of mediocre minds centered in an upperclass core, and the indifference of an administration which must toady to the alumni."[18] The challenge was to analyze those educational assumptions and recognize that they made Yale less able to produce the leadership of trained intellects the nation most needed.

Posner was one of ten students chosen his junior year to be a Scholar of the House in his senior year. Scholars of the House took no classes and instead wrote a thesis of at least 250 pages of publishable quality that "must justify by its scope and quality the freedom that has been granted" the scholar, who took at the end of the year an oral examination.[19] The program had started in 1946 and had been successful in selecting students up to the challenge of complete freedom in their senior year. By the time of Posner's participation in the 1958–59 year, there had been 115 Scholars of the House, and only four had been unable to satisfy the program's requirements. In a very clubby tradition, the year's scholars and the faculty advisers met on alternate Wednesdays during the school year, in the evening, first for sherry, then for dinner, and then for presentations by some of the scholars of their ongoing work, with critiques following.

Under the direction of Cleanth Brooks, Posner wrote "Yeats' Late Poetry: A Critical Study," a 321-page effort. Cleanth Brooks was one of the leading critics in the country, practicing the New Criticism that he helped found and popularize. The approach emphasized the importance of the text itself, playing down, if not avoiding, biographical excursions as a way to understanding a text's meaning. It was as though the connection between the writer and what he had written had been broken, so that the writer had no more insight into the text than any other reader might have. The method saw literature as self-contained and self-referential. It looked to understand literature's aesthetic properties. The goal was to consider the way the text was constructed, in what explicators of the approach described as the text's formal properties, such as tone, irony, paradox, polysemy, complexity, and, above all, metaphor. Brooks as a New Critic was especially interested in metaphors, symbols, and paradoxes. Application of the method led to an aesthetic appreciation of a text. It was not read for ethical or moral or philosophical values. Those interests were left to philology or literary history. These were interests external to the text, as opposed to the formal properties that were internal to it. The method had been first and perhaps most famously applied to seventeenth-century English poetry, resurrecting the reputations of Marvell and Donne, for example, but the method had also been applied to drama and fiction. Brooks's finest essay in the New Critical mode, some might argue, was "The Naked Babe and the Cloak of Manliness" from *The Well Wrought Urn* (1947), which not only made sense of all the clothing imagery in *Macbeth* but demonstrated that it rested at the play's core.

Posner's thesis took on the later poems of William Butler Yeats, which, despite Yeats's stature as one of the leading poets of his generation, had not yet been carefully studied. Individual poems had been discussed and praised, but the volumes from which the individual poems came had not been looked at as books, something especially true of the last books as a group. Driving the inquiry into the individual books of late poetry as an interconnected group was Posner's deployment of the New Criticism in close readings of the individual poems. To study the later period was to study more than just the best-known poems, such as "Sailing to Byzantium" and "Long-Legged Fly," for example, though Posner had lengthy close readings of these poems. He sometimes went outside the method—to what he would later call eclectic New Criticism—and considered biography, autobiography, and other of Yeats's prose writings to strengthen the argument that the interconnectedness he was teasing out of the books had Yeats's implicit backing. This was Posner's angle of entry, arguing for a cohesiveness and building and deepening exploration of nonreligious meditation—the poetic imagination—all leading to the assertion of metaphor as the core of that poetic imagination. Metaphor, he ultimately argues as part of its connection to the imagination, helps the poet—and us—live in the world by mediating between the subjective and the objective. Metaphor becomes the gateway to what he calls "the intelligibility with the objective world."

The Scholar of the House thesis is notable for at least two reasons. One is the level of Posner's sophistication as a reader, writer, and researcher. Not only were his close readings often subtle, imaginative, and original, but when he was working with critical commentary from the leading critics he demonstrates that he understood it deeply enough to give the reader every suggestion that he was their peer. The second is that, as impressive as Posner's reading and writing skills are in the thesis, it is his embrace and disciplined application of the New Criticism that most catches our attention. He wrote in his introduction that to take the usual approach to Yeats's poetic corpus "through his biography, letters, and other published opinions can be of only limited value. It may give us clues; it will not reveal the basic pattern. If instead, the critic approaches Yeats' poetry resolved to attend in the first instance to the text itself; and to attend to it by reading sensitively and tenaciously and by inspecting large clusters of poems with a view to uncovering form and order, patterns of recurrence and continuity, then, I believe, he is in a far better position to realize what's going on in Yeats' poetry."

Posner in his contribution to his class's twenty-fifth-anniversary supplement credited his study of literature with contributing to his excellent grades at Harvard Law School. But he went further in his contribution and connected the New Criticism interpretive approach to his work as a judge, explaining that the approach "treated a work of literature as an artifact, more or less complete in itself, rather than as a psychological, biographical, historical, or political manifestation or emanation. This implied the centrality of close reading stripped of the crutches furnished by biography and history—in short, the social context of the literary work's creation. And imaginative close reading is almost the definition of legal reasoning, as we judges strive to make sense of complex statutes and difficult (whether because turgid or vague or cryptic or equivocal) judicial opinions."

Posner's interest in Yeats and in the New Criticism stayed with him for the rest of his career. He became something of a Yeats devotee. Thirty years after college he wrote to a college friend, who was congratulating him on the publication of his book on law and literature, and remarked both that he still read Yeats every year and that the book on law and literature had its origins in his study of literature at Yale, so much so that he recycled a paper he had written in freshman year discussing the false tale in the *Odyssey*'s third chapter.[20] He also provided an amusing observation in a 1994 letter on his interest in Yeats in college and the economically inclined thinker he later became. He explained in the letter that he knew in the summer of his junior year when he was visiting Europe for the first time that he was going to be writing on Yeats but that he nevertheless did not expand his travel to include Ireland to see the haunts of Yeats's poetry. "It did not even occur to me to visit Ireland," he continued, "so denatured was my interest and limited my curiosity. I kick myself to think that it did not occur to me that seeing Thor Ballylee, Lissadell, Ben Bulben, Sligo, Galway, Coole Park, etc.—these mysterious place names that recur in his poetry and that meant nothing to me—might deepen my understanding of the poetry." As an almost throwaway conclusion he writes, "I was not empirical in those days."[21]

Harvard Law School and the *Harvard Law Review* (1959–62)

Though he had considered going to graduate school to study English literature, Posner applied to law school his senior year at Yale. In what might be thought of as bad form, Posner in his contribution to the *Yale Class of 1959 50th Reunion Class Book* explained, "I chose Harvard Law School over Yale Law School because everyone said Harvard was more challenging and I didn't like the idea of flinching in the face of challenge." In a 2012 interview he added a bit to the story. "I only applied to Yale and Harvard Law School," he explained, "and was accepted by both. I interviewed at Yale, but Harvard just seemed so much more challenging. Yale seemed so lax; it seemed to me you had to go to Harvard—go to the tough place, don't go to the easy place."[22]

Posner took classes from well-known and famous professors, such as Henry Hart for Federal Courts, Albert Sacks for Legal Process (years later he would write to a correspondent that the course was worthless), and Austin Scott for Trusts. Only a few were good teachers, though. The best courses tended to be in the first year. Barton Leach on Property and John Dawson on Contracts were two examples. Dawson's for most was an especially challenging and frustrating class. One former fellow student said that the nickname for the twelve o'clock class was "Darkness at Noon," a reference to Koestler's novel. It was not until February or March, the anecdote continued, that the light of understanding began to shine in.

The instructors used the Socratic method, not as it is used today, but more brutally. Cold-calling was the standard of the day. Perhaps because he did well at it, Posner became an enthusiast of the method. In *Reflections on Judging*, Posner wrote that he loved his first year at Harvard Law School, "in all its brutishness."[23] The first-year teachers were "superb, though cold, demanding, and at times nasty."[24] The effect of that year, he wrote, was that he had "the strange feeling that I was markedly more intelligent than I had been a year earlier."[25] In an interview he elaborated. Yale had been lax, he said, and there wasn't a real method used there. In contrast, Harvard became the greatest educational experience of his life. "It was really Socratic, they really hid the ball. They told us at the beginning not to look at secondary stuff; it wouldn't do you any good. The case books themselves had very little interstitial material; they had a little, but it was mostly just cases and the professors would not give you any answers. They would just call on a student and ask a question about a case. The student went through the questions and then they'd ask another student." As an enthusiast of the Socratic method, he rebuffed a correspondent who had recently been to Stanford and had been impressed by the use there of the Socratic method. "The Socratic method is dead—deader at Stanford than anywhere," he wrote back. "Don't believe anyone who tells you differently. The Socratic law school method involves 'cold calling' on students, pressing them hard, hiding the ball—the sort of thing for which Socrates was executed, after all. I believe that no teacher at Stanford calls on students who do not raise their hands. Many *nouveau*-style law professors are incapable of the Socratic method."[26] Then, in the paragraph's conclusion he returns to Harvard and his experience. "It was law's single contribution to education," he writes. "I experienced it in its heyday."[27]

Posner's attitude as a student had not changed in the transition from Yale College to Harvard Law School. Part of him, as he put it, "was very peculiar—a teacher's pet and very grade conscious, very grade conscious." Another part was rebellious. But while the Yale professors had not been bothered by Posner's acts of rebellion, "they were very sensitive about it at Harvard. The Harvard professors were displeased by it, though not all." Derek Bok, after mentioning that he still recalled exactly where Posner sat in his class, said that he fondly remembered Posner as "a brash young man." But others felt challenged by what they considered to be impertinence. When he later worked for Erwin Griswold in the Solicitor General's Office, Griswold complained to him that his manner in the tax course Griswold taught him at Harvard had been very disdainful. Sneering was involved, Posner recalled. He admitted that he was sure that his manner had in fact been disdainful and explained the behavior by pointing out that Griswold was a terrible teacher and that he felt neither malice nor hostility toward him.

Posner made an impression on at least a few students. Nancy Eastham Iacobucci, who with Posner was in one of the four 140-student sections their first year, remembers that Posner distinguished himself early on: "It was quite obvious during the first few weeks of questions from the professors and answers from the students that we had at least one very clever member in our group. Unlike many of us, Dick was not shy about volunteering to answer questions and he invariably gave a good answer, often an especially memorable one. One of his offerings that I remember from that first intimidating year was his comparison of a lengthy continuing obligation of a party (probably to a contract) as 'an albatross around his neck'—a rather more colorful interjection than most student comments at that time, and one perhaps arising from his undergraduate English major at Yale." She added, "We all knew that when he spoke we should listen and take notes." Sandy Weiner, also in the section, tells a similar story and adds a touch of drama. When Posner was called on, everyone in the room went quiet. His "answers had the quality of written prose about them," he explained, "shaped in perfect paragraphs." Pierre Leval of the Second Circuit was a year behind Posner and also a member of the law review. He took classes with Posner and in a 2005 tribute to Posner described in a full paragraph worth quoting the phenomenon of Posner speaking in class. "When Dick spoke in class, what had been obscure and confusing would suddenly become clear. It was amusing to see an entire classroom of students, many of whom had been dozing, suddenly poised over their notebooks, pen at the alert, ready to write as Dick started to speak. The Harvard Law School faculty in those days had a high opinion of itself. It was amusing to witness a customarily smug professor's unsuccessfully concealed alarm when Dick raised his hand to speak. Why alarm? A professor accustomed to veneration could be quite chagrined to hear the school's most brilliant student say, in Dick's mild, mellifluous way, 'I don't see how anyone could reasonably hold that view'—and then to watch the entire class taking careful notes of Dick's methodical demolition of the professor's exegesis."[28] Classmate

Theodore Collins recalls something similar and describes Professor Dawson in the Contracts class "summing up a section of the course, in April or May, by saying: 'To sum up, I would just like to repeat what Mr. Posner said last February.'" Collins sat next to Posner in the first-year Torts class, in the second row to the left of the professor's podium. "It was a great place to sit," he writes, "because Posner always had his hand up to answer whatever question was being discussed, and as a consequence if I leaned back just a little I never got called on because the professor couldn't see me at all."

Posner did not know at the start of the first year how he would do on the exams that would come at the end of the second semester. He did know, though, how two friends from Yale who had been a year ahead of him had done on their exams. Future federal appellate judge Richard Arnold had ranked first in his class at the end of the first year, but Arnold, Posner knew, had a steel-trap mind of the sort that he did not have. A second friend, Robert Rifkind, Posner knew to be terrifically smart, but Rifkind had not placed in the top twenty-five after the first year and had not made the law review.

The first results were not what Posner wanted or expected. Professor Dawson in the first-year Contracts course gave a practice examination several weeks before the final examination and graded it. Getting a B sent Posner scurrying to find ways to improve. Believing himself rusty at taking examinations, since Yale had preferred seminars and papers, he began going to the library every night to take the past examinations that were on file. He took all the available examinations, not just for Contracts but for all his other courses that first year. This, he believed, gave him a big advantage over the other students. Then, to prepare for the end-of-year examinations, Posner built on his active class participation and familiarity with the cases studied through the year and followed the suggestions of the instructors to create outlines and to form study groups. He was part of a four-man study group.

These efforts paid off. After his first year Posner earned the Sears Prize, which went to the highest-ranking first-year student. It was worth $500 in 1960, at a time when tuition for a year cost $1,250. His first-year average was 81. An A required a score of 75. More to the point, ranking first gave him a leg up on his ambition. As he put it in an interview, he "really wanted to be president of the *Harvard Law Review*."

Law review selection was based on academic merit as measured by class rank. Ranking atop the class qualified Posner for the law review, which offered membership to the top twenty-five students at the end of the first year. They served with the students chosen from the class a year ahead of them. Some of the third-year students were members of the editorial board, while the rest served as staff. All second-year students served as staff. The editorial board was headed by the president of the law review, who had been chosen by the outgoing editorial board.

One of the first tasks for second-year members was to research and write up a preliminary note. James Springer, the president of the law review when Posner was a second-year staff member, explains: "We had a process of doing what we called prelims, in which somebody would do sort of an initial survey of the area that the note editors would sometimes think about. And one of the second-year people would just go out and see what was there." Posner was assigned the topic of space law, which, Springer explains, "back in 1961 was really a pretty far-out thing, and it was something he had a couple of weeks to do, and usually people would come in with five or ten pages to sort of say what they think. Dick apparently read everything in the field and came in with something thirty or forty pages long, which was pretty nearly a treatise on the state of the law on the subject at that point. And I remember we all said wow. I mean, there's nobody who had ever done anything like that that we knew of."

The note when fleshed out produced the same kind of response. Tom Farer, one of the note editors, remembers that "it was a remarkable work. There was virtually nothing to do. The average edit could go on for weeks—six, seven, eight hours a day until we had produced a second draft, maybe sometimes a third draft. In Richard's case the first draft looked like everyone else's final draft—there wasn't much to do." Note editor Bernard Nussbaum, who forty years later served as President Clinton's White House counsel, was the editor for Posner's note and reports that they had editing sessions that went long into the night and the early morning but that on almost every contested point Posner won out. He jokingly noted that Posner wore him down to get his way. What was perhaps most interesting about the note, another member of the editorial board commented, was that writing it was apparently not a big event for Posner. It did not require any significant effort to produce. Tom Farer thought that this was because Posner "was a professional already."

There were obstacles standing between Posner and the presidency of the law review. One was a stumble in cite checking caught by the treasurer (otherwise known as the managing editor), Peter Edelman. "He was quite savage in his criticisms," Posner recalled in an article written nearly fifty years later, "and I worried, though it turned out unnecessarily, that his criticisms would result in my being passed over for the presidency of the law review."[29] Another was a complaint made by one of the second-year members to the president of the *Review* that the student had seen Posner in Harvard Square take an apple from a fruit stand and not pay for it. The fellow *Review* member took a moralistic position and argued that the event should preclude Posner from consideration for the presidency. Posner was fast to deny the allegation, and nobody could confirm it, so it had no effect.

Springer, as the *Review* president running the selection process, thought that it was not much of a contest and that Posner was just head and shoulders superior to everyone else. Posner was smarter than the others, making it almost a given that he would be the president. Case editor Jack Levin agreed with the "head and shoulders above" assessment and added that Posner "was extremely competent, smart, good writer, and had great breadth. Posner was clearly a standout guy, and we selected him as president of the law review because he was such a standout guy." Nussbaum thought Posner was an intellectual giant but noted that he had an unusual personality. Other editorial board members also mentioned aspects of Posner's personality. Springer said that Posner knew that he was smart. "For want of a better word, he had a certain amount of arrogance." Farer thought that Posner was "about the opposite of warm and fuzzy. He was kind of cold, a cold fellow." For Farer, Posner was aloof, "distant, not someone who connects readily to the flesh and blood of other people. It's like having a computer. You think of your GPS voice who directs you from one place to another. That'll be my analog to Richard."

Certainly those who worked closest to Posner in his year as president thought well of him. Springer remained friends with the *Review*'s secretary, Jenny Wright, and reported that over the years she had often spoken, in Springer's words, of "what a wonderful guy he was to work for. She was very fond of Dick on a personal level." Robert Gorman was the treasurer of the *Review* and had an office in Gannett House, the home of the *Review*, next to Posner's. He wrote that Posner was "quiet, not outgoing, but warm and friendly." "We worked together every day, in immediately adjacent offices throughout our year together as officers of the *Law Review*. He was quiet, unflappable, with a soft sense of humor, and he never showed off that he was the smartest guy in the room. He read everything that went into the *Review*. The team of a dozen or so officers were very hardworking and very bright, but I do believe that Richard was indisputably the leader." Michael Horne, the developments editor, said that he had gotten along very well with Posner. Three years after graduation Posner attended his wedding. As to the work itself, he offered that Posner ran operations carefully and helped edit everything that went into the *Review*. There was "a tremendous amount of rewriting of the developments note for the Supreme Court," and Horne remembers Posner rewriting on an old electric typewriter. Posner, he said, "wanted the *Review* to be more readable and imposed that style on everything on which he did the final editing."

Others on the *Review* had different assessments of Posner. One of the staff members remembers that Posner was "a very unusual guy." He was not very personable in relationships and not very easy to approach, though he was "very, very good" in his role as president. "He was very businesslike and very well organized." Giving his view of Posner's personality some context, this staff member explained that while Posner could be difficult, the same was true for others on the *Review*: "They were all very bright guys and very ambitious, and very energetic."

Posner's year as president was eventful. A handful of issues that arose were not handled particularly well. Hindsight was not needed in these instances to show this truth. The first was Posner's overriding the decision of the book review editor to publish the favorable review he had solicited from Charles McCormick of a revision of Wigmore's *Evidence in Trials at Common Law* edited by Harvard Law School professor James McNaughton. Posner favored an unsolicited review of the book submitted by Frederick Bernays Wiener, a flamboyant, eccentric appellate lawyer who had worked in the government and retired from the army with the rank of colonel. The review was deeply critical of McNaughton's revision. Ultimately, a compromise was struck and both reviews ran, Weiner's first and McCormick's second. There was fallout from Posner's decision to publish Weiner's review, as it seemed to be in bad taste to publish a review that so criticized a Harvard Law School faculty member. Posner's decision to run the review caused problems on the editorial board itself. He was seen as acting with a heavy hand and humiliating the book review editor with his intervention. In describing the incident in a 2012 interview, Posner noted that he had been tactless in the way he handled the problem with the book review editor.

Wiener, an outspoken critic of Communism and Communists in the United States, also played a role in a second embarrassment for Posner as president. The school had decided that, since this was the seventy-fifth anniversary of the *Review*, the annual banquet should be a bigger than usual to-do. It was a grand affair held at the Harvard Club of Boston. Dignitaries had been invited, such as Justice Felix Frankfurter. Paul Freund of the faculty had wanted Frankfurter to speak at the banquet, but according to Freund, Frankfurter didn't want to be seen taking over the banquet, so Freund solved the problem by making himself the master of ceremonies and having additional speakers to go along with Frankfurter. The speakers were supposed to represent different generations at the *Review*. They included, in addition to Posner, Professor Emeritus Edmund M. Morgan, Elliot Richardson, Dean Erwin Griswold, and Wayne Barnett, who had been at the *Review* a few years before. Unfortunately, Frankfurter took ill and could not attend. Posner suggested that Freund invite Wiener to speak. He remembers saying to Freund, "What about Colonel Weiner? He seems like a colorful guy." This description did not do Weiner justice and did not fully capture what lay ahead for the banquet. Freund indeed invited him, not knowing that Wiener would use the occasion of his speech to go after Communist sympathizers and single out Alger Hiss. It was considered bad form to do this to Hiss, a former member of the *Review*, even though Hiss was considered to be a traitor. The Wiener cock-up redounded onto Posner, though technically it was Freund who had invited him, but Posner's embarrassment was not yet complete. Posner had been writing a column in the *Review*, in a manner not practiced by earlier presidents, and had irritated Professor Morgan in the process. Morgan took the occasion of his speech at the banquet to, as Posner put it in a 2012 interview, whack him for what Morgan called bad writing.

On this big stage, it could be argued, Posner had flopped, embarrassingly so. Posner in that 2012 interview took pains to say he did not act out of malice in suggesting the invitation to Wiener. It does not seem to be a stretch, though, to think that attendees such as Griswold might have blamed him, given the prior episode of the harsh review of McNaughton's revision.

As dean of the Law School, Erwin Griswold had a special interest in the *Review*. He had been a member in his days as a student at Harvard and had also been instrumental in the idea and execution of the *Bluebook* of citation practices for which the *Review* over the decades would gain a fair measure of fame. Tradition held that the president of the *Review* delivered a freshly printed copy of the latest issue to Griswold personally, as a way of showing that it had met the publishing deadline. It always did, something that was a matter of pride to Griswold. That Griswold was an odd and difficult man likely contributed to the difficulties Posner had with him, but Posner surely did his part in the strained relationship, as when treating Griswold disdainfully when he took his taxation class.

Complicating matters was Griswold's hatred of drinking, social or otherwise. One longtime Law School faculty member recalled that certain faculty, when invited to a party at Griswold's house, would be sure to stop at a bar or liquor store beforehand so as to have filled up, so to speak, ahead of time. The aversion to drink in the relationship between Griswold and Posner caused some strain because one of Posner's innovations as president was to begin Friday cocktail hours for the editorial staff. Some members thought that Griswold was angered by *Review* money being spent on drink, but the truth lay hidden more deeply. Griswold was apparently convinced that *Review* members were raiding a refrigerator stocked with snacks for the faculty. He brought the complaint up with a board that met occasionally to consider the financial investments held on behalf of the *Review*. Posner as the current president attended these board meetings and recalls Griswold telling the board about the grave problem of snack pilfering. Posner tried to maintain a suitably grave face during a moment that sounds like a Captain Queeg and his strawberries moment, but couldn't. The face he made likely went with the sneer he had shown during the taxation class.

Posner's problems at the *Review* and especially with Griswold might well have affected his future career. It is an oddity mentioned by many interviewed that Posner did not end up teaching at Harvard or even being offered a professorship there. It was and still is Harvard's approach to attract if not poach academic stars from other law schools. Not Posner, though. Donald Turner, a Harvard Law School faculty friend of Posner's from his student days, was able to give Posner an insider explanation that there was not a good fit between Posner and the Law School. Turner told him that he had talked to people about the offer that never went out to Posner, despite his preeminent academic standing, and that, as he put it, "personal factors" were involved. He said that Posner had offended the faculty. Posner was once offered and turned down a position at Harvard in 1979, but it was as a visiting professor for one quarter.

That Griswold was likely set against Posner finds support in another move by Griswold to block him, which came when Posner was being considered by Stanford for a faculty position beginning in the 1968–69 year and Griswold wrote to Stanford and urged the school not to hire him.[30] Things had apparently changed for Griswold by 1990, however, when he wrote to Posner praising him for an article he had published on Robert Bork.[31] In his concluding paragraph he asks how Posner can find the time and energy to write as much as he does and remarks, "I can only say that I am one of your faithful readers and admirers."[32]

Posner graduated first in his class from Harvard Law School in 1962. His experience there was connected to much of what later happened in his life. There was the negative connection of being blackballed by Harvard. But there were of course the usual results of having been the president of the *Review* and having graduated first in his class, such as being asked by Freund, who chose Justice William Brennan's clerks for him, if he wanted to clerk for the Justice. Doors opened for Posner throughout his career in part because of his performance at the Law School. No surprise there. But beyond this, Posner's note on space law led to his first publication, a book review in the *Harvard Law Review* in 1964.[33] He also relied on an article by Derek Bok on bank mergers in the *Review* that he had cite-checked in his second year for an important opinion he wrote when clerking for Justice Brennan on the same subject.[34] And his work on the law review led him later to argue against the persnickety sensibility of the *Bluebook* and to work while teaching at Chicago for a new approach in the *Maroon Book*, a less arcane system of citation. More generally, his law review experience also led to articles in 1995, 2004, 2006, and 2009 attacking the very nature of student-edited reviews.[35] His familiarity with Donald Turner's antitrust article led to his first law review article while at Stanford, in which he began his assault on the thinking of the Harvard antitrust school by squarely refuting Turner's analyses of oligopolies.[36] It also led, paradoxically, to Posner's friendship with Turner and an interest in economic analysis.

Posner's future was affected in a different way by attending Harvard Law School. He met his future wife, Charlene, who had graduated from Radcliffe but returned to Cambridge, during his second year as a result of living in the same apartment building. Posner somewhat jokingly blames dropping from first in his class after the first year to fourth after the second year to meeting Charlene and spending time with her. He righted whatever had been out of balance for his third year and got back to being first in his class. He graduated with a 79.9 average and missed graduating summa cum laude by a tenth of a point. He instead graduated magna cum laude. Having in his third year worked out a better balance between school, the *Review*, and his personal life, Posner spent some of his remaining free time teaching Freshman Composition at Harvard College.

Friends recall going to his apartment, conveniently located across the street from Gannett House, the home of the law review, for meals and, on at least one special occasion, to watch television. Robert Gorman recalls going to the apartment and watching the Nixon-Kennedy debates in 1960. Others recall going to the apartment and being struck by Posner's near total absence of domestic skills. One remembers opening the refrigerator and finding only a lemon in it. Nancy Eastham Iacobucci, the only woman on the *Review*, says that Posner had two Siamese cats and that they "were decidedly not cuddly."

Clerkship with Justice Brennan (1962–63)

Posner clerked for Supreme Court Associate Justice William Brennan for the October 1962 term, which, for the law clerks, extended from the summer prior to the summer following. Justice Brennan was not the leader, intellectually or otherwise, of the Warren Court, but his chambers, in Posner's words, were "the cockpit of the revolution."[37]

Justice Brennan hired two law clerks for the October 1962 term, as did many other Justices. Today each Justice hires four clerks for each term. Posner's fellow law clerk for Justice Brennan was Robert O'Neil, who went on to a career as a law professor and then president of the University of Virginia. He had graduated from Harvard Law School in 1961 and was a few years older than Posner. The two clerks usually worked six days a week and occasional Sundays in busy times. Posner has described the clerkship job as a nine-to-five job and as the lightest he has had. The hours left him with a lot of free time, which he filled with reading literature, especially novels. The emphasis when he studied English at Yale was poetry and drama, favorites of the New Critics. Now he was reading classic British and American fiction, from Dickens to Faulkner. Brennan was a good boss to have, according to Posner. "He was very friendly, a really nice person, a nice boss." He encouraged Posner to take trips during the Thanksgiving and Christmas holidays, and when Posner got to the office late one day and explained that he had just gotten married, he was told to take a week off for a honeymoon. Letters between them show what seems to be a genuine affection for each other. When Brennan announced his retirement in 1990, Posner wrote, "You have earned a rest; no Justice has served with greater distinction, or greater influence, or more good-natured tenacity, since your appointment, than have you. With your retirement you join a select pantheon of great figures in the history of law and the history of the United States."[38] Brennan wrote back to say that the note meant something very special to him.[39]

The two clerks initially divided the cases between themselves in an ad hoc fashion, though some patterns emerged. O'Neil, for example, tended to handle cases with First Amendment issues, while Posner's area was criminal procedure and habeas corpus. They simply divided the work on petitions for certiorari, that is, requests for a review by the Court. All unpaid petitions (those filed by parties without the means to pay the filing fee) were handled by Chief Justice Warren, who had an extra law clerk, while the other Justices handled the paid petitions. This work on certiorari petitions took on average one day per week. The balance of the time was spent writing Brennan's opinions. In the 1962 term, Brennan contributed thirteen majority opinions. He did not like to concur (agree with the majority decision but for reasons different from those given in the majority opinion) and did so only when the circulated majority opinion did not seem up to the job. Brennan dissented only five times, a fact he was proud of. The clerks also prepared interchambers memoranda when the Justices were negotiating over language in an opinion or were trying to switch a Justice's vote. Lastly, the clerks also wrote speeches for Brennan.

The clerks did not consider it their place to make recommendations on Brennan's decisions. Posner's politics at the time were liberal and roughly consistent with Brennan's. As he put it in his 1990 *Harvard Law Review* tribute to Justice Brennan, he "was a political liberal back in the early 1960s, and therefore assisted Justice Brennan with enthusiasm, indeed with relish." In later pieces on Brennan, Posner noted that his politics changed dramatically some years after clerking for Brennan but that the change, pushing him to the right—sometimes to the hard right—did not get in the way of his ongoing friendship with Brennan. That their views roughly coincided at the time, though, was not why Posner did not seek to influence his Justice. The governing rule was to facilitate. As Posner described it, he did "whatever Brennan wanted to do. I just thought I was working for him." Nor, he added, did the clerks from the different chambers ride in ideological packs. There were no cabals among the law clerks. They talked with each other, some being more friendly than others. Only Justice Douglas's clerk—Douglas hired only one rather than the usual two—tended not to be particularly friendly with the clerks of the other chambers. This, that clerk told me, reflected the sensibility of the chambers, of the Justice himself.

At the same time, once a case had been assigned to a Justice to write a majority opinion, the clerks worked with a free hand in shaping the opinion. Brennan left the jurisprudential niceties to them, though he studied what the clerks produced and could engage on the finer points of an opinion with his colleagues. He rarely made changes to what the clerks drafted, in part because the clerks consciously sought to give Brennan opinions written in language he preferred. The clerks became shameless Brennan mimics and used words or phrases such as "plainly" and "plain" because they were Brennan favorites.

Posner in fact did persuade Brennan to follow a particular path in one case, but the result was accidental, not deliberate. Brennan had come back from conference having been assigned by Chief Justice Warren to write the majority opinion in *Sanders v. United States*, affirming the lower-court decision not to afford the petitioner a hearing as part of his federal habeas corpus petition.[40] He directed Posner to write it, but Posner misunderstood the directive and wrote an opinion reversing the trial court and remanding the case for the hearing that the petitioner had been denied. Brennan read through the opinion and was sufficiently impressed that he changed his mind. He circulated the opinion and found that others were similarly persuaded and wanted to change their votes. What had been a majority to affirm now became a seven-to-two majority to reverse.

The two clerks for Brennan drafted their assigned opinions quite differently. O'Neil went draft after draft after draft. Posner, on the other hand, polished a first draft. Posner acknowledged that he wrote only one draft and added that he was likely acting irresponsibly. This approach came about because Brennan's secretary (who later married him) did not like typing for the two clerks. O'Neil responded by typing his own successive drafts, while Posner took the attitude that if the secretary did not want to type several drafts, then he would produce just one.

Posner wrote some of the 1962 term's most important opinions, most notably *Fay v. Noia*,[41] a habeas corpus case holding that a prisoner had not with the necessary intelligence and understanding waived his right to appeal; *NAACP v. Button*,[42] holding that the activities of the NAACP and its affiliates are modes of expression protected by the First and Fourteenth Amendments; and *United States v. Philadelphia National Bank*,[43] which held that a proposed merger was forbidden by the Clayton Act and was required to be enjoined. He was irritated to learn after it was too late that Justice Brennan, after he had approved his opinion in *NAACP v. Button*, had acceded to Justice Black's request and taken a chunk out of the opinion, interrupting its flow, without giving him a chance to repair the problem.

The two clerks stood in equal favor with the Justice. It was something of a daily ritual for them to meet with Justice Brennan in his office to discuss the day's work. Brennan's chambers could be a busy place, as befits the cockpit of a revolution. Brennan was the consensus builder for changes wrought by the Warren Court, using an impressive array of interpersonal skills to get other liberal-minded justices to shift the direction of the Court. Chief Justice Warren frequently visited Brennan in his chambers, as did Justice Tom Clark. Both Warren and Clark on occasion in that 1962 term turned to Brennan when their respective chambers were struggling with particular opinions. Chief Justice Warren brought *Townsend v. Sain* to Brennan, for example, and explained that he was having problems with it.[44] Brennan told Posner that Warren was struggling with the opinion and asked if he would write something. Warren got an opinion back written by Posner that went into the *United States Reports* bearing Warren's name.

One feature of the clerkship experience was meeting the other Justices. Lunches during the year were arranged so that the eighteen clerks would have a chance to engage with each one. Clerks would, of course, have occasions to encounter and perhaps speak to a Justice not their own, but the lunches were designed so that all the bases—or Justices—were covered. Posner reports that the most interesting Justices to lunch with were those "who had been around a lot and had a lot of personality," people like Black and Douglas. Douglas was handsome and glacial. He was very smart, Posner explained, and he was an excellent academic, writing very good articles. His problem was that he found the Supreme Court boring. "So it was sad because he was a really able person, and although he was a sourpuss, he had a lot of charisma. He was the kind of person who I think had tremendous leadership potential. I don't know what it was. He had these flashing eyes. Of all the Justices when I was there, he made the strongest personal impression even though he was not a 'sweety.' "

Posner first wrote about Brennan in 1981 and described his "complete freedom from self-importance that high office induces in so many of its holders, his many personal kindnesses not only to me but to my family, his modesty and warmth, and his unassuming friendliness."[45] He returned to Brennan's personal characteristics in his 1990 *Harvard Law Review* tribute. He drew a connection between Brennan's personality and his political liberalism, which bypassed doctrine. He wrote that "the political liberalism that is the salient feature of Justice Brennan's judicial opinions is, I am convinced, not the product of commitment to doctrine. It is the emanation of a warm, generous, and good-hearted person."[46] Brennan, he argues, has not pretended that the changes wrought by the Warren Court had the support of the text of the Constitution or the intentions of the framers, which for Posner places Brennan in the American pragmatic tradition. It was too early, though, in the 1990 tribute, to make judgments about whether the changes wrought by the Court's liberal experiment under Warren and spearheaded by Brennan had improved American life. By the time of Posner's next assessment of Brennan, occasioned by his death, Posner was willing, perhaps to the surprise of some, to provide some preliminary judgments.

Posner knew his "In Memoriam" contribution to the *Harvard Law Review* might be shocking to Brennan's admirers. When the president of the law review wrote to say that Posner in a few pages had compellingly and comprehensively challenged the way Brennan was ordinarily considered, Posner replied that he was "sensible of the shock that my piece must have given you and your associates," though he noted that he did not *intend* to elicit shock.[47] Posner was more concerned about the piece's "perhaps ungracious or inappropriate tone."[48] Posner, who had begun to write about jurisprudence in 1990, was in his contribution taking his foundational experience with Brennan in the 1962 term, linking pragmatism to results, and testing its success by asking the tough questions about whether the changes wrought had succeeded. He put it bluntly: Brennan's achievement in the law needed to be determined by "whether his influence was good or bad."[49] It's true, he noted as an example, that because of the constitutionalization of criminal law it was more difficult to convict an innocent person, but at the same time punishments under the new regime were more severe than previously. What had been assumed to be good under the liberal Warren Court was now being questioned, as with pornography and with affirmative action in education and employment. The scorecard was not impressive. "It's as if the fundamental constitutional law promulgated by the Warren Court were the law of unintended consequences."[50] Reputation and influence were a function of the "long-term social and political consequences" of the Court's decisions, and here history might judge Brennan harshly.

Philip Elman and the Federal Trade Commission (1963–65)

Posner had not been excited by his clerkship or the law and discovered that he really did not have much interest in practicing law,[51] though in

the spring of his clerkship year he applied and was accepted for a position with the Wall Street firm Paul, Weiss.[52] He thought about pursuing a graduate degree in English but quickly abandoned the thought.
He was interested, though, in what John French, a former president of
the *Harvard Law Review*, told him—that he was leaving his position as
assistant to Federal Trade Commission commissioner Philip Elman, that
the job had been a great experience, and that he should talk to Elman
about working for him. Elman, French explained, was very smart and
very good to work for. French, who had clerked for Justice Frankfurter
after Harvard, had taken the job with Elman because Frankfurter had
spoken so highly of Elman, who had been Frankfurter's clerk for the
1942 and 1943 terms. Posner talked to Elman and was impressed. Posner
wrote to Paul, Weiss to explain that, because of the Elman job, he was
not going to work for them. The firm responded with a tart letter sar-
castically wishing him good luck in his government career. Posner took
the job with Elman and found a mentor.

Elman, as a former star of the Office of the Solicitor General with
disappointed ambitions for the Office of White House Counsel, had
settled for the only job the Johnson administration could offer. He
brought to the Federal Trade Commission a kind of resistance movement into which he drafted his assistants, a movement against business
as usual and the pols on the FTC.

Much of Posner's work for Elman was opinion writing, and
because Elman was such a frequent dissenter, Posner wrote many
dissents. Elman thought that publishing a dissent—going public—
was the only way to get the other commissioners to pay attention
to him. To their displeasure and irritation, Elman would describe
in his dissents the small-mindedness of the commissioners and the
trivialization of the work the agency should otherwise be doing.
Joel Davidow, who for nearly a year was Elman's other assistant,
explained that Elman's irritation and frustration with his fellow
commissioners combined with Posner's ability to write so quickly
and so trenchantly meant that Elman did not have to wait a few days
to see if his heat cooled before dissenting. However, having access to
a loaded gun while irritated and frustrated, as Davidow put it, was
not necessarily a good thing for Elman. Some especially aggressive
and alienating dissents followed Posner's joining the team.

One example of Posner's ability to write quickly and well came when Davidow was drafting a speech for Elman to present at an evening dinner function. Davidow worked on it for a week. At noon of the day when Elman was to deliver the speech, Elman asked Posner to look it over. Posner reported that it did not include enough economic theory to be persuasive. Elman asked if Posner would take a crack at the speech. Davidow was in the room with Posner while he in three and one-half hours produced a thirty-page speech from scratch, relying on no notes or secondary materials. The speech, Davidow reports, was perfectly typed and precise in language and ideas. Elman gave Posner's speech and later sent it to the *Yale Law Journal*, where it appears in volume 74 as "A Note on Administrative Adjudication."[53]

Davidow thought that Elman and Posner were two peas in a pod. Neither suffered fools gladly, and both were socially awkward. Both lacked what Davidow termed "social warmth" and "social skills." Posner was mild-mannered but brutal in his critical responses. He made no effort to soften his criticism. He did not raise his voice but had no tact in delivering cutting judgments. His manner was to criticize when there were errors, as in vocabulary choices, for example.

Elman gives great credit to Posner for the FTC's success in fashioning a rule requiring health warnings on cigarettes. The much-anticipated report from the surgeon general in 1964 on the health effects of smoking led the FTC commissioners to believe that they should require on each pack of cigarettes a warning about the health hazards of smoking. Within a week the FTC had issued a notice of rule-making for hearings that would begin within two months. The commissioners conducting the hearings for several days heard from medical experts, industry experts, and consumers. Posner then "drafted a report on the proposed rule which summarized everything in the record, which drew conclusions, made findings, and gave a legal basis for the rule."[54] In doing so, Elman says in his memoir, Posner relied on "his ability to turn out work that's first rate, and quickly. He has the great capacity to absorb masses of facts and arrange them in his brain, and out it comes. And his first drafts are like other people's last drafts, only better."[55] Posner remembers that "in addition to justifying our rule-making authority, with help from an economist and a statistician in the Federal Trade Commission I assembled quite a lot of empirical data about smoking

and advertising for smoking cigarettes." Posner became friends with
the chief economist, Willard "Fritz" Mueller, and work on the project fed his growing interest in economics. The Unfair or Deceptive
Advertising and Labeling of Cigarettes in Relation to the Health
Hazards of Smoking rule that the FTC put in place never became
effective, however. President Johnson did not want one agency taking
the lead, and before the start date of the FTC rule Congress inserted
itself and passed the Federal Cigarette Labeling and Advertising Act,
which replaced the FTC's warning, "CIGARETTE SMOKING IS
DANGEROUS TO YOUR HEALTH AND MAY CAUSE DEATH
FROM CANCER AND OTHER DISEASES," with the far less potent
caution, "CIGARETTE SMOKING MAY BE HAZARDOUS TO
YOUR HEALTH."

Elman also credits Posner for writing the opinion in the *Procter &*
Gamble merger case that attracted both attention and admirers.[56] The
merger case presented a particularly vexing problem in merger law as it
was evolving. There was, as Elman explained it in his memoir, analytic
processes for mergers that were not strictly horizontal or strictly vertical,
but there wasn't much that had been decided or even figured out about
mergers between firms in different industries, which was the situation
in the Procter & Gamble merger. Elman tells us in his memoir that his
opinion in the case made a large contribution to the analytic process
that should be applied, and in the same breath generously explains that
the opinion was largely written by Posner. He goes further and quotes a
1965 letter he received from Thurman Arnold, an intellectual leader in
the field, in which Arnold describes the opinion as "the clearest exposition of the merger problem that has as yet been written, either by any
other court or in any other literature on antitrust laws."

The work Posner did at the FTC helped shape his interests in law and
economics. On a personal level, Elman was an important influence on
Posner. In an interview, he said that Elman "was a great force. I really
learned a lot from him. He was also a really good editor. I learned a
lot about writing from him, and it was quite significant." He is quoted
in the Elman memoir as saying that his job with Elman at the FTC
changed his life and that he learned about compromise from Elman.[57]

Elman also helped Posner get his next job in Washington, after he
had been at the FTC for two years. The FTC wanted Posner to stay on

as the agency's solicitor—its principal courtroom lawyer. Elman, on the other hand, wanted Posner to work for the solicitor general. Elman called people he knew from his long tenure in the office. The office asked Posner to come over for an interview and offered him a job.

Office of the Solicitor General (1965–67)

The Office of the Solicitor General at that time was a high-powered, nine-lawyer office headed by Archibald Cox, on leave from Harvard Law School, who had been appointed in 1961 and who would go back to Harvard to teach soon after Posner arrived.[58] This was the first time Posner was working as a lawyer in his own right, not as someone's assistant. In an oral history Cox explained that the lawyers in his office "were people who had been the quality of top Law Review editors at the top law schools, that had appellate experience and demonstrated their ability either in private practice or government."[59] They were the best and the brightest, which was only fitting for a solicitor general appointed by Kennedy.

Posner worked for Cox a few months before Cox was replaced by Thurgood Marshall. Posner served under Marshall throughout his tenure as solicitor general, which ended two years later when Marshall was appointed to the Supreme Court to replace Tom Clark. Erwin Griswold was then chosen to replace Marshall in October 1967. Posner served under Griswold for a few months before moving over to act as general counsel to the President's Task Force on Communications Policy, where he stayed for about a year before heading west to teach at Stanford Law School. All three of these solicitors general were easy to work for, in the sense that each gave the assistants latitude to exercise their own judgment on files. Their work was initially reviewed by the deputy in the office, otherwise known as the first assistant solicitor general. Ralph Spitzer was this first assistant. He reviewed the briefs carefully, though ordinarily he did not make substantive changes. Dan Friedman was the second assistant, and Louis Claiborne the third. Spitzer was considered to be the best courtroom advocate by far, always smooth and compelling. Claiborne was the more stylish advocate, both in court and on the page. As part of a long career practicing before the Supreme Court, Claiborne spent fifteen years in the Solicitor General's Office in two stints. His entry in *The Yale Biographical Dictionary of American Law* notes that "if he was 'known for the wry eloquence of his oral arguments,' his gift for the written word was if anything rarer still. . . . The solemn opening of the *Griffin v. Maryland* brief holds echoes of Lincoln."[60] Dan Friedman served as acting solicitor general in 1977 and later became a judge on the US Court of Appeals for the Federal Circuit.

Posner argued six cases before the Supreme Court while at the Office of Solicitor General. Colleagues report that Posner's strength was in the briefs he wrote more than the arguments he delivered, though he was an effective advocate. He was not the courtroom performer that Ralph Spitzer or Louis Claiborne was. Reports are that he was very confident, though unflashy. He was solid and very helpful to the Court. He was able to clearly explain the position he was taking. As a general matter, one colleague told me, he would not let the Justices get out of hand, and he would answer the questions well. "He would be very low-key. You know, he's not an emotional person at all. He wouldn't rant and rave, raise his voice or anything like that." Robert Rifkind reports an interesting detail, saying that Posner admitted that he practiced his oral arguments to his cat—to what response he did not say. It is likely, though, that these arguments had as much influence on the Justices as they had on the cat, since Posner later wrote that one reason he left the Office of the Solicitor General after two years was that he did not think "that the government's briefs or oral arguments swayed decision—whatever drove Supreme Court decisions, it wasn't the lawyers' advocacy."[61]

Lawyers in the Office of the Solicitor General are usually thought of as arguing cases in the Supreme Court, but the primary job of assistants is to review cases from the various divisions of the government and make recommendations as to whether the government should appeal. Appeals can be taken only with the approval of the Office of the Solicitor General. Posner had unsurpassed talents for such work. Paul Bender describes how Posner proceeded. "Dick was very, very smart. And you could talk to him about anything. And he was a very fast worker, I mean, astoundingly fast. He would do in a couple of hours what would take me a couple of days to do. You know, he would read a draft brief in opposition and digest it and know what was wrong with it and make the changes and say 'give me another one.' He was just amazing in his ability to do a lot of work and at a very high level. He was a wonderful person to have in the office because if there was too much work, he would take it and get rid of it." Robert Rifkind similarly reports, "The thing I remember most about Richard at that stage—I had known him both in college and in law school—was that every Monday the clerk in the office would come down the corridor dumping piles of briefs, files and petitions or whatever on each of our desks, sort of the week's work. I would look at this pile on my desk and begin to plow into reading it. I would scarcely have gotten through the decision below when in the next room, which was Dick's, I could hear through the partition his typewriter going. By the end of the week, sort of an early Friday, when I was still looking at a pile of stuff and realizing that Saturday was going to be devoted to finishing the week's work, Dick would come down the corridor and show up on your door and say, 'You got any extra briefs to work on?'"

Some of Posner's colleagues in the office report on Posner's personality, temperament, and attitudes. One explained that Posner "came with a more developed, what shall I say, ideological perspective in which to trend his thoughts than most people had. He had thought a lot about the problems of government and the law. He had views about what the antitrust laws ought to mean. In that sense he was intellectually more rigorous and certainly more thoughtful, more philosophical. In that respect I think he wasn't a smart aleck." Another colleague thought that Posner was content to describe what he thought was the right way to do something and leave it at that: "I've never sensed in Dick a deep eagerness to demonstrate his brilliance. I think he never thought it was necessary. I just think he was doing what he was doing, and not only did he not have to demonstrate that he was the smartest guy in the room, he was the smartest guy in the room. I never felt any particular arrogance except a certain self-confidence. He could be snippy with people, but it wasn't in a self-promoter sort of way." Added to the mix, this same colleague reported, was something of a mean streak in Posner. "One illustration of it that I saw, he would disparage any displays of tenderheartedness," though this colleague, who remained friends with Posner, went on to note that this personality trait had waned over the years. He worried, though, that there might be a streak of cynicism that lurked beneath the surface.

Posner left the Office of the Solicitor General after a little more than two years on the job. He had accepted an offer to teach at Stanford Law School. He wrote in *Reflections on Judging* that he left for two related reasons. One was that he did not want to continue to work for others. The other was that he did not want to have to defend positions that were not his own. It did not matter whether the position was that of a boss (as in the Office of the Solicitor General or the Federal Trade Commission) or a client. Neither obligation appealed to him.[62] In an interview Posner reports that Erwin Griswold thought he was the reason that Posner left, not long after Griswold took over as solicitor general, remembering the way Posner had responded to him at Harvard. Posner assured Griswold that he bore Griswold no ill will and that his departure was solely due to wanting to pursue other interests. When I had a chance to talk with Griswold in the early 1990s, he chuckled after explaining that Posner had left the office a few months after he had become solicitor general, saying that he "always had the suspicion that [Posner] wanted the place [position of solicitor general] himself."[63]

But before going to Stanford, Posner spent the next year working as general counsel to the task force for the President's Commission on Communications Policy in Washington.

President's Task Force on Communication Policy

Alan Novak as the head of the task force recruited Posner in 1967 to work on his smallish (fewer than ten full-time members) task force for the President's Commission on Telecommunications Policy.[64] Posner's title of general counsel meant nothing. The task force fell under the aegis of Eugene Rostow, Undersecretary of State for Political Affairs; Novak, a Yale Law School graduate, was Rostow's personal assistant. Rostow was the former dean of Yale Law School. The broad mandate of the task force was to consider communication policy against a background of emerging technologies and in the context of regulation of the private sector. The task force was the action following President Johnson's August 14, 1967, "Message on Communication Policy,"[65] which stated that he was "appointing a Task Force of distinguished government officials to make a comprehensive study of communication policy."

Novak had complete freedom from a hands-off Eugene Rostow to choose his staff. More important, he could ask departments in the government to loan him people, Posner being loaned by the Office of the Solicitor General. He was able to recruit a number of former Supreme Court law clerks, either full-time, such as Posner, or part-time. Novak could also recruit from industry and the academy, which he did with great success, getting economists Leland Johnson and Roger Noll. As Novak put it in an interview, "The task force had a lot of brainpower." Industry leaders were also keen to provide their perspectives, which led to a parade of corporation heads meeting with the task force and lobbying for their ideas on regulation.

Staff members took different approaches in trying to solve problems. Posner's approach, according to Novak, was to solve all of them with economics. One reason for this was that Posner worked every day with Leland Johnson, a very good price theorist. "He was excellent," Posner later wrote, "and I learned a lot from him."[66] Another reason might be that it was while working on the task force that Posner first read Ronald Coase's work.[67] Posner was the principal writer of the final report, though others also pitched in. That final report, which had a recurring theme of deregulation, was published at the end of Johnson's presidency and was promptly disavowed by the Nixon administration, which "in no way endorse[d] the recommendation of the Task Force or its analysis of the issues."[68]

Though the task force's mandate did not extend to questions about AT&T's possible antitrust violations, Posner, musing on the idea one day, wrote a forty-page memorandum explaining that AT&T was violating antitrust rules on vertical integration and that the company should be broken up. Novak recalled that the memorandum within twenty-four hours had somehow made its way to AT&T headquarters and the desk of the company's president. Unhappy with what he had read, the president of AT&T called President Lyndon Johnson to complain about the report. President Johnson then called Walt Rostow, Eugene Rostow's brother, who served as a special assistant to the president for national security affairs, and directed him to bury the memorandum. Walt called Eugene and relayed the message, which was then given to Novak, and the memorandum did not become part of either the final report or the working papers supplementing the final report. Roger Noll in an interview recalled the story the same way.

Stanford Law School (1968–69)

Posner had thought of an academic career to follow his years in Washington but was not persuaded it was right for him until he met with Bayless Manning, dean of Stanford Law School. In the spring of Posner's second year with the Solicitor General's Office, Manning had contacted him, and the two met in early June when business brought Manning to Washington.[69] To counter Posner's worry that he was not right for an academic career because he did not see himself writing academic articles, Manning explained that professors made contributions other than academic writing.

The hiring gauntlet at Stanford required that the entire Law School faculty (about twenty at the time) interview Posner. Then the entire faculty, not just tenured faculty, voted. In this age in which personal recommendations more than published work mattered, the hiring committee asked Erwin Griswold what he thought of Posner for the Stanford job. One faculty member described Griswold's response as an extraordinary letter advising Stanford not to hire him. He recited both the McNaughton book review when Posner was president of the *Harvard Law Review* and the details of the seventy-fifth *Harvard Law Review* dinner. He mentioned Posner's sneering treatment of him in class and argued that his behavior demonstrated a lack of respect for the faculty.

Posner during the full faculty interview was asked about Griswold and the events that had so troubled him. The conservative faction of the faculty, then a minority, was troubled by what Posner had done and argued against the hire. The rest of the faculty, which was committed to increasing the Law School's status, interpreted Griswold's complaints as cutting in Posner's favor. They liked that he had stood up to authority and, relying on Bayless Manning's strong support, voted to hire him.

One of Posner's colleagues at Stanford described him upon arriving at Palo Alto as a man on a mission. Posner by that time knew that his interest was in applying economic analysis to law. What he had done while clerking for Brennan in writing the *Philadelphia National Bank* opinion, at the Federal Trade Commission in working with the economist Fritz Mueller, at the Solicitor General's Office in specializing in antitrust matters, and at the President's Commission on Telecommunications Policy working with economist Leland Johnson all led him to want to explore and explain the relationship between law and economics.

Stanford had two professors in particular interested in law and economics generally and in antitrust specifically, Bill Baxter and Edwin Zimmerman. Zimmerman had been an assistant attorney general in charge of the Antitrust Division of the Department of Justice in the Johnson administration, and Baxter would go to hold the same position in the Reagan administration. Of greater importance were two economists linked with the University of Chicago, George Stigler and Aaron Director, who also had ties to Stanford. Stigler, who won the Nobel Prize in Economics in 1982, visited at Stanford during winter quarter each year. Director had retired as a full-time Chicago faculty member and moved to Palo Alto in 1965. Stanford provided him with an office at the Law School as a courtesy, allowing him to remain active in his field. Posner met each of them early on. Bill Baxter introduced Posner to Stigler, and Posner discovered Director on his own. As for Director, Posner comments, "When I started at Stanford I was walking to my office and I saw the name on the door so I just went in and introduced myself. And I realized within minutes this is a really smart guy. He was very smart, very, very smart. . . . Director's great. I learned a lot from him."

Stigler and Director had achieved significant success in economics, but in different ways. Stigler's was the traditional approach, influencing thinking principally through books and articles. Director, on the other hand, published little and instead gained influence as a teacher of both students and colleagues. Sometimes his ideas appeared in print only in the writing of others, though Posner believed credit should be given when the occasion presented itself, as when Ronald Coase sent him a draft of his entry on Director in the *New Palgrave Dictionary of Economics*. While generally praising the draft, Posner intervened, so to speak, on Director's behalf, telling Coase, "You do not mention any of the ideas that Aaron produced, for which he is entitled to credit despite the fact that they were written up by others. You might also add somewhere," he continued with reference to other of Director's personal qualities that had affected him, "that Aaron's personal influence rested to an important extent on the *integrity* of his conversation. Most of us both hear and repeat a lot of stuff that either we don't believe or have never thought to examine, just to be polite and convivial. Aaron had the disconcerting habit of not allowing his interlocutors to get away with unconsidered statements. But because of the old-world courtesy that you mention, he did not cause offense."[70]

Director and Posner made a perfect pair as teacher and student, so to speak. One colleague, whose office was next door to Posner's, said the two spent hours discussing law and economics, Director lecturing and Posner, the intellectual sponge, taking it all in. Director would come to Posner's office at least weekly, often daily, and the two would talk for hours at a time. Posner was at his desk, his electric typewriter clacking furiously as Director talked, sitting atop a row of filing cabinets. Posner would occasionally ask questions, but for the most part it was, for hours on end, Director explaining and Posner typing.

Posner had a busy teaching schedule for the two semesters he was at Stanford. He taught telecommunications, regulated industries, an antitrust seminar, and a seminar on distributive justice. The antitrust seminar must have been a treat, or at least a new experience for the six or so students who took it. Every week Stigler and Director came, and often Zimmerman and Baxter also, thus presenting the students with a freewheeling discussion among the five antitrust experts of different approaches to antitrust regulation. James Atwood, who took the seminar, told me that the students just sat back and listened. Another student, James McIntosh, commented that the " 'free-for-alls' were fun, sort of like Milton Friedman's *Free to Choose*, with Baxter playing Friedman's role, and all of us free to chime in. Disagreeing with Baxter was perilous, at least for law students (not because he was disagreeable, but because he would take your argument apart in a way that brooked no response). Posner was gentler, but persuasive." William Hoffman, another student in the class, described Baxter as a "vivid intellectual personality."

Posner's Regulated Industries class was a big success, at least if Vaughn Walker, who later went onto the federal trial bench in San Francisco in the Northern District of California, is to be believed. "Going into Posner's seminar on regulated industries," he told me, "was like going into a dark room and having someone turn on the lights." James Selna, class of 1970, also took the Regulated Industries class, and he too became a federal judge, in the Central District of California. He told me that the class was so oriented to the problems that practicing lawyers would encounter that, as a young lawyer, he was able to confidently move through a matter for a client by addressing the very problems discussed in the seminar. Other former students from the various courses Posner taught report that the smaller the class, the better Posner presented the material. James Atwood, who took three of Posner's courses, said that in a small seminar Posner sat with the students as equals. With larger classes, he was on the dull side and struggled to keep the attention of the students. In a small class, though, he was low-key, unassuming, and compelling.

Though he had told Bayless Manning that he didn't see himself writing academic articles, Posner took to the task as soon as he arrived at Stanford. Posner published his first two major articles in the *Stanford Law Review*. James Atwood, who went on to a distinguished career as an antitrust litigator, was the articles editor of the *Stanford Law Review* at the time. He said that Posner's two articles came to his office perfect and ready for publication. The same colleague who thought Posner was a man on a mission reports that Posner did not have much of a sense of humor about how others saw what he was doing. Because their offices were not far apart, Posner had asked him one day what was expected of young faculty members to get tenure. "I responded," the faculty member wrote to me, "that it was expected that non-tenured faculty members would write scholarly articles, but, I added, no one expected they would write, write, and write—as he had done. A sense of humor was not among his qualities at the time, and I recall he did not think this was worth a smile. Some years ago, he and I were speaking to the same group. I told this story about him and, once again, he failed to reveal the hint of a smile."

"Natural Monopoly and Its Regulation,"[71] the first article published, was rooted in Posner's own experience with regulatory matters as general counsel for the President's Task Force on Communication Policy. That experience, he wrote, made him skeptical of the assumed premise that regulation was "fundamentally inevitable, wise, and necessary." His study of natural monopoly and its regulation had convinced him "that in fact public utility regulation is probably not a useful exertion of governmental powers; that its benefits cannot be shown to outweigh its costs; and that even in markets where efficiency dictates monopoly we might do better to allow natural economic forces to determine business conduct and performance subject only to the constraints of antitrust policy."[72] This answered the question posed at the conclusion of the article's opening paragraph: whether natural monopoly provides an adequate justification for the imposition of regulatory controls. The article was an examination of first principles and a reconsideration of the basic soundness of regulation, something that had not been attempted to date. Aaron Director, not surprisingly, is acknowledged in the article as having played an important role in clarifying and enlarging Posner's thinking. Also acknowledged in the same way are William Baxter and Leland Johnson.

Posner's second article was "Oligopoly and the Antitrust Laws: A Suggested Approach."[73] It fundamentally questioned the assumptions that undergirded the prevailing approach to oligopoly monopoly pricing, which treated the two types of collusion, explicit and tacit, as two parts to a dichotomy in what was described as "interdependence." The solution for Posner did not come in the form of new legislation, that is, legislation beyond the Sherman Act. What was missing in the prevailing view was recognition of the ways in which the two drags on competition resembled each other. Once that was understood, he argued, it was easy to see that nothing more than available enforcement powers was needed. To make his argument Posner had to dismantle the prevailing view, as set out by Donald Turner of Harvard, who had also served as the chief of the Antitrust Division in the 1960s. Posner's insight, that explicit and tacit collusion had more in common with each other than had been previously recognized, had come with Aaron Director's help, a point Posner made clear in his first footnote, writing, "The suggested approach is a product of collaboration with Aaron Director, who, in addition, first suggested many of the ideas that are developed in it." He elaborated on this acknowledgment in an interview: "I said to Director that this is really your idea, so we should be coauthors. I'll write it, but it's your idea. He was adamant against that, so I thanked him and put him in the footnote, but he was very modest."

Director was also the leading force responsible for Posner leaving Stanford after the 1968–69 academic year and going to the University of Chicago Law School. Director had taken it upon himself to call the dean of the Law School, Phil Neal, and tell him that he needed to add Posner to his faculty. Neal was aware of Posner, aside from what Director was telling him, because Posner had gone to a meeting of the Industrial Organization Workshop at the University of Chicago

Law School, where he delivered a paper based on an earlier version of his article "Oligopoly and the Antitrust Laws: A Suggested Approach." Neal offered him a very big raise from his Stanford salary and a full professorship, as opposed to the associate professorship that Posner held at Stanford. Bayless Manning, the Stanford dean, did not compete to keep Posner. One faculty member there at the time said that Manning thought that he could not come close to what Chicago was offering Posner. Aside from the promotion and the extra money, the important economists at Chicago helped decide the matter for Posner. The ties that he and his family had to the West Coast were not great, and being in Chicago put them closer to his wife's family in Dayton, Ohio. George Stigler was at Chicago. So were Ronald Coase and Milton Friedman, who, coincidentally, was Aaron Director's brother-in-law. Director, though retired, would frequently return to Chicago to teach, often with Posner.

2

University of Chicago Law School Professor (1969–1981)

POSNER ARRIVED AT THE University of Chicago in 1969 against the back-drop of Aaron Director's influence in the law and economics movement and with an interest in proselytizing for economic analysis the likes of which Director and others at Chicago had never imagined. The prevail-ing influence model, that is, making one convert at a time, was not for Posner.[1] Once at Chicago he moved purposefully with a variety of strategies—or one large strategy with several constituent parts—to push the economic analysis of law. He was hardly joking when he referred to his "relentless effort to proselytize for the economic approach to law"[2] and to "propagandizing for law and economics."[3] Posner combined his missionary zeal with a strategy that included books and articles as well as lectures and conferences to argue that economic analysis of law should be taught and studied because the approach yielded insights by identify-ing and explicating the role of efficiency in law. Everything he did in his twelve years at Chicago sought to spread the word of economic analysis of law. He worked out the language of the economic analysis of law in his seminal book of the same name early in the 1970s and spent the bal-ance of the decade helping others to learn to speak that language.

The figures Posner has at various times recognized as the founding forces of law and economics—Stigler, Coase, Director, and Becker—were all at Chicago in varying degrees when Posner arrived in 1969. Only Guido Calabresi of Yale was absent. Director was still based in Palo Alto, but he returned to Chicago in the first years of the decade for a quarter each year. Stigler, in contrast, was at Chicago except for the winter quarter, which he spent each year at Stanford. Coase was at the Law School and editing the *Journal of Law and Economics*, while Becker was in the Department of Economics. But there were others doing important work, such as Harold Demsetz, who held joint appointments in the Business School and the economics department. He would overlap with Posner for only two years before he migrated to the UCLA economics department in 1971. In a development that would affect Posner throughout his career, Becker, not long after Posner arrived in Chicago, encouraged him to become involved with the National Bureau of Economic Research, and at a New York meeting of the NBER in 1971 Posner met Becker's protégé, William Landes, who two years later left the NBER to take a position at the University of Chicago Law School as an economist in residence, so to speak. Thus Posner's frequent collaboration with Landes over the years had its start. The law faculty itself through the 1970s was made up of several older faculty members—such as Allison Dunham, Phil Kurland, Harry Kalven, Ronald Coase, Bernard Meltzer, and Phil Neal—a few others in their forties, and the majority younger than forty. These included (most throughout the decade but some for shorter stretches) Gerhard Casper, Edmund Kitch, John Langbein, Geoffrey Stone, Stanley Katz, Franklin Zimring, Kenneth Culp Davis, Robert Burt, Owen Fiss, Kenneth Dam, William Landes, and Richard Epstein. Posner was thirty when he started at Chicago at the rank of full professor.

Posner taught all manner of courses over the next twelve years. In the first years he taught an antitrust seminar with Aaron Director during Director's quarter at Chicago. He taught Economic Analysis of Law and classes on regulation, torts, civil procedure, contracts, and the history of legal thought, among others. One year he taught a seminar on Blackstone, Bentham, and Smith. He used the Socratic method and thought that this approach was best suited for students to learn the ways of the law and to prepare them to respond to judges in courts and to clients in offices. Posner in an interview published in the *University of Chicago Law School Record* in his second year at Chicago said that law school taught students two basic skills, "those of identifying legal questions and then predicting how courts will react to a question that hasn't come up a hundred times before."[4] For him this was the essence of legal education. Asked if he would change anything for second- and third-year students, he said that he wanted law school to be "more practical, realistic, and concrete."[5] Adding courses that brought in the social sciences more systematically would be one way to do this. He taught with his expressed goals of legal education in mind and even in his first years at Chicago brought economic analysis into courses, such as torts, that had not been associated with the economic approach.[6] Douglas Laycock, who went on to a distinguished teaching career, recalled his Torts class with Posner in his first year, 1970, and Posner casually leaning against the blackboard while handling a sixty-five-minute class of 180 students, questioning Socratically. Laycock was astonished at Posner's ability to always come up with the right hypothetical question. Posner had a seemingly bland demeanor in the class, which was in stark contrast to its extraordinary substance. One exasperated student complained that the class should be more about black-letter law to help students pass the bar examination than about provocative hypotheticals built upon a core of economic analysis. Posner showed some irritation and shot back that the students were at the University of Chicago, a great school, and that as lawyers they would need to solve complex problems. Theirs would not be a world of simple slip-and-fall cases. The student might not be getting the rules he thought he should be getting, Posner explained, but he was getting the rules and ideas of economic analysis, and it was with economic analysis that lawyers would be able to solve complex problems to predict how courts would react. About the leading tort law hornbook and its author, William Prosser, he said, "That's hack work."

Posner pushed to expand law and economics at the Law School in a variety of ways. He proposed a formal link between law and economics, suggesting that the Law School ask the economics department about the possibility of offering a joint law-economics degree,[7] a proposal that came after discussing it with Gary Becker. He pushed an initiative to add another economist to the Law School faculty.[8] The school was offering so many law and economics courses, he argued in a memorandum, that a second economist was needed. He tried to interest Charles Meyers of Stanford Law School, a law and economics man with whom Posner had worked on a water rights project, to come to the Law School as its dean,[9] and he tried to get the Law School to make an offer to Robert Bork when he decided to leave Yale in the mid-1970s.[10] Posner argued that Chicago's reputation was increasingly identified with its powerhouse law and economics programs and professors but that other schools were catching up and that to maintain its preeminence Chicago needed to make a dramatic move by hiring Bork. He encouraged his former student Frank Easterbrook to consider an academic career when Easterbrook was in the Office of the Solicitor General, and Posner was generally on the lookout for talented newcomers to teaching.[11] In an exchange with Harvard's Phillip Areeda, who had asked what Posner knew about various Chicago graduates Harvard was interested in hiring, Posner provided remarkably candid evaluations, and closed with, "In return, could you rack your brain for recent Harvard graduates that we should be interested in?"[12] And when he encountered a particularly bright young lawyer, such as James Atwood, a former student of his at Stanford, he encouraged him to think of teaching at Chicago.[13] He urged new law and economic programs at the Law School and tried to secure a continued and expanded role for Stigler.[14] He wanted to increase financial support to the Law School and pursued an idea to bring short law and economics programs to law firms to train lawyers in the ways of economic analysis.[15] He wrote a detailed memorandum outlining strategies to increase fundraising generally,[16] and another on corporate fundraising in particular.[17]

He spoke his mind and delivered blunt criticism. This was the way of the school when he arrived, and it remained a distinguishing trait while he was there. The tough-guy approach played out in faculty meetings and even when colleagues met for roundtable lunches at the faculty club. Posner certainly didn't mind the school's confrontational style. In a 2002 blog entry for *Slate* Posner recalled the Industrial Organization Workshop, a cousin to the roundtable lunch, run by George Stigler, the school's leading tough guy. "George set the tone [at the workshop] of brutally candid criticism, pounding me so hard once when I gave a paper that another professor made him call me up and apologize, which he did with rather an ill grace—but he needn't have bothered, because I thrived in that atmosphere."[18]

Robert Burt of Yale Law School, who overlapped with Posner at Chicago in 1970, tells a Posner man-on-the-street story with economic analysis overtones and personality implications. Explaining that Posner was a regular attendee of the roundtable lunch, he recalled that "on one occasion he arrived and told the group about an encounter he had just had on his way to the club. A stranger had stopped Dick on the street and asked the time. Dick related that he had said, 'Sure. For a nickel.' Dick continued, 'The man seemed confused by my response but I explained to him that he could have had his own watch but didn't and was trying to 'free ride' on mine. I was willing to charge him for the use of my watch and a nickel seemed about the right price.' The man walked away, Dick told us. Dick didn't give him the time."[19]

Posner, observers report, usually displayed equanimity at Chicago faculty events, such as when visiting professors presented papers, usually as a type of tryout for their own ambitions in joining the Chicago faculty, but beneath the usual calmness in Posner was a viperish streak that cut to the quick. His questions would be asked without rancor, hostility, or irritation, but invariably they aimed for the core of the presenter's ideas to dismantle or gut them. One former colleague explained that Posner was not a fast talker, and that he would pause to select the right adjective or adverb that did the heavy lifting in the cutting remark.[20] And while he was not the only offender, Posner's performance sent some of those who had come to deliver a paper fleeing home, hoping to erase the memory. This caused problems when the Law School wanted the person to come back, possibly to join the faculty. Dean Gerhard Casper described having to make phone calls, trying to explain that Posner was not really that bad, that the criticism was not meant personally, and that Posner would be better next time.[21] There were times, the dean admitted, that he needed to take Posner aside and ask him to tone his questioning down. "Can't you be more restrained in the way you express your views?" he would ask.[22] It was, he said, a genuine problem. Posner took no prisoners. As the dean remembers it, Posner never needed to demonstrate he was the smartest person in the room, "and I never understood his interventions to come from such a desire. It was just his incredible tendency to be controversial and quickly cut to the weakest point of a lecture or of a paper."[23] Others on the faculty read it differently. Another faculty member from the 1970s noted that for a time in the workshop settings Posner came across in his questioning as disrespectful. He thought that Posner was impatient with what he considered wrongheadedness and that, once riled, he could be very dismissive. While others on the faculty, such as Frank Easterbrook, got imperious and condescending as they sent their messages of superiority, Posner took to cross-examining the presenter. Matters improved, he noted, after Dean Casper took Posner to the woodshed a couple of times for his behavior.[24]

Perhaps underlying it all is that what Posner did not like got a comment from him, critical but not necessarily hostile. He thought, for example, that the Salzburg Seminar he attended for six weeks in the summer of 1976 was not as well planned and executed as it should have been, especially on the faculty selection and performance fronts. This led to a three-page letter to the seminar's director setting out the problems, possible solutions, and a list of proposed faculty who would better engage the seminar's students.[25] And when the University couldn't seem to find its way to clearing, during winter snowstorms, a path across the famous Midway that he took to get to the Law School, he sent two letters describing his outrage.[26] A second was needed when the first went ignored. When the school responded and agreed to keep the path clear, Posner circulated a memo to the faculty displaying the result of his complaint.[27]

Commenting on papers sent to him by law professors seeking his opinion, he delivered with typical Chicago toughness knockout punches, but without any personal edge. He pointed out both where he disagreed with an argument and when arguments had been missed or misunderstood, but all in a matter-of-fact tone. He gave Duncan Kennedy, for example, brutal commentary in a two-page response to a paper on Ronald Coase, but as critical as the assessment is, it comes across objectively. He wrote, "You are, of course, not the first to try to refute the Coase theorem. It is a task with the same fascination that squaring the circle used to have. With respect, and having your best interests to heart, I believe your attempt is prolix, labored, and technically and conceptually flawed."[28] Perhaps the references to respect and Kennedy's best interests take the sting out of the verdict. A certain definitiveness marks his comments, as when he writes to James Boyd White that he "found the last sentence of the first paragraph florid and obscure."[29] This tone appears again in his summing up: "I think the paper is too long, and the style rather plethoric."[30]

He takes after Bruce Ackerman's prose after reading the first chapter of his manuscript on social justice, writing that Ackerman's style is irritating in two respects. "The first is striving for 'gender neutrality' in which in your hands has reached an absurd extreme. The constant alteration between 'he' and 'she' is extremely distracting." He then explains, "I don't think you realize that in English the masculine gender is unmarked and the feminine marked. That is, the masculine gender is used *when gender is not in issue*. The use of the feminine gender implies that attention is being drawn to gender. That is why your gender alteration is so distracting. It is, quite simply, wrong grammar."[31] (Posner was pushing against the historical tide, since the masculine gender was in the process of becoming marked.) But he is not done. "Second, you are awfully fond of cute phrases—really cliches: 'heart that beats within,' 'shock of recognition,' 'thought-experiment,' and many more. You give the impression that you are trying to write impressively, arrestingly. Well, it is nice to have an impressive, arresting style, but when effort to achieve it is perceptible, you've failed. People not gifted with a sense of style, you and me for example, should strive to write unaffectedly and plainly. (That's how Rawls writes.) There is a bumptious quality to the style of Chapter One."[32]

Academics with great reputations (Ackerman had not yet achieved his) got off no more easily. Ronald Coase, for example, sent Posner his paper "The Market for Goods and the Market for Ideas," later published in the *American Economic Review*,[33] for comment. Posner began, "I have some specific comments on the paper, set forth below, and one general comment: the tone is rather acerbic, even bitter in places. The paper would be more effective, in my judgment, if it were somewhat more gentle."[34] The published paper does not have the tone of which Posner complained.

Posner's sharp comments occasionally made their way into print, but only when a paper of his had been challenged and he was asked to reply. This happened when Richard Markovits published a four-part article in the *Stanford Law Review* on oligopolies that explicitly challenged Posner's 1969 article on the subject. The journal's editors asked Posner to respond. He does this by first providing a historical overview of legal control of oligopoly pricing and then a detailed summary of Markovits's particular positions. This summary is required, he slyly, wittily, and aggressively notes, not just because of the length of the four articles—152 pages in total—but because of their challenging prose style, a style, he writes, "to which I react as did one reader to Bentham's prose: 'I felt as though I had been asked to masticate an ichthyosaurus.'"[35] In the accompanying footnote he explains that his objection to Markovits's style is not that he relies excessively on economic jargon or on geometrical or algebraical formulations. "The problems with Markovits' style are different. They include the proliferation of new and unfamiliar terms and acronyms (POP's, SOP's, CA's, CCA's, BCA's, etc.), abstractness, prolixity, and a lack of clear organization. His style presents enormous difficulties even for the economically sophisticated reader. The difficulties are unnecessary since his ideas are basically quite simple, as I have tried to indicate in my summary of the article."[36]

Economic Analysis of Law

Posner marked the influence of Stigler, Director, Demsetz, and others in the papers he wrote once he was at Chicago, and as the 1970s progressed, references to Director became fewer, while Stigler remained a constant. Demsetz had also gotten effusive acknowledgments in Posner's papers—and in *Economic Analysis of Law*—but the mentions became fewer after Demsetz escaped Chicago winters for the warmth of Los Angeles. The acknowledgments of appreciation and thanks went increasingly to Gary Becker, Bill Landes, and Bernard Meltzer, one of the few older faculty members. Ronald Coase less frequently makes his way into the group of those whose influence is mentioned.

Coase and Stigler had engaged in something of a battle for Posner's intellectual soul. Stigler had won out, and Coase was not happy. Both possessing intellects of the highest order (Stigler winning the Nobel Prize in Economics in 1982 and Coase winning it in 1991), the two men represented different approaches to law and economics. Coase wanted to use law and economics to see what it could reveal about economics, while Stigler's empirical interests looked to the effect of economics on law.[37] This was the interest Posner developed. Posner, who has said that Stigler was the smartest person he ever met, ended up spending more time with Stigler, to the dismay of Coase, who, while he would publish Posner's papers on the economic analysis of law in the *Journal of Law Economics*, did not think his journal was the right place for them because they advanced an approach that rivaled his own. Coase suggested to Posner that he start his own journal for the kind of law and economics he wanted to develop. Thus Coase, ironically, gave Posner the idea for the *Journal of Legal Studies*.

Coase was also sensitive to the idea that the University—with Friedman, Stigler, and Posner in the lead—wanted to push Stigler's (and Posner's) approach to law and economics through the establishment of a center at the Law School named for Stigler that would do National Bureau of Research and Economics–type empirical studies. The center could be seen as the victory monument for the economic analysis of law instead of the law and economics approach Coase favored. Posner, in short, could be seen as the driving force in replacing what Coase had worked to erect. Coase argued forcefully and successfully against the center at a faculty meeting in the mid-1970s, but the damage had been done.[38] Coase on at least two occasions advised Law School faculty members not to work with Posner. He told William Landes that Posner, with his greater reputation, would get all the credit for cowritten articles. There is perhaps no ill motive that can be attached to this advice.[39] Not so with the advice Coase gave another faculty member. As that faculty member describes it, "At one point I remember Ronald warning me in a mentoring way to be careful about sharing ideas with Dick. His concern was that if you discussed a promising but not yet fully worked-out idea with Dick, he would quickly ingest it and incorporate it in his own torrent of output. The problem was, Ronald said, that Dick would get the details of the execution wrong, but the idea as he presented it would be absorbed into the literature and it would be impossible to ever get it corrected. And because of the flaws in execution, the idea would end up having little long-lasting influence."[40]

Some years later, in 1993, Coase and Posner got into a barbed exchange at a conference on new institutional economics prompted by a paper Posner gave on Coase's lack of interest in economic theory and dismissal of the law and economics movement, premised as it is on an empirical, social-science approach and a rational model of human behavior.[41] Coase, as he writes in his response, was not amused by Posner's take on him.[42] In the published response, Coase writes that he is not what Posner describes him to be. He is not against abstraction, and he does not object to econometric studies. And he does not want, he emphasizes, to go back to what Posner described as the "earlier, simpler, looser, non-mathematical theory of Adam Smith." Going beyond specific attempts at refutation, Coase at the meeting and in the paper makes plain his unhappiness at Posner's effrontery. This was of course not lost on Posner. He later wrote to Aaron Director, enclosing a copy of the conference paper, and explained that Coase "didn't like it at all."[43]

The jagged exchange between the two must have stayed with Posner, because nearly twenty years later he returned to it in a paper on Keynes and Coase which he gave at a 2011 conference honoring Coase and his one hundredth birthday. Here he retracted some of the criticisms he had made of Coase in 1993.[44] The retractions, however, were outdone by a repetition of the main charges: that Coase was not interested in theory and held no truck with the cornerstone of economic, rational maximization. Posner reassessed the importance of Coase's approach to economics while referring to the resurgence of Keynes in reaction to the economic crisis of 2008. His resounding conclusion seems to cut both ways, as both criticism and retraction. "The firmness of his conclusions does not appear to be based on a theory of government but instead appears to reflect the confidence with which he rejects formal theory and formal empirical methods in favor of a stubborn adherence to the illustrious tradition of what might be called commonsense economics, which is the economics of Adam Smith, of John Maynard Keynes, and of Ronald Coase—economic geniuses all, and to which our current economic troubles invite renewed respect."[45]

An explanation for the sharp exchange might lie in Posner's reaction to the extent that Coase was willing to take credit for the insight driving economic analysis of law, that judges in their opinions use the common law to promote efficiency. Posner thought the insight was original to him, with some qualification. He was asked in a 2001 interview about the insight and responded, "[i]t was pretty original." He further explained that "there are hints of it in Ronald Coase's article on social cost. He wasn't too clear about it, but the implication that I drew was that he thought the English judges had been trying to make an economically sensible law of nuisance. And Harold Demsetz, one of the Chicago economists now at UCLA, wrote something which hinted at this."[46] Having this view of the insight's origin, Posner might have been surprised by Coase's lecture at the University of Chicago on April 7, 1992, on the history of law and economics at the school,[47] published the next year and before the conference where sparks flew, in which Coase took credit for the insight.

Journal of Legal Studies

Posner in 1971 established the *Journal of Legal Studies*. Its first issue appeared in January 1972, and Posner remained its editor for ten years, until he went onto the bench. It was not conceived as a competitor to the *Journal of Law and Economics*, started by Aaron Director in 1958 and later edited by Ronald Coase. Posner used the *Journal of Legal Studies* to distinguish between the two branches of law and economics. In a 1978 draft letter seeking additional funding for the journal, he explained that the *Journal of Law and Economics* emphasized "the relevance of legal and institutional factors to understand and improve the operation of the economic system," while the *Journal of Legal Studies* emphasized "the application of economics to the understanding and improvement of the legal system."[48] The latter journal applied the theories and empirical methods of the social sciences, especially economics, to questions about the legal system. He wrote in an afterword to the first issue that the aim of the journal was "to encourage the application of scientific methods to the study of the legal system."[49] He saw his version of legal studies—the economic analysis of law—as endeavoring "to make precise, objective, and systematic observations of how the legal system operates in fact and to discover and explain the recurrent patterns in the observation—the 'laws' of the system."[50] Studies that might be too technical and scare off law review editors could find a home in his journal. The journal would be a place where scholars of different disciplines interested in this branch of legal studies could go to see what others were up to. For this new field the journal would help create a sense of identity. In a draft of an undated but likely 1977 letter in which he sought funding for the journal, he went beyond what he had said in his afterword, writing, "Because law has become so pervasive—even threatening—a force in American life, the need to subject it to rational, scientific study has become a matter of urgent concern, and not merely of intellectual curiosity."[51]

The *Journal of Legal Studies* was very much Posner's journal. There was an advisory committee of eight faculty members for the first few years, but later it was just Posner on the title page. The journal did not within its covers bill itself as a refereed journal and likely was not one, strictly speaking. The reason, according to some familiar with economic analysis of law during the 1970s, was that there were not enough experts available to conduct peer review of the articles that came in.[52] Posner was probably the most knowledgeable person on the scene, certainly as to economic analysis applied to the wide range of subjects and topics within the law. Moreover, all journals, even refereed journals, gave their editors editorial discretion when needed. This developing field of legal studies—economic analysis of law—created a constant need for that editorial discretion to be exercised. The articles that Posner published in his journal helped begin the foundational buildup of economic analysis of law. Terms such as "economic approach," "efficient," "economic analysis," "economic basis," "economics of," "economic theory," "empirical," "law and economics," and "statistical analysis" appear frequently in the titles in the cumulative index of the journal's first ten years. The articles covered the full range of topics both in areas of the law and in the legal system, including judicial administration. Posner by himself or with coauthors contributed fifteen articles to the journal in his ten years as editor.

Foundations to the theory

His first article on economic analysis of law, "Killing or Wounding to Protect a Property Interest," was published in Coase's *Journal of Law and Economics*.[53] The second article, published in the first issue of the *Journal of Legal Studies*, was "A Theory of Negligence."[54] These two articles were important in demonstrating what economic analysis of law could do, what it was based on, and why it was needed. "Killing or Wounding to Protect a Property Interest" explored what seemed to be a simple case involving the collision of two readily identifiable interests, the right to protect property you own and the right not to have deadly force used upon you when the facts do not warrant it. There had been a case much in the news at the time involving an Iowa farmer who had rigged a spring gun to protect valuables in his farmhouse. A burglar tripped the spring gun, was injured, and successfully sued the farmhouse owner for damages. What triggered Posner's article was his disappointment when he went looking to sort out the applicable law. He found it was in a mess. There were few reported judicial opinions on the doctrine of using deadly force to defend a property, and what the *Restatement of Torts*—published by the American Law Institute and summarizing common law tort principles—reported was confusing, inconsistent, and contradictory. The reason scholars had not been able to successfully detail the law on the doctrine of deadly force came from the "limitations inherent in a certain type of scholarship and in the attempt to restate the common law in code form."[55] Those trying to restate the common law in code form had "a propensity to compartmentalize questions and then consider each compartment in isolation from the others; a tendency to dissolve hard questions in rhetoric (for example about the transcendent value of human life); and, related to the last, a reluctance to look closely at the practical objects that a body of law is intended to achieve."[56] "Indeed," he continued, "the preoccupation with completeness, conciseness, and exact verbal expression natural to codification would inevitably displace consideration of fundamental issues and obscure the flexibility and practicality that characterize the common law method."[57] Judging, he stressed, is about the practical. Judges think of cases in highly practical terms before deciding them, in that "they consider the probable impact of alternative rulings on the practical concerns underlying the applicable legal principles."[58] He then invokes Holmes as a pragmatist in his essay "Common Carriers and the Common Law," writing that Holmes must have been thinking this way when he wrote that "the very considerations which the courts most rarely mention, and always with an apology, are the secret root from which the law draws all the juices of life. We mean, of course, considerations of what is expedient for the community concerned."[59] Holmes would have likely agreed with Posner's next observation, that it is a mystery why judges, having made a practical decision, nonetheless write it up in "pompous, stilted, conclusory prose that the layman derides as legalistic."[60] In manifesto-like language, he continues that "the task of legal scholarship is to get behind the prose and back to the practical considerations that motivated the decision. Yet scholars often seem mesmerized by the style, terminology, and concepts of the judicial opinion; they confuse their function with the judicial."[61] To the question of what to do, Posner points to economic analysis. He writes, "[a] possible way of avoiding this danger is to take an economic approach to questions of legal interpretation."[62] To do this is to break free of judicial opinions as the text of the law and to look at the underlying facts and the economic factors and in any analysis to begin with them.

The spark for Posner's "A Theory of Negligence," the second article, was what Posner considered to be wrongheaded thinking that tried to explain the shift in the nineteenth century in the world of torts from the strict liability standard to the negligence standard.[63] The usual reasons given for the shift—that the negligence standard acted as a subsidy to expanding industries, that the dominant purpose of civil liability for accidents is to compensate the victim, and that negligence is a moral concept—broke down when examined closely. A better explanation was needed, though it turned out it was already there. That explanation was the Hand negligence formula, which was a distinctly economic theory. The idea had been used by judges going back to the nineteenth century and waited for Hand to give it a name and a memorable algebraic equation assigning values to the cost of preventing accidents, the magnitude of loss if the accident occurs, the probability of the accident occurring, and the burden of taking precautions. If it were true that the roots of Hand's economic meaning of negligence lay in the nineteenth century, then the best explanation for the shift in the nineteenth century from strict liability to the negligence standard would be an embrace of the economic theory of tort law, though the embrace was never explicit or reported in the judicial opinions as such. It was going on nonetheless, as Posner sought to show in his article. He did this by going back to the cases themselves and reading 1,528 American appellate court decisions on accidents from the period 1875–1905. This represented a sampling in which Posner read every published opinion from the first quarter of 1875, 1885, 1895, and 1905, and by his estimate represented "one thirtieth of all appellate accident opinions issued during the period."[64] With his sample in hand, he did what no one had thought to do before—he culled the opinions for the negligence doctrines and recognized that the cases were decided based on economic factors. Economic analysis, it turned out, got closer to the heart of the predictability theme of the common law than the traditional approach based on judicial opinion language. That language gave way to a method of understanding the relationship of economic factors to each other.

Economic Analysis of Law

Now in its ninth edition and extending to 1,056 pages of text, *Economic Analysis of Law* in the first edition of 1972 ran to 395 pages. All told, the various editions have sold some one hundred thousand copies.[65] Posner wrote *Economic Analysis of Law* in the summer months of 1972 and sent the manuscript to eleven fellow academics for comment. He singles out economist Harold Demsetz for special acknowledgment for the contributions he had made in conversation with Posner and in a 1970 seminar on property rights that Demsetz had given at the University of Chicago. In a like manner, Posner acknowledges Director's influence for the analysis found in the antitrust chapter. His greatest debt, according to the preface, "is to those who through their writings and conversation have enriched my general understanding of economic theory and of the relationship of economics to law: Gary S. Becker, Ronald H. Coase, Aaron Director, and George J. Stigler."[66] The book explores the application of economic theory to the legal system and considers a wide range of topics, such as property rights and liability rules, contracts, antitrust and public utility regulation, price controls, corporations, the regulation of capital markets, taxation, strategies for reducing poverty, racial discrimination, freedom of speech, the criminal sanction, legal procedure, and the administrative process. Its method asks two questions of each topic. The first is whether economic theory explains the relevant legal rule or practice. The second is whether economic theory can suggest worthwhile reforms in the law. The book engages readers in a way of thinking about law, about what animates it. The preface states that he wants to force readers, most of them law students, "to confront economics not as a body of abstract theory but as a practical tool of analyses with a remarkably broad application to the varied problems of the legal system."[67] His textbook approach is better suited for the task of teaching economic analysis of law over a book of readings in the subject, he explained in a letter, because, beyond the incompleteness of the field itself, "many of the best things in the literature are unreadable by law students."[68] What he had tried to do in the book, he explained, "was to give the field a sense of coherence and perspective by attempting to fill in—often superficially to be sure—some of the conspicuous gaps in the existing literature." Lastly, he added that "in teaching from readings it is awfully easy to get deflected from talking about the problems to talking about the authors."[69] His book, in contrast, as he declares in his preface, seeks to weave "exposition of the relevant economic principles into a systematic (although necessarily incomplete) survey of the rules and institutions of the legal system."[70]

Posner acknowledges in his preface that there are limitations to the economic analysis of law. In a paragraph on how the book should be used by instructors he explains that, because the text is likely to be sufficiently clear, instructors will not need to take classroom time to translate ideas into simpler terms and spend class time probing the students' understanding. Instructors will "also want to use class time to explore the limitations of economic analysis as both an interpretive and normative tool."[71] He gave a further explanation as to what he meant by limitations when he wrote to former Stanford colleague Charles Meyers that one of the book's goals was to provoke. He expected "a major portion of class time to be devoted to challenges by students and in some cases by the instructor, to the utility, decency, etc. of using economic analysis and to the soundness of the policy proposals with which the book is so liberally sprinkled. The book is intended to be provocative, and I predict that many students will find it provoking. I have deliberately downplayed the limitations of economic analysis (although I concede it has many), in order to give students and/or instructors an attractive target for classroom discussion."[72] The book's appeal was not limited to law students with little or no knowledge of economics, though. He was writing as well for lawyers and economists, since his book went beyond a summary of the literature of economic analysis of law, in places adding to it.

The book was reviewed in a variety of journals.[73] Peter Diamond, an economics professor, objected to the shortage of economics in the book.[74] Gordon Tullock, who had himself written a book applying economics to law, complained that he could not find himself in the index, though he acknowledged that his book, which sought to apply welfare economics "to a deduction of the basic principles of a desirable law code," might not have helped Posner much.[75] Malcolm Feeley pointed out that the argument that common-law judges seek efficiency in their analyses overlooks the limitations of judges, who are not well equipped to handle the intricacies of cost-benefit analysis.[76] Economist A. Mitchell Polinsky argued that Posner failed to grapple adequately with transaction costs that affect his efficient rational man premise and that he ignored redistribution costs. The assumptions Posner builds into his competitive market paradigm are likely to fail, he writes, and one should proceed with caution lest the reader believe all that Posner has declared to be part of the efficiency theory. This leads Polinsky to unkindly title his piece "Economic Analysis as a Potentially Defective Product: A Buyer's Guide to Posner's *Economic Analysis of Law*."[77] The book's premise, that man is a rational maximizer of his self-interest, was too much for Arthur Miller, as was Posner's complete conviction about the assumptions animating his analysis. "The efforts of the Posners of the law school world to reduce the buzzing, booming confusion of life to their neat little economic categories simply will not wash," Miller writes.[78] Lastly, Miller notices the mere two-page concluding chapter in which Posner develops the idea that, in Posner's words, "it may be possible to deduce the basic formal characteristics of law itself from economic theory," and writes, "What chutzpah."[79]

Arthur Leff in his review like Miller derides Posner's two-page chapter, quoting the same sentence from the conclusion and snarks, "What bliss." But there is far more than snideness to Leff's view. Leff likens Posner's tour of the legal countryside to a picaresque novel, with Posner following his hero, economic analysis, from one town to the next, from one adventure in economic analysis to the next. Though not noted, this insight into the book's structure juxtaposes the buoyant, comic tone of a picaresque novel such as Henry Fielding's *Tom Jones* with the despair that Leff sees at the core of Posner's *Economic Analysis of Law*. While Leff seems to admire, on one level, what Posner has done, what Posner is advancing troubles Leff and leads him to hold him up for ridicule, even personalizing the attack. He complains that Posner looks only at empirical economic data and ignores other disciplines such as anthropology, psychology, and sociology. This leads to what Leff describes as "four hundred pages of tunnel vision."[80] There is for him a circularity at the heart of the value system Posner promotes. "Thus what people do is good, and its goodness can be determined by looking at what it is they do." Leff rejects the efficiency- or wealth-rationalizing man because, as he puts it, "we all know that all value is not a function of willingness to pay." Posner's "grievous mistake" is "to use a tone which implies (while the words deny) that it is."[81] "If economic efficiency is part of the common law," he writes, "so is *fiat justitia, ruat coelum*"[82] ("May justice be done though the heavens may fall").

Posner did not seem to see whatever darkness others might have seen in Leff's review, or if he did, it did not trouble him. A friend wrote to express sympathy at Leff's negative judgment, to which Posner responded that the review seemed flattering.[83] "I am delighted that the book has caused a stir," he wrote back, "and the sorts of criticism to which it has been subjected, both in print and in conversation, are not the sorts of criticism that disturb an author."[84]

Strategies

Strategies for converting those beyond Chicago's walls involved getting the word out, both written and spoken. Beyond Posner's strategies for founding the *Journal of Legal Studies* and for writing and pushing *Economic Analysis of Law*, he seems to have had a fully worked-out publication strategy. Part of that strategy was to avoid law reviews for the most part and publish in faculty-edited journals, especially those at the University of Chicago, including his own *Journal of Legal Studies*. He turned down an invitation to give the Marx Lectures at the University of Cincinnati in 1980, for example, because his lectures would be published in the school's law review. He wrote to the school's dean and explained that that would not be advantageous. "My work," he explained, "is addressed at least as much to economists as to lawyers, and economists are not able to obtain law reviews other than those published at a handful of the best-known law schools. Even many law professors nowadays largely confine their literature searches to the major reviews. That is a fact of life, regrettable as it may be. While in the past I have given some 'tied' lectures—tied to publication in the law review of the school sponsoring it—I have decided that this is, at least for me, an unwise publication strategy."[85] The exception to the rule about law reviews was the *University of Chicago Law Review*, with nine articles in the 1969–81 period. He published a total of forty-two papers in University of Chicago faculty-edited journals during the same period. His favorite non-Chicago faculty-edited journal was the *Bell Journal*, edited by Paul McAvoy, where he published four times. Posner's strategy was also linked to the economic analysis he was doing with Lexecon, his consulting firm. Studies conducted for two clients had sufficient academic appeal that revised versions were published, one in the *Bell Journal*[86] and the other in the *Harvard Law Review*.[87]

Articles

There was much to be written at Chicago. First Posner needed to complete the work on antitrust and regulatory issues he had started at Stanford with his articles on oligopoly and natural monopoly. In 1969 Posner was part of an American Bar Association commission to study the Federal Trade Commission. The commission concluded that the FTC was badly run(there was not enough planning and too much petty infighting among the commissioners themselves, and staff members were not up to the challenges of the job) but that its structure and statutory objectives were sound. This was not enough for Posner and led him to put into the commission's report a separate statement that had "nothing good to say about the FTC."[88] Some of the members of the ABA commission wanted to suppress his separate statement. Posner built on it later that same year for an article in the *University of Chicago Law Review*.[89] The article noted that the FTC had long been a target of criticism that had failed to ask fundamental questions about whether the work that the FTC did—the goods that it produced, so to speak— was worth its costs. Posner looked at a year's worth of the FTC's cases to argue that in antitrust and restraint-of-trade matters the Department of Justice was the better-suited enforcement arm of the government and that on fraudulent conduct cases the FTC was doing nothing that the courts could not do—if, Posner suggests, anything needs to be done at all. "If the analysis presented in this article is correct," he concludes, "there is no salutary role for a federal trade commission. What is required is not redirection, but reduction."[90] "I would urge," he continues, "that more attention be given to reliance on market processes, and on the system of judicial rights and remedies that provides the framework of transactions in the market, as an alternative to the Trade Commission."[91] Looking to the market and to the Department of Justice rather than the FTC would not, however, eliminate all restraints of trade or all frauds. That the market and the Department of Justice cannot promise complete success is no argument, though, for an administrative agency as an alternative, especially given the evidence available of the FTC's performance. "On what evidence we have, the costs of having a federal trade commission appear to exceed the benefits."[92] In 2005 he revisited the FTC—and by extension the ABA commission's report and his law review article—and was delighted to note that the report had been effective in getting higher-quality commissioners appointed, a higher-quality staff hired, and even a change in ideology that made the FTC fonder of free markets.[93] His assessment was that the FTC could continue so long as it did not "become complacent and cease striving to contribute to the nation's prosperity."

Continuing with regulation, in 1970 he considered cable television and the problem of local monopoly in a thirty-five-page discussion paper that assessed the costs and benefits of local regulation and considered the idea that there should be no regulation at all.[94] He consulted with the Department of Health, Education and Welfare and wrote a paper on cost and demand for the department, revised for publication in a law review, analyzing five of the thirteen bills pending before Congress on national health insurance plans.[95] Another paper, written with Charles Meyer of Stanford, resulted from a study funded by the National Water Commission to consider transfers of water rights in the American West. It argued, not surprisingly, for allocations to be made as a function of market forces and their interest in efficiency, in contrast to allocations determined by administrative systems.[96]

He published articles in 1971 and 1974 in the *Bell Journal*.[97] The later article built on the earlier and considered the progress empirical studies had made in the promising theory of economic regulation. The economic theory, unlike so-called public interest theory and capture theory, would gain validity only to the extent that empirical studies of various industries and their regulation supported it. Regulation had to be explained as "the outcome of the forces of demand and supply. Outcomes that cannot be so explained count as evidence against the theory." George Stigler was the first to propose the economic theory of regulation in 1971 and to argue, as Posner describes it, that regulation is to be understood "as a product allocated in accordance with basic principles of supply and demand."[98] In sorting through the empirical studies Posner found reason to think that the economic regulation theory had legs. More studies needed to be done. In an amusing aside, the editor sent Posner a letter complaining that he had too often cited himself in the article. Posner answered that he pretty much had to cite himself because he had written most of the secondary literature. He relegated himself to footnotes, he said, while discussing Stigler and others in the text. Acknowledging though that he understood the editor's point, he wrote that he would try to comply in the future.[99]

He contributed in 1971 to a symposium on the regulation of the burgeoning interest in computers and its implications for telecommunications, presenting his no-regulation approach, to the surprise of fellow participants.[100] His direct challenge and crisp economic argument against regulation led to an apparent bristling of egos and temperaments.

Not much was different at a 1972 conference titled "Regulating Health Facilities Construction," the proceedings of which were published under the same title.[101] Here the major issue was so-called state-issued certificates of need, much in vogue at the time, necessary for new hospital construction. Posner provided, unsurprisingly, a dissenting view. It was unsound, he argued, to treat healthcare providers as public utilities and regulate them as such. Public utilities regulation had been a failure, so it made no sense to repeat the mistake with healthcare providers. More to the point, healthcare providers were sufficiently unlike public utilities to essentially guarantee regulatory failure. It had been assumed at the conference that there must be controls over hospital construction. No case had been made for construction controls specifically or for other relevant regulation generally, Posner argued, so the matter should die there, while market forces lived on. As was true in the conference on the computer industry and regulation, in the discussion period Posner was again brutal in exposing weak arguments, as when he says of one participant that if you strip his "comments of their endearing, jocular tone, there is no logical or factual core."[102]

The last two forays into regulation were pamphlets published by the American Enterprise Institute as part of its Evaluative Studies in Government Regulation series. Ronald Coase and Milton Friedman of Chicago were on the advisory board of the AEI. Posner published *Regulation of Advertising by the FTC* in 1973 and argued, as he had elsewhere, that in matters of advertising specifically the FTC was not suited for the regulatory task and that advertising as an original matter did not need to be regulated.[103] In 1976 he wrote on federal regulation of price differences in the Robinson-Patman Act (legislation passed in 1935 to fight the menace of downward price flexibility after the Supreme Court had struck down the National Industry Recovery Act) which had been used to curb deflation.[104] Posner considered the utility of the legislation and concluded that it should either be repealed as ineffective or, if left on the books, not enforced. Posner's contribution to the voices of repeal was to attempt an evaluation, even though there was not much hard data available, of the Act and its enforcement. His view was that price discrimination issues fell within the Sherman Act's jurisdiction and that "repeal would allow the problem of price discrimination to be approached in the incremental and evolutionary fashion of judicial interpretation of the Sherman Act."[105]

On antitrust, one article was a statistical study of antitrust enforcement he had taken on at the suggestion of both Director and Stigler.[106] It looked at all the antitrust cases instituted by the Department of Justice since 1890 as reported in a series of volumes published by Commerce Clearing House. Posner analyzed them along many fronts—the number of cases, won-loss record, choice of civil or criminal remedy, and length of proceeding—as part of a damning analysis criticizing the division for being inefficient and for ignoring the prerequisites—especially statistical prerequisites—of serious planning. His conclusion was that the division should be run as a business but wasn't.

The argument Posner had made in 1969 against the FTC, when he all but called for its dismantling, took on whirlwind proportions when in "A Program for the Antitrust Division" just a year later he set out a program to clean house and reorient the mission of the Antitrust Division.[107] He wanted to reorganize it along the lines of an enterprise applying a cost-benefit analysis, an approach that "may be viewed as seeking to maximize the efficiency of antitrust enforcement by discovering and implementing those policies whose net social product is largest.[108] Like his study of the Federal Trade Commission, this analysis of the Antitrust Division reflected a marked tone of *the author knows best*. Its premise, as he acknowledges, is presumptuous, an assessment reinforced by a footnote in the section of the paper outlining possible reforms stating that the discussion relies heavily on the author's personal experiences in government, in which his various assignments "provided an opportunity to observe the Antitrust Division from several perspectives, always somewhat detached."[109]

Giving himself the role of writing as a Supreme Court analyst, Posner looked at the Court's antitrust jurisprudence in six articles from 1975 to 1981. All evaluated the Court's performance in antitrust cases, three explicitly so and three as part of larger topics. The two articles from 1975 are larger and speech-adapted versions of each other.[110] He tracked developing jurisprudential doctrines and criticized the Court's work for not being animated by theory and for not giving the bar the guidance that comes with precise opinions. Judging by the remarks of the moderator thanking him, Posner seemed to have surprised the audience with his candid comments that the Justices seemed to be out of their depth in antitrust cases and that they compounded their ignorance by relying on law clerks to write their opinions, making it difficult for the bar to know what each Justice actually thought about antitrust. The plaintiff-leaning decisions of the Warren Court made matters worse, with one exception, Justice Brennan's opinion in *Philadelphia National Bank*.[111] That opinion was grounded in an understanding of oligopoly and economic theory and set out quantifiable measures of forbidden concentration to guide the bar: "[o]ne must have clear rules, and they will inevitably have a quantitative dimension."[112] He sharply criticized the Supreme Court for ignoring the government's arguments in *United States v. Von's Grocery Co.*[113] (a case he had argued for the government) and fashioning a result unrelated to what the government suggested.[114] That it was more than the government had asked for did not justify the result. In the article that went with Posner's talk at the 1978 annual meeting of the antitrust section on the Burger Court and antitrust,[115] Posner gave good marks for the improved craftsmanship of the Burger Court antitrust opinions and for recognizing that antitrust was not related to Jeffersonian democracy. The problem the Burger Court faced, he explained, was that it had not had many antitrust cases in which to beat back any of the Warren Court's plaintiff-oriented approaches. If nothing else, the Burger Court was trying to give lawyers what they wanted in judicial opinions—"consistency, candor, proper deference to precedent and legislative history, and awareness of the limitations of the judicial branch."[116]

Holding up the *Philadelphia National Bank* decision as the high-water mark of right-minded antitrust jurisprudence might have raised eyebrows if it had been disclosed that Posner had written it. His declaration that the Court had gotten it right in *National Bank* and that the decision should have become a model for the Court's antitrust jurisprudence to follow suggests, of course, that Posner had figured out the right path to follow. The suggestion is compounded with his description of the Court's ruling in *Von's* and his irritated bewilderment that the Court had not followed the path that the Solicitor General's Office—the office in charge of shaping the government's antitrust policy—had set out in Posner's brief and oral argument in the case, since it was far better suited than the Court for analyzing antitrust. It seems that Posner in the mid-1970s articles on antitrust was saying that we would not have all these problems in antitrust if the Court had just followed what he had done in *Philadelphia National Bank* and then what he told the Court to do in *Von's*. That he delighted in "flaying" the High Court,[117] as he put it, gives away the intention. Posner stayed with the personal, it should be noted, in his next article on antitrust, a reflection on the *Sylvania* per se vertical restrictions decision that had overruled *Schwinn*,[118] a case which he also had briefed and argued for the government. That he had been involved with *Schwinn* was only part of his personal interest, though. He had changed his views in the year following *Schwinn* on when nonprice restrictions on dealer competition as part of a sales contract would be illegal per se and was pleased to report that the Supreme Court in *Sylvania* had followed his lead by citing his academic writing and coming around to his new point of view that such restrictions are not per se illegal.[119]

More and Somewhat Different Economic Analysis

Posner returned to economic analysis themes and arguments beginning in 1975 with an article arguing for the benefits of economic analysis of law and indicating ways in which it could be more fully integrated in the law school structure.[120] He recited the history of economic analysis, described some of its basic insights, suggested areas for future research, argued for its place in a student's law school education, and responded to major criticisms of the economic approach. He did not use the phrase "wealth maximization" in the article. He recognized nonetheless that economic analysis might be strong stuff for lawyers to stomach and that "the idea that the logic of the law is really economics is, of course, repulsive to many academic lawyers, who see in it an attempt by practitioners of an alien discipline to wrest their field from them."[121]

Posner used the term "wealth maximization" in "Utilitarianism, Economics, and Legal Theory," his contribution to the 1979 symposium

"Change in the Common Law: Legal and Economic Perspectives," hosted by the *Journal of Legal Studies*, as part of an argument or explanation that economic analysis of law is different from much-discredited utilitarianism.[122] The goal of economic analysis, wealth maximization, was different from utilitarianism's single goal of promoting happiness. "Wealth is the value in dollars or dollar equivalents of everything in society. It is measured by what people are willing to pay for something or, if they already own it, what they demand in money to give it up. The only kind of preference that counts in a system of wealth maximization is thus one backed up by money—in other words, that is registered in a market."[123] Ronald Dworkin, also a participant in the symposium, rejected Posner's approach, giving his essay the title "Is Wealth a Value?" and arguing that it is not and that the only person who would make such an argument would be the kind of person who thinks that the person with the most money is the happiest.[124] Those present at the conference describe the exchanges between Dworkin and Posner as an epic battle, waged for high stakes. Some say Dworkin handily won the impromptu debate, dazzling the attendees with his smooth, courtly, and urbane debating skills. Richard Epstein, who might have been cheering Dworkin on as he took on Posner, a rival of sorts for him, noted in writing a tribute upon Dworkin's death in 2013 that he had attended the 1979 conference, "where these two giants squared off on the issue [of wealth maximization]. Dworkin's skill and daring in argument carried the day, I thought, in a rhetorical feat that I have rarely seen equaled anywhere else."[125] Dworkin had a knack for the apt, even if familiar, analogy. Stephen Williams, now a senior judge on the District of Columbia Circuit Court of Appeals, was at the conference and remembers Dworkin saying that "Posner was like a man looking for his lost keys under the lamppost because that's where the light is best."[126] Law professor Randy Barnett was also at the conference and notes that Posner did not recognize he was losing and just kept coming at Dworkin.

The next year, the two presented papers again in the symposium setting to argue, helmets flashing, as Homer might say, one more time about wealth maximization. Posner began with a reference to his Chicago symposium paper, writing, "In a recent article I argued that a society which aims at maximizing wealth, unlike a society which aims at maximizing utility (happiness), will produce an ethically attractive combination of happiness, of rights (to liberty and property), and of sharing with the less fortunate members of society."[127] Then comes the dismissive, "Evidently, I did not explain adequately why this combination was ethically attractive."[128] He seems both bored and irritated to have to go through the arguments again, but go through them he must. The critics, though, remained unimpressed.

Having staked himself to this battle rather than to a more general one about the usefulness of economic analysis, despite its limitations—as described in the preface to the first edition of *Economic Analysis of Law* and in correspondence of the time about the book—Posner was forced to retreat, or modify his claims somewhat. He acknowledges in *The Problems of Jurisprudence* that he had been wrong and wants to consider the dimensions of what he had been wrong about. He opens with the idea that "the normative theory has been highly contentious in its own right" and then gives full credit to his opponents, writing that "most contributors to the debate over it conclude that it is a bad theory, and although many of the criticisms can be answered, several cannot be, and it is those I shall focus on."[129]

He is even more explicit in acknowledging that Dworkin in the wealth maximization debate had been very convincing. In an interview published in 2012 as part of James Hackney's *Legal Intellectuals in Conversation* Posner was asked about the change with regard to rights theory from the time of his early writings to when he became a pragmatist. He answered that he had been "very dogmatic about the application of economics in a very pure form" when he first started off and that he modified his views, "partly because I got very good criticism from Dworkin in his article 'Is Wealth a Value?' That was pretty convincing." He goes on to say that "being a judge, now for twenty-five years, has taken off some of the hard edges of my thinking."[130]

Books

There were more books following *Economic Analysis of Law* and more book strategies. One was to bring out an expanded second edition of *Economic Analysis of Law* in 1977. Though it updated the first edition of just four years earlier, an apparent change in Posner's view toward

Bentham's utilitarianism—which links morality to the greatest happiness of the greatest number—marks perhaps the biggest difference between the first and second editions. In the first edition Posner had written that "Bentham's utilitarianism, in its aspect as a positive theory of human behavior, is another name for economic theory."[131] This sentence was deleted in the second edition, allowing Posner to distinguish his wealth maximization approach from Bentham's utilitarianism. A second strategy was to publish in 1979 with Little, Brown and Company (which had published Posner's *Economic Analysis of Law*) *The Economics of Contract Law*, a collection of essays by various authors on different contract doctrines along with essays on the economic basis of contract law that would supplement a contracts casebook that a law student might be using.[132] Posner contributed essays to the volume that he had written or cowritten on gratuitous promises, unilateral and implied contracts, and the impossibility doctrine.

The last and perhaps the most important strategy for spreading the word of economic analysis via books came in the publication of *Antitrust Law: An Economic Perspective*[133] in 1976 and the publication in 1981 of *Economics of Justice*.[134] In both Posner used the strategy of taking already published articles, rewriting them to some extent, and fashioning them into theme-based books.

ANTITRUST LAW: AN ECONOMIC PERSPECTIVE

This was the first of many books in which Posner recycled but also rewrote previously published articles. Posner recognized in the antitrust articles he had been writing for seven years that he had a "thorough dissatisfaction with the existing state of antitrust" and that his book represented "a reasonably detailed blueprint for its overhaul."[135] The proper purpose of antitrust laws, he asserted, was to promote competition, as competition is defined in economics. His book was about economics and its relevance to antitrust law and its administration. He was asserting sometimes surprising implications of economic analysis, leading to proposed fundamental changes "in antitrust principles governing collusion, mergers, exchanges of information among competitors, restrictions on competition in the distribution of products, monopolization, boycotts, and other traditional areas of antitrust doctrine."[136] If nothing else, the proposals needed to be reckoned with. He explicitly wanted to reach a larger audience than the scholarly audience his various articles had reached and reworked the articles to make them more accessible, a fact noted by nearly all of the many reviews, though with at least one reservation. "We must acknowledge that unlike some in the field, he knows how to write," noted Thomas Kauper, himself head of the Antitrust Division from 1972 to 1976, in the first paragraph of his thirty-six-page review in the *Michigan Law Review*, "although his style has a pontifical quality from time to time."[137] Another important antitrust figure to weigh in was Bill Baxter, a future head of the Antitrust Division under President Reagan, whose review stresses the book's readability and its sophisticated presentation of both legal and economic positions.[138]

That the book is a revision of collected articles on antitrust poses a problem for some readers more than others. Terry Calavini in his review begins with what seems to be a lament that the book incorporates articles that have already been published, but then he sees them as representing Posner's collective scholarship on antitrust, which he considers to be the book's major value.[139] Others are more critical. The book's treatment of its topics is uneven, Kauper points out, yet the reader deserves to have each be developed thoroughly. According to Kauper, this flaw stems from the choices Posner made in developing some ideas in article form and leaving others to cursory treatment in the book.[140] Peter Steiner writes that the book is not the cohesive discussion Posner wants us to think it is, but "bold, uneven, and idiosyncratic."[141] He blames Posner's prodigious output, noting that he is an "indefatigable writer, and, less laudably, a relentless publisher of what he writes."[142]

ECONOMICS OF JUSTICE

Posner in *Economics of Justice* brought together fourteen previously published articles, some with revisions but most without. He gave a broader scope to arguments on wealth maximization by including, along with his conference papers and response to Dworkin on wealth maximization, a lengthy paper on Bentham and Blackstone on the issue of people as rational maximizers of their satisfactions in all that they do. The second section broadens the scope of economic analysis historically and applies it to ancient and primitive cultures to show the economic theory at work. The operating facts of ancient Greek society are culled from Homer's epic poems and then pushed through the processor of economic analysis to show its application. Papers on an economic analysis of privacy and on the Supreme Court's jurisprudence on privacy make up the third section, while papers on *Bakke* and *DeFunis* are put together with a chapter from *Economic Analysis of Law* on the economics of discrimination to make up the fourth and last section.

The book was widely reviewed,[143] with many reviewers struggling with the book's organization and with Posner's wealth maximization argument. Posner saw "the meaning of justice, the origin of the state, primitive law, retribution, the right of privacy, defamation, racial discrimination, and affirmative action" all as issues fit for an economic approach that could not be cabined into studies of markets and their concepts or activities.[144] Reviewers, though, were skeptical. They were not persuaded by the argument of the introduction—that the "economist's basic analytical tool for studying markets will suggest the possibility of using economics more broadly"—was sufficient to fit together the disparate articles into a cohesive book.[145] Others thought the collected nature of the book had advantages despite weakening its cohesiveness and thematic unity. Not all reviewers thought Posner's forays into other disciplines were well taken. One reviewer considered Posner's explanation of the social and political order in Greek society as found in Homer, to say nothing of ancient and primitive societies generally, and remarks that such an explanation shows "remarkable academic chutzpah."[146]

Most reviewers in their substantive criticisms followed the lead of Dworkin in pointing to flaws in the wealth maximization idea that undergirds Posner's approach. But the reviewers presented criticisms on multiple fronts. Some were not for the faint-hearted. One reviewer concluded that "parody is always somewhat unfair. But Posner certainly invites it, with his vigorous, roughhewn exposition. There are no doubts here, no hesitation about the capacity of his approach to explain and prescribe. This is a book for the True Believer."[147] Another noted that Posner displayed a "flippant attitude towards substantial critiques," which the reviewer believed was explained by Posner's "deep belief in economics not just as a method but as a description of the world.[148] The book's sensibility was also an issue. Izhak Englard in the *Harvard Law Review* noted that "Posner's book displeases by its saddening soullessness. It knows nothing of human emotions, of laughter or of tears, of joy or of sorrow. Its cold intellectuality exhales a freezing chill onto the delicate fibers of human relations."[149] Aware of this response, one reviewer refers to the "virulence of the reaction" to Posner's articles on wealth maximization and their collection in *Economics of Justice*, noting that the reaction is "intriguing."[150] Posner is an "attractive target," the reviewer notes, because he has "an apparently willful coldness in assessing, among other things, the sometimes forbidding consequences of his own theories,"[151] such as his denial that "there is a broad social duty to support people who cannot support themselves. Some nonproductive people might therefore starve in a system guided by wealth maximization."[152] One reviewer writes that Posner "delights in his role of provocateur,"[153] and to be sure he makes assertions worthy of the provocateur. In a single paragraph Posner asserts that "an implication of the wealth maximizing approach . . . is that people who lack sufficient earning power to support even a minimum decent standard of living are entitled to no say in the allocation of resources unless they are part of the utility function of someone who has wealth" and that "if [a person] happens to be born feeble-minded and his net social product is negative he would have no right to the means of support even though there was nothing blameworthy in his inability to support himself."[154]

Proselytizing in Person

Another aspect of Posner's overall strategy as a proselytizer was to hit the road during the 1970s to give talks, to participate in conferences, to teach, and sometimes to schmooze. Published articles often followed. Aside from events already mentioned in passing, he attended in 1971 the annual meeting in Washington of antitrust section of the ABA. In 1972 he gave a talk at UCLA based on a draft *Economic Analysis of Law* chapter on constitutional law and got useful comments from Harold Demsetz. He also participated in a conference on government policy and the consumer put on by the University of Rochester Graduate School of Management and Henry Manne.[155] In 1973 he gave a talk on the economic theory of administrative regulation at the Kennedy School of Government. In 1974 he delivered a paper at Stanford. He delivered a paper at Columbia University as part of a conference on the problems of policy deconcentration.[156] He met with Irving Kristol in New York, which led to Posner agreeing to serve on the American Enterprise Institute Advisory Council. He delivered a talk to the Illinois Bar Association on proof of liability in price-fixing cases, went to the Association of American Law Schools meeting held at Harvard, and participated in a seminar for Norlin Music on compliance with antitrust laws.

He was even busier in 1975. He gave a lecture at Gonzaga University School of Law and a talk to the Philadelphia Society. He participated in the American Enterprise Institute roundtable on affirmative action in Washington.[157] He delivered a lecture at the University of Texas Law School on economic analysis.[158] He went to an AT&T seminar in New York and delivered a talk to the ABA meeting on antitrust.[159] In 1976 he met in Washington with the American Enterprise Institute Advisory Council. He addressed the Harvard Law School. He taught law and economics at a summer session at the University of Miami in a program run by Henry Manne. He participated in the Conference of Law and Economics Studies at Columbia University and presented a paper.[160] In 1977 he again taught at the University of Miami in the Miami Law and Economics Center. He presented a paper at the Boalt Law School's Law and Economics Workshop on the doctrine of impossibility in contract law.[161] In Washington he participated in an Antitrust Division seminar series, and also in Washington he participated in the Antitrust Law Briefing Conference sponsored by the Federal Bar Association.[162] In 1978 he delivered the John A. Sibley lecture at the University of Georgia.[163] He attended a conference on law in Sweden. He delivered a lecture at the University of Buffalo.[164] He taught again during the summer at the University of Miami School of Law, Law and Economics Center. At an antitrust conference at the University of Pennsylvania he delivered a paper.[165] In 1979 he gave a talk to the Jurisprudence Section of the American Association of Law Schools on economics in law.[166] He participated in a Hoover Institute conference on regulation, and he delivered an address to the Antitrust Law Section of the New York Bar Association.[167]

Consulting/Practice

With the success of his books, articles, lectures, and participation in conferences, Posner developed a busy practice and consulting sideline. This too was part of his proselytizing strategy.[168] As a consultant, he could be called in by a law firm to make sure that it was on the right path and not ignoring any legal land mines. As an appellate advocate he wrote the briefs and argued the *National Broiler* case in the Supreme Court.[169] There were many clients and many legal memoranda, briefs, and the like. He wrote a memorandum for Wells Fargo Fund Advisory Group explaining that the prudent-man rule should not be considered a bar to trustees' investing in the fund; he wrote a memorandum for American Airlines on capacity-limitation agreements arguing that the regulating agencies should not dismiss as unsound such agreements as part of a broader strategy to shake the Department of Transportation's confidence in its economic reasoning. For AT&T, the client for whom he did the most work, he wrote in 1975 a detailed memorandum entitled "The Government's Case against AT&T: An Exercise in Devil's Advocacy." He wrote memoranda on legal issues, such as jurisdiction, for AT&T, and in 1976 he wrote a twenty-nine-page trial brief for AT&T making the most of what he knew about antitrust to argue the case for AT&T. His work for AT&T continued once Lexecon was formed.

As reflected in his invoices, Posner worked for more than two dozen clients who were billed for more than 2,500 hours in his consulting work and legal practice between the beginning of 1974 and the first few months of 1978.[170] He worked 363 hours in 1974, 1,056 in 1975, and 429 hours in 1977. These last hours in 1977, the year in which Lexecon started up, were non-Lexecon hours. Hours were billed out at $75 per hour in the beginning and topped out at $100 per hour in 1977. In his hardest-working months, Posner averaged more than 200 hours per month, with 188, 197, and 267 hours in June, July, and October, respectively, of 1975 and 230 hours in December 1976. All told, Posner earned $35,930 in 1975, $99,821 in 1975, $79,189 in 1976, and $42,950 in 1977. The 1976 figure for billed hours does not include a fee of $10,000 for testimony before Congress on behalf of a client.

Lexecon

By 1977 Posner and Landes were both consulting with AT&T as part of its antitrust litigation with the federal government, though separately. Posner suggested they form a consulting firm together with Andrew Rosenfield, a recent University of Chicago Law School graduate who was also doing graduate work in the University's economics department.[171] Posner and Landes met with George Saunders, AT&T's top litigator—at a bar, no less—to check that starting the consulting firm would not jeopardize the consulting contracts that Posner and Landes each had in place. Getting the all-clear from Saunders, the three new partners met at Posner's house one night in the summer of 1977, and each wrote a check for $700. Landes came up with the name. They filed incorporation papers as Lexecon with the state of Illinois, using for this legal task Milton Shadur, later to become a federal district judge but at the time a partner in Devoe, Shadur & Krupp, a Chicago firm for which Posner had done extensive consulting for a few years. At first the partners worked out of their homes and their offices in the Law School, though once the consulting firm got sufficiently busy, they moved into small, modest office space adjacent to the office Rosenfield's father used for his law practice in downtown Chicago. There had been some talk of having an office in Hyde Park, but the consensus was that the firm needed a downtown presence.

Lexecon was one of the first consulting firms to offer clients economic analysis on antitrust and regulatory matters. The partners pitched their services not to companies, though, but to law firms handling antitrust and regulatory litigation, offering them assistance they could not find elsewhere. As William Landes in an autobiographical essay explains, "We could figure out what economic studies should be done, direct and supervise them efficiently, and, when needed, bring in other academic economists who had expertise and specialized knowledge in the areas being litigated."[172] These experts working with Lexecon entered into agreements in which they could charge whatever they saw fit as an hourly rate and be able to keep all of that rate minus a certain amount that went to Lexecon. In a 1978 agreement, for example, the amount was $25 per hour that Lexecon used to pay expenses and also for bonuses that might go to people working on a project. Using contacts Posner had developed in law school and then in his government work, the fledgling consulting firm set up presentations with the big law firms in the Northeast, Washington, and Chicago doing antitrust and regulatory litigation to explain not just that what Lexecon offered was unique but how it could help in litigation. Best of all from the point of view of the law firms being pitched, Lexecon posed no threat to them. Lexecon was not a law firm looking to poach clients. They were consultants with whom the firms could develop ongoing relationships, something that became important once the firm's effectiveness was shown. Law firms, as Lexecon's clients, understood that they were getting Posner. What he and Lexecon were offering was something no one else could—putting the power of economic analysis, with Posner as its voice, to unlock the core of a case with Posner's talents for clear exposition clarifying for jurors what would otherwise be an incomprehensible and jargon-filled fight between experts.

Lexecon was able soon enough to hire staff economists and others to work on the ever increasing number of projects needing analysis. Along with the experts who sometimes worked with Lexecon, a particular project could be worked on by staff, by one of the principals, and perhaps by George Stigler or another occasional expert with a staggering reputation. For client Pinny Dock in a monopoly case, for example, Lexecon conducted a study that provided the needed economic justification regarding allegations of exclusionary conduct. And in another example, Lexecon conducted an economic study for client Bayok Cigar to support, on the regulatory front, Bayok's merger with Outman Cigar. Lexecon would sometimes conduct analyses or studies and provide the client with a report or memorandum. For one regional airline, for example, Lexecon prepared a cost-benefit analysis of the airline's pending merger before the Civil Aeronautics Board considering how the airline industry would realign itself after national airline deregulation went into effect. In another example, Lexecon for a delivery service client prepared an economic study of the anticompetitive characteristics of the client's main rival, the US Postal Service's Express Mail service. The memorandum considered what happened when the postal service entered new geographic markets with the advantage it had in not having to comply with regulations that Lexecon's client needed to comply with. Lexecon analyzed just how big an advantage that gave the postal service. For AT&T Posner and Landes wrote a forty-one-page memorandum on tying issues, which occur when a seller conditions the sale or lease of one product or service on the customer's agreement to take a second product or service, in the government's case against AT&T. Posner also wrote a detailed explanation addressing the weaknesses in the AT&T case, which he and Christopher DeMuth, a Sidley Austin

lawyer working on the case for AT&T, presented to the Sidley litigators who would be trying the case, to no avail. It had been DeMuth,
a former student of Posner's at the University of Chicago Law School,
who had recruited Posner to work as a consultant to AT&T. They made
the argument that AT&T's case was not nearly as strong as the litigators
thought it was and that settlement was the best option, but the advice
was declined. Later Posner resigned as a consultant for AT&T.

Posner supported clients with expert testimony in different ways
while at Lexecon from 1977 to 1981. Sometimes he provided affidavits
on behalf of a client in support of a motion in the federal trial court.
Mostly, though, either by himself or with others from Lexecon, he gave
statements or testimony to congressional committees or regulatory
agencies on behalf of a client.

A great success for the three principals and for a market that needed
the kind of work it did, Lexecon did cause some problems for Posner.
Because Lexecon sometimes hired University of Chicago students who
were also working on projects as research assistants for faculty members
Posner and Landes, at one point the issue of whether the Law School
was paying for Lexecon work came up. Correspondence and supporting
documents in Posner's archive suggest that this was just an accounting
issue handled to everyone's satisfaction. A different type of problem was
caused by the very success of Lexecon, which was making a substantial
amount of money. This caused some tension among Law School faculty
members, with some thinking that it was bad form to make so much
money consulting.[173] One faculty member remembers having lunch in
the late 1970s with Edward Levi, former dean of the Law School and
president of the University of Chicago who had recently served as US
Attorney General in the Ford administration. Levi expressed fury at
Posner for his involvement with Lexecon and for a paper he had written
with Elizabeth Landes on an economic analysis of the infant adoption
market.[174]

Conflicts with the Law School occurred in a different way before
Lexecon had moved to its downtown office. That Lexecon was being
run out of the homes of the principals and out of Posner's office at the
Law School got the attention of administrators and led to a meeting in
which the associate dean told Posner he could no longer use his office to
conduct Lexecon business.[175] Nothing ever came of it for Posner—aside

from the disapproval of some colleagues, who were perhaps motivated by jealousy or resentment (traits that run fairly fast in academic circles).

Within a few years of starting Lexecon, Posner left full-time teaching to go to the Seventh Circuit. To take the bench, he needed to sever his connection with the firm, which was accomplished when his two partners bought out his interest for $400,000.[176] When Posner left at the end of 1981, Lexecon had about thirty employees and annual billings of about $5 million.[177]

Nomination

Making what he described as "a great deal of money" at Lexecon mattered when in the summer of 1981 Posner was approached by the Reagan administration about a circuit judgeship, with a substantial reduction in income from his consulting practice. He could accept a lower income in part because he would continue to teach and thereby supplement his income. He was also bored with consulting by the middle of 1981, with so much more of his time devoted to rainmaking than to working on projects, making the acceptance of the judgeship relatively simple. The offer had come by way of Bill Baxter, who had been named by Reagan as the head of the Antitrust Division of the Department of Justice and been given the special charge of trying to get high-powered conservatives on the court as a way of putting into practice the president's vision of the judiciary. Baxter sold Attorney General William French Smith on Posner, describing him as a libertarian, "a nineteenth century liberal." Posner and Baxter, we know, went back at least a dozen years, from the time they were on the Stanford faculty together for one year. That Baxter sat in on Posner's antitrust seminar at Stanford suggests that he saw something special in Posner. They stayed in touch and even worked together once Posner went to Chicago. Baxter reviewed Posner's *Antitrust: An Economic Perspective*. They exchanged papers they were writing for the other's review, worked together on one consulting project, and competed with each other to be hired on another, with Baxter prevailing. When Baxter was appointed head of the Antitrust Division, Posner wrote in February 1980 that he was "delighted—overjoyed, really—to read that you are going to be head of the Antitrust Division. Reagan couldn't have made a better choice." Then in June

1981 Baxter agreed to come to Chicago and speak at Posner's antitrust class. Baxter's call to Posner inquiring about his interest in joining the Seventh Circuit came the next month.

Another connection Posner had made at Stanford then also entered the picture, so that the decision to accept the offer was not just about financial considerations. Posner had met Aaron Director at Stanford in his 1968–69 year there and had enlisted in the good fight of law and economics that Director was part of. Posner took the fight to Chicago with a new strategy and with a missionary's zeal. He wrote to Director at the end of July 1981 and explained that he had been offered the slot on the Seventh Circuit and that it was likely that he would be confirmed. In a key, revealing passage reflecting his ambition, he says that he "was intrigued at the prospect of being a federal circuit judge and measuring myself against Learned Hand and Henry Friendly, better lawyers, but with less economics." Posner then writes that he hopes Director does not think of him as a deserter—a deserter to the cause of law and economics, we have to assume.[178] Awaiting confirmation, Posner read opinions by Oliver Wendell Holmes, Learned Hand, and Robert Jackson.[179] He took his seat on the Seventh Circuit on December 1, 1981.

For Posner, who believed he understood a way that law could work better, the opportunity to go onto the bench was fortunate. He would have the best of all worlds. He could continue to contribute his scholarly voice, writing books and articles, since judicial work not would monopolize him. More important, he could assume the role of active participant and directly affect, through votes and opinions, the law as it was being shaped. And because he wanted the world to come to his view of the importance of economic analysis, he could seek to persuade his new judicial colleagues to follow him, so as to further shape the law as he saw it—in his own image.

3

Making His Judicial Mark and Challenging Others (1982–1989)

THE THEN NINE-SEAT (IT now has twelve seats) Seventh Circuit in December 1981 when Posner joined it was not a particularly distinguished court. It was still reeling from seeing one of its members, Otto Kerner, who had formerly been governor of Illinois, led off to prison in 1974, the result of a bribery conviction. The court resembled those of the other circuit courts in the average age of its active members (sixty-three); the fraction of judges who had, prior to their appointment, served on federal district courts (between a third and half); and in the percentage of judges coming from elite law schools such as Harvard and Yale (about 30 percent). The Seventh Circuit when Posner arrived was also like all the other circuits, save one, in that its active judges were all men.

Posner was by far the youngest judge and was the only one without experience in private practice or as a district court judge. He was also the only academic on the court. Richard Cudahy, appointed to the Seventh Circuit by President Carter in 1979, was for about a decade Posner's chief ideological nemesis, with Luther Swygert, appointed way back in 1961 by President Kennedy, coming in second. Of the others, Joel Flaum, appointed the year after Posner, has most resisted Posner's push to have the Seventh Circuit feature economic analysis (this even though Flaum had also been appointed by a Republican president), while Frank Easterbrook, a former student of Posner's at the University of Chicago appointed in 1985, has followed Posner in style and substance. Today the court, with all of its changes over the years since Posner first joined it, divides between judges with law school teaching backgrounds and those with prior experience as district judges.

Starting In

Posner's first clerks describe the way work was handled within chambers.[1] For many years Posner had only two law clerks, each hired for one year, though circuit judges could have three. He expanded to three clerks in 2003, though circuit judges are now allowed four. Both law clerks read the briefs of the cases assigned randomly to Posner and set for oral argument as part of an appellate panel of three judges or, in the rare instances of en banc arguments before the court, the full complement of the circuit's active judges. This practice would continue when the number of clerks increased to three. The clerks did not write bench memos, which, after stating the facts and issues of a case, summarize the arguments of the lawyers and suggest questions to be explored at oral argument. Posner read the briefs and other supplementary submitted material, and like his clerks did not write bench memos. The law clerks did not talk between themselves about the briefs, waiting until they met with Posner to discuss the cases. This happened a week or so before argument. Each of the two law clerks would present his position as to how the case should be decided and then Posner would give his position. Then the three would debate the issues, with Posner insisting on a "no holds barred" approach to discussion. The clerks report that he could be swayed by their arguments. As one of the first clerks put it, Posner "absolutely welcomes free thought." That Posner insisted that his clerks call him "Dick" helped facilitate the free thought value. After the cases had been discussed, Posner and his clerks would read the bench memos that had been produced from the other chambers.

The clerks, who would attend the oral arguments, give some information on how Posner got on with the other circuit judges. Posner sometimes met with resistance from fellow panel members, while others were intimidated by him. He would not infrequently surprise the other two judges on the panel in argument with his questions. Other judges had a mocking nickname for Posner, referring to him as "The Judge of First Impression" because of the frequency with which he used that phrase in his opinions. In his first year he asked the chief judge for extra work but was told no.

One of the clerks from the 1980s described the sight and sound of Posner at work at the keyboard writing opinions assigned as a result of the meeting the judges had immediately following oral argument.

He would come in the day after an argument, walk through our offices with a wave to say hello, hang up his coat and hat. Then I would hear him sit down in his seat and turn on his word processor. A minute or so later, I would hear him start to type—the clicking of the keys at a steady, extraordinarily fast pace creating a steady whirring sound. Then he would pause. I could hear him take one of the casebooks off the rolling shelves we would stack around his desk in which he would flag cases and key passages. Silence for a few moments or minutes, then I'd hear him throw the book back on the shelf and another slide off, then another pause, then he'd throw that book back on, and this would continue for however many cases we had placed on the shelf, in rank order of importance. Then, the chair would squeak as he swiveled back around toward the word processor, and the steady whirring clicking of keys would start again. He worked in discrete, focused blocks of time. He would continue on a task until it was completed. So the morning might be spent on one of the opinions, and then a similar block of time on the second opinion assigned to him, before he would turn to working with some of the opinions which were now ready for expansion and editing.

Larry Lessig, who clerked for Posner at the end of the decade, relays Posner's position on where to draw the line between his judicial and academic lives. In a C-SPAN interview Lessig noted that Posner's ability to compartmentalize was "actually quite revealing about him, because you know he is the founder of the law and economics movement. I remember when I clerked for him, there were a number of times where there was a law and economics theoretical answer to the problem, and he would brush that aside and say, "The question for me is what the law requires, not what law and economics requires."[2] Posner's habit now was to write his opinions at home the evening of oral argument. "So he goes home," Lessig explains, "and comes back the next day with two thirty-page opinions with citations in them. He gives them to you, and your job is to write a critical memo. So I would write, you know, ferociously critical memos page by page, line by line, criticizing what he'd say. He'd take the note, he'd take his opinion, he'd do another draft, and we'd do this four or five or six times."[3]

Henry Friendly

In 1982 Posner began a correspondence with Henry Friendly that would develop into a friendship, approximately twenty years after their paths had crossed at Harvard when Friendly had delivered the Holmes lectures and Posner as president of the *Harvard Law Review* had published them there.[4] Friendly in the nearly twenty-five years between his appointment and striking up the correspondence with Posner had become the gold standard in federal appellate judging and was with Learned Hand one of the two judges against whom Posner wanted to measure himself as an appellate judge. He was a towering legal and intellectual figure, now in his early eighties. "He was the greatest appellate judge of his time—in analytic power, memory, and application perhaps of any time," Posner later wrote as part of his *Harvard Law Review* tribute. "His opinions have exhibited greater staying power than that of any of his contemporaries on the federal courts of appeal."[5]

Friendly was impressed by Posner from the beginning, and his regard for him and his work only increased as the correspondence developed. It starts modestly enough when Friendly writes of the first opinion Posner sent him that it "seems to me to be very surefooted, thoroughly reasoned and well written."[6] Two months later Friendly begins to indicate that there is something quite special about Posner's opinions. "The two opinions which you sent me," he writes, "were fascinating to me, particularly so since they dealt with problems with which I have long been concerned.... Please keep sending me these fine opinions."[7]

Then, two months later, Friendly struggles for the right description of Posner's style. The style is not quite breezy and not quite colloquial, he writes. "Anyway, it is 'distinctive.'"[8] At the close of 1983 he delivers the assessment from which he never withdrew. "Every one is a masterpiece of analysis, scholarship, and style," he wrote. "About a year ago I said you were already the best judge in the country; having uttered that superlative, I am baffled on how to better it. If I could think of a way, I would use it."[9] "How would we get along," he asked, "without judges who have the understanding of such matters that you do?"[10] About five months before his death, Friendly gave Posner what must be one of the greatest compliments a judicial writer can get, especially given Friendly's discerning taste. "As usual," he writes, "when I receive a letter from you with some of your opinions, I put an evening aside and turn to them as a welcome relief from the dullness of Law Weeks and most Second Circuit slips," referring to the slip opinions containing the most recent work of his colleagues.

The relationship that developed through correspondence after a few months sufficiently thrived that they began to meet every few months, or whenever Posner went to New York, where he had family. By May 1985 matters had intensified, such that Friendly suggested that a lunch would not be enough, writing, "your letter of May 9 and the enclosures require more than a letter in response. We ought to have not simply a luncheon but a day or two."[11] Lunches and sometimes dinner followed every few months. Their last lunch was on November 15, 1985. In his letter following it, Posner wrote, "I hope things are going well with you. I look forward to seeing you in March when I will be in New York next."[12]

Posner last saw Friendly a few days before Friendly committed suicide on March 11, 1986. Friendly lost his wife of fifty-five years in 1985, his health had continued to deteriorate, and by 1986 he worried about keeping up with his judicial work because of failing eyesight. His spirits were flagging and the prospect of seeing Posner brightened him. The last letter to Posner was written not by Friendly but by law clerk Tom Dagger on Friendly's behalf. Friendly by now had retreated to his apartment, which makes his eagerness to see Posner all the more poignant. "Judge Friendly asked me to send you this batch of his latest opinions, with the comment that he is fearful of rebuke from you over [one of them].[13] Judge Friendly is still at home while he waits for some eye trouble to clear up, and he would very much welcome a phone call from you if he is still at home when you come to New York in March."[14]

Posner might have been the last person to see Friendly alive. They met at Friendly's apartment, Posner recalls, "because he was suffering from dry eye and could hardly read and because of that impaired vision didn't want to go out."[15] As Posner was leaving, Friendly perhaps gave him a clue that he was going to commit suicide. As Posner describes it, "[Friendly] said two things that got me thinking. First, I noticed an odd photograph of a couple, with the woman holding a chimpanzee in her arms, and I said jokingly, Was that their child? Friendly didn't respond to the joke, but said that they were old friends of his, and that they had committed suicide together (I think he said because one or both of them were very ill, but I'm not sure), and that 'wasn't a bad idea.' The other thing he said was, when I was leaving and said I was looking forward to seeing him the next time I was in New York, he said he wasn't sure he'd be there, or he may even have said it wasn't likely he'd be there." "As I thought about what he'd said," he continues, "I began to think that maybe he was thinking of committing suicide. After thinking it over a few days, I was about to call his son-in-law, Frank Goodman, whom I knew, when I received the call from Friendly's clerk that he had died." Friendly biographer David Dorsen reports that Friendly had planned the suicide well in advance and had in fact told his family of his plans.[16]

Posner's Style and Approach to Law as Expressed in His Opinions

Little Posner had written as a professor, lawyer, or consultant prepares the reader for the whirlwind Posner appearing in the pages of the *Federal Reporter*. His academic work had generally followed the conventions followed by other law school professors for either law review or faculty-edited journals. But with judicial opinions he paid no attention to the recommended regimented structure, which in its traditional five-part structure moves an opinion from stating the issue to its conclusion, to the dispassionate if not objective tone that is considered necessary to give an opinion authority, and to the footnotes believed to denote scholarship. He has never used footnotes in his opinions. Opinions are for him about his engagement—his personal engagement—with the law as presented to him in the facts, issues, and case given to him to write about. On all fronts—from style, to tone, to his take on the issues—Posner's opinions are singularly his.

Posner's opinions show a flair for casual language, even slang. We find expressions such as "a shot in the dark,"[17] "goof-offs,"[18] "the joker in the deck,"[19] "having made his bed, [the taxpayer] must lie in it,"[20] "slice the bread awfully thin,"[21] "fought tooth and nail,"[22] "to reap where he has not sown,"[23] "a Mexican stand-off,"[24] "smoke out,"[25] "the roof caved in,"[26] "cuts little ice,"[27] "scotch the tactic,"[28] "the proof of the pudding was indeed in the eating,"[29] a "one-man band,"[30] "in cahoots,"[31] and "mumbo-jumbo,"[32] to list just a few examples.

The flair for casual language finds further expression with an interest in animals, so that we learn about "the tail on a large multiparty anti-trust donkey,"[33] a "tendency to cry wolf in judicial dissents,"[34] a party that "having swallowed the camel ... has strained at the gnat,"[35] "a choice between this bird in the hand and more than two birds in a very remote bush,"[36] "the equity tail wagg[ing] the legal dog,"[37] a cat that "had been out of the bag for a year,"[38] "another way to skin this cat,"[39] and a party "thrown to the dogs."[40]

Posner uses the full battery of allusions—literary, historical, cin-ematic, philosophical, and popular—though he is fondest of literary allusions. He uses them for color, authority, and even some flash. He uses them to support a joke, as part of a simile, as a hyperbolic example, and as shorthand when the allusion has widespread, recognized mean-ing. Occasionally he uses them to show life imitating art. He uses the academic wars of Mary McCarthy's novel *Groves of Academe* to illus-trate the phenomenon in a university employment case of professors using students in vendettas against other faculty members[41] and invokes Gertrude Stein and paraphrases her in a diversity jurisdiction analysis for the proposition that a corporation is a corporation is a corpora-tion.[42] He uses the grapes of Tantalus to explain that while expansions in habeas corpus help prisoners, the harmless error rules takes away any gains,[43] while Heraclitus's river ("always changing, yet always the same") helps explain that, while rosters may change from year to year, a professional sports team retains its essential identity.[44]

Then there's Shakespeare. In one representative example he wittily uses a well-known line from *Hamlet* to illustrate the point in an anti-trust case about what level of competition antitrust law is designed to maintain.[45] He explains that competition is not defined by keep-ing all competitors alive, as the plaintiff argued, but by only keeping a sufficient number alive for the best interests of the consumer. That a competitor (the sparrow in the allusion) withers, meets its fate, and leaves the competitive landscape is not cause for antitrust concern if sufficient competition remains. Put differently, "that 'there's a special providence in the fall of a sparrow,' *Hamlet,* Act V, sc. II, line 232, is not the contemporary philosophy of antitrust." In another he jolts the reader in a case involving a murder-for-hire plot in which a husband instructed that his wife be shot below the neck so as not to preclude an open-casket funeral.[46] "Thus," Posner writes, "does life imitate art; for Othello had told the sleeping Desdemona, 'Be thus when thou art dead, and I will kill thee, / And love thee after.'" Another allusion flashes illumination on one of the issues in a civil rights case brought by an Illinois resident against a police officer. The issue was whether the tort of false imprisonment applied as a result of the plaintiff's bond terms requiring him to remain in Illinois during the pendency of his case. Posner framed the issue by looking to Hamlet, explaining that, since the false imprisonment tort in Illinois does not require close confinement, it is possible that not being able to leave the state could have turned Illinois into a sort of prison for the plaintiff. "If Denmark was a dungeon to Hamlet (as the latter claimed), we suppose Illinois could be a prison to [plaintiff]."[47] But since the plaintiff could have left the state with leave of the court, having his own key to the prison door, so to speak, he was not sufficiently confined to trigger application of the false imprisonment tort.

He can be epigrammatical,[48] as in "Although the path to judicial review is strewn with thorns, it is not quite the impassable thicket that the government makes it out to be,"[49] and "Feelings of solidarity do not confer standing to sue."[50] Other examples include "The motto of the Prussian state—that everything which is not permitted is forbidden—is not a helpful guide to statutory interpretation" and "Tears wept for adversaries are crocodile tears."[51] "Correlation is not causation,"[52] we learn and "The Fourth Amendment does not expand accordion-like to fill what may be a gap in the privacy law of a particular state."[53]

Then there's evocative descriptive language of a sort not often seen in judicial writing. He writes in a criminal case, for example, of a "horrifying glimpse of the sordid and lethal world of modern prison gangs."[54] Describing a case that has gone on too long, he writes of "the leisurely manner in which the judge decided the case."[55] He captures in another a trial judge's tone and mood when he writes that his "exchanges with defense counsel show an occasional asperity"[56] and catches our eye in what should be a yawner with an opening assertion that the "facts are surprisingly lurid for a bankruptcy case."[57] He captures the scene in a tort case when he writes of "a gruesome accident, when plaintiff stepped into the corn head of a combine."[58] Ditto for facts in a criminal case that reflect "a lurid mixture of corruption and murder in a west suburban Chicago setting."[59] Strip joints in a zoning case are described as "tawdry enterprises."[60] In an Individuals with Disabilities Education Act case an unmanageable student with profound behavioral problems is described as "this unfortunate child."[61] He writes in a civil rights case about a prisoner who refused meals and smeared walls with blood and feces that "his behavior was disgusting."[62] A defendant is described as having a "frightening criminal history."[63] And an overwritten and overpleaded complaint is described as having "252 paragraphs which sprawl over 66 pages."[64]

In the manner of an essayist, Posner pauses to explain or define concepts, doctrine, or principles that he is discussing in the opinion at hand, giving the discussions additional grounding. The definitions can bear traces of his understanding of the relationship between law and economics, though of course not always. He explains in the 1980s, for example, abstention ("promoting a harmonious federal system by avoiding a collision between the federal courts and state (including local) legislatures")[65] and the difference between collateral estoppel and res judicata ("purpose is to reduce cost of litigation to all involved by forcing closely related claims to be combined in a single lawsuit").[66] His typical approach looks to history, purpose, and context to educate the reader as to the law as a function of a set of interrelated ideas.

And with an essayist's voice, Posner provides commentary for the reader to heighten the immediacy he seeks and the impression he wants of tracking his thinking process. It is not quite a stream-of-consciousness approach, and perhaps not metacommentary; it is commentary that stands out from the exposition and analysis that otherwise distinguish the opinions. Some commentary comes across as offhand, so that, for example, when the issue is the imperfect method by which prisons process inmates' name changes, he remarks parenthetically, "But all human institutions, indeed all human undertakings, are imperfect."[67] When stating that the purpose of jury instructions is communication and that spontaneity has a role in making the instructions more effective, he notes that "any lecture goer knows how deadly it can be to listen to someone reading a text word for word."[68] The issue of the similarity of maps to each other in a copyright context prompts him to observe about the case at hand that modern maps depicting the same area are not much different from each other, adding that "it would be most unsettling if, like medieval maps, they did not!"[69] And when the issue is the rough draft of a letter to be produced in discovery, it leads to the thought that "many rough drafts, like the unedited thoughts that run through people's minds, are pretty strange."[70] After describing how uncomfortable a deposition cross-examination can be, he notes that "the transcripts of depositions are often very ugly documents."[71]

He also comments on law revealingly, with free-wheeling reactions. His most general observations are that law "like politics is the art of the possible and often requires imperfect compromises" and that "the glory of the Anglo-American system of adjudication is that general principles are tested in the crucible of concrete controversies."[72] Mostly he is critical of American law as it is practiced. He writes about the ideal of the profession, which is to make law certain, and promotes stability as an important value in law.[73] Not shy with his criticisms, he notes "the fouled-up character of modern American criminal procedure."[74] The most repeated complaint is that American law is too complex and "should where possible be simplified,"[75] though simplicity in law is "perhaps a lost cause in the United States."[76] We read that the American system of criminal procedure has a "baroque structure."[77] As specific examples, we learn that the Fourth Amendment "abounds in fine distinctions, perhaps more than necessary,"[78] that "the law of habeas corpus is subtle and intricate,"[79] and that the jurisprudence of constitutional criminal law is confusing.[80] When an elderly woman is automatically jailed for a minor offense, he writes that "given the overcrowding of American jails, we venture to suggest that a practice of automatic incarceration of all arrested persons, regardless of circumstances, is as wasteful as it is uncivilized."[81]

He even addresses the reader on occasion. He is aware of times when he gets sucked into tedious analysis and, aware of what must be the reader's impatience, apologizes for being tedious.[82] His awareness of the dynamic between writer and reader shows in a case featuring both equitable tolling and equitable estoppel, for example, in which he comments, "We said that statute of limitations law is confusing, and now you'll believe us! And we're not through."[83] Going even further, in a slip-and-fall case in which the defendant, Wal-Mart, had in the district court tried to keep the opinion from being published, lest it set other plaintiffs' lawyers to thinking about suing, he addresses the company directly with a stinging rebuke: "And Wal-Mart, this decision, a reported appellate decision, unlike the decision of the district court, will have precedential authority."[84]

Commentary about oral arguments, an important part of the appellate process, shows lawyers sometimes succeeding but mostly failing and both irritating and occasionally astonishing the judges with what they say or fail to say. Premium praise is given to lawyers who are candid and recognize that it is better to be straight with the panel than to defend their clients at all costs. Lawyers are described as helpful when they answer questions, even though the answers cut against their arguments.[85] A lawyer's sin of refusing to acknowledge a damaging point is equaled by not knowing the case well enough to answer questions that go to facts not in the record. One lawyer, not knowing her case thoroughly, read in the published opinion that "counsel should come to an oral argument in this court prepared to supply all information material to our consideration of the appeal."[86] Lawyers caught out when trying to mislead the court come in for frequent comments. Sometimes the criticism is mild, as when the opinion states only that a particular assertion made by the lawyer was not supported by facts appearing in the briefs or record. On other occasions Posner goes to the record itself and reproduces that which the appellate lawyer had tried to pretend did not exist. Lawyers giving excuses not rooted in fact as to their performance do not fare well either. Some commentary goes to what might be called atmospherics, as when, as part of an argument to show that a company's "head of household" eligibility rule discriminated against women, a lawyer likened the effective bias to the fact that baldness affects men more than women. Jumping off the page is the description that in making the argument the plaintiff's lawyer was "staring fixedly at the members of this panel."[87] That the panel members, including Posner, were soldiers in the bald army did not need to be mentioned. Lawyers heeding intellectual honesty in argument receive fulsome praise. We read of a lawyer who conceded a point "with a frankness as refreshing as it is commendable"[88] and of another lawyer who answers with "captivating candor" when he acknowledges against his interest that a particular jury instruction should not have been given.[89] Lawyers only grudgingly conceding points nonetheless receive praise for bending.[90] But we learn of lawyers answering incoherently, evading questions, and being at a loss to answer questions. The highlight of the decade might be a bankruptcy lawyer asked a fundamental question about which creditors in his bankruptcy proceeding would be paid if additional money surfaced. "He surprised us (he is a bankruptcy lawyer, after all)," Posner writes, "by saying he didn't know."[91]

As he encounters the law in his cases Posner with a seemingly if-I-ruled-the-world sensibility either asserts his take on what the law should be or questions the reasoning that has led the law to develop in a particular way, all under the cover of the well-established phrase—a term of art almost—"as an original matter." In a group of cases, for example, he struggles with the litigiousness of prison inmates and the burdens they place on the federal courts under the "as an original matter" umbrella. In a free speech case in which an inmate claimed that his warden refused to transfer him to a lower-security facility as retaliation for letters he had written complaining about racial discrimination in disciplinary sanctions, Posner prefaces his analysis by doubting, as an original matter, "whether convicted criminals should have much if any freedom of speech within prison walls" but recognizes that the Supreme Court seems to take a different view.[92] He writes in a 1987 civil rights suit over the nature of a prisoner's confinement that "as an original matter one might question whether prisoners should be allowed to bring lawsuits complaining about prison discipline and the conditions of their confinement."[93] He acknowledges that there should be some control over what is in effect the unlimited discretion of prison officials and balances that control against the strain prisoner suits place on the federal courts, noting that in the prior year (1986) nearly twenty-one thousand prisoner civil rights suits were filed in the federal district courts. The implicit answer to the question he has asked "as an original matter" is that prisoners' complaints belong someplace other than in the federal courts. "However," moving to the submissive act of deference, he writes that "unless and until either Congress or the Supreme Court changes the ground rules that have evolved for this type of litigation, all judicial officers in this circuit must exert themselves to handle prisoner cases in conscientious compliance with these rules, complex as the rules have become."[94] In another case he questions whether prisoners validly convicted should be able to complain about disciplinary sanctions that affect what he describes as "the amenities of confinement."[95] And in a last case he writes in dissent to record his amazement that so many prisoner suits are filed, that counsel was appointed for the plaintiff inmate, and that it might seem bizarre, as an original matter, "to allow lawfully imprisoned convicts to spend their time bringing damage suits again their jailers, so that instead of reflecting on the wrongs they have done to society our convicts—exchanging as it were contrition for indignation—prosecute an endless series of mostly imaginary grievances against society," an observation followed by the necessary concession that the jurisdiction of the federal courts over the type of prisoner rights suit at issue is too well established to question.[96]

Not surprisingly, given his long-standing interest in pointing out a better way to do things, he makes suggestions to the responsible parties. In one case he tackles the issue he thinks needs consideration, even though resolution of the case before him does not require it, so that the Supreme Court will be in a better position to decide if it wants to take such a case.[97] If the Court does, his analysis can guide the Court. In an antitrust case he thinks it would be useful if the government put more effort into studying price concentration in the hospital industry.[98] He frequently has suggestions for Congress. He wants Congress, for example, to close a loophole in the Bankruptcy Code that could lead to mischief when the lien avoidance provision for tools of the trade interacts with the state exemption for the same. He suggests that a loophole in the code on tax avoidance be closed,[99] and he suggests that Congress or one of the federal rules committees clear up the ambiguity in the sentencing guidelines concerning multiple, piecemeal sentences and whether such sentences necessarily run concurrently with each other.[100] And unhappy, as we have seen, with the volume of prisoner litigation filed under the Federal Tort Claims Act, he suggests to Congress that it might want to make the mandatory administrative appeal first step required by the act be the exclusive remedy for prisoners when they bring claims that should be resolved in some version of small claims court.[101] The cases, of course, kept on coming, with Congress not having acted, and when another one came his way, this one for $50, the alleged value of a tennis shoe and some personal hygiene items, including toothpaste and baby powder, he ups his complaint, telling Congress that it "should give serious consideration" to the exclusive administrative remedy he had written about earlier. The $39.20 that was at issue in yet another case prompted the observation that "no rational system of government burdens its highest courts with a class of litigation dominated by petty cases typically brought for their nuisance value by persons on whose hands time hangs heavy."[102]

Posner takes advantage of opportunities to provide specific guidance to improve the performance of others. There is to be sure a customary appellate court practice when remanding a case to the trial court to offer guidance on issues that would be likely to come up,[103] but Posner takes the idea of guidance for the benefit of the district judges further and will identify issues that had not been raised on appeal that might crop up, and if there is a Supreme Court precedent that the district judge needs to consider, Posner will point it out.[104] He provides general guidance for district judges on a variety of issues. He advises them to approach claims of hypochondria in tort claims against the government "with a healthy skepticism necessary to prevent excessive and unfounded damage awards."[105] In an attorney's fees case being remanded to the district court, he makes some observations not just for the lawyers and judge in that case but for the bench and bar generally.[106] Still on attorney's fees, Posner offers district judges guidance on determining attorney's fees in class action cases, suggesting that the process could be simplified if the inquiry turned not on hourly rates but on the value for "the ensemble of services" that the lawyers provided.[107] When a jury instruction in one case is the issue, Posner gives a full explanation of what the instruction should accomplish, stopping short of writing the instruction himself.[108] And when an employment discrimination case is remanded for a new trial and requires an instruction on the issue of disparate impact, Posner provides a complete instruction for the judge to use if he chooses.[109] Going further, Posner in a debt collection case in which the issue was what is known as "safe harbor" wording in a collection letter so that collectors can avoid liability under the applicable federal statute, his opinion contains a complete letter for debt collectors to adopt, including salutation and closing. Debt collectors using the letter were not getting assurances that they were complying with other parts of the statute, but about the safe harbor provision they could feel pretty secure.[110]

As a distinguishable if not signature trait, Posner often moves off from the center line of the opinion to follow a related issue he had raised in a burst of explanation, only to return to the center line. These bursts of related explanation are dicta in that a case's holding does not flow from them, but they might also be called explication discursions, stream-of-consciousness musings, or spinnings. They share DNA with the many examples of explanation that we find in the opinions and sit upon the essay skeleton of his opinion structure.

He has done this hundreds of times, with no attempt to disguise these adventures in dicta as anything but what they are. That they veer away from the holding-related issue is signaled often by reference to alternatives and extensions of the thought at hand. Often we find an explicit signal taking us back to the opinion's center line. With metareflexiveness Posner will exhort himself back to the point. "Enough of the mysteries of laches," he writes in one case after wandering off, attracted to what he sees as a mystery. "But enough of this," he writes in another case, "no one questions the validity of the doctrine [of prioritization] in this proceeding."[111] "Enough! Damages are not the issue,"[112] he barks in another case—at himself, we have to assume.

Posner's "Enough!" reminds us that exclamation marks used to convey a judge's emotions are rare occurrences in judicial opinions. We encounter them fairly often in the pages of the *Federal Reporter*, almost always in two general ways: when a transcript is being quoted and when the exclamation mark is part of an entity's name, as in the E! Television network. Exclamation marks conveying a judge's emotion are rare because judges do not want to show emotion, certainly not excitement. But that is how Posner uses the exclamation mark, though the emotional level recorded is on the low side and is the written equivalent of arching an eyebrow. The mark helps us follow along in opinions that track his thinking process and, via the exclamation marks, his reactions to the subjects at hand. What is a rarity for others is commonplace for Posner. Over the years he has used the exclamation mark to convey emotions more than three hundred times. Others judges barely make it into double digits for a career. Henry Friendly used an exclamation mark once. Learned Hand never used one. The only other judge to use exclamation marks often is Frank Easterbrook, who in many ways follows Posner's approach to writing. He often writes opinions without footnotes in the manner of Posner, and he too is known to use engaging and less than formal language. Easterbrook, who joined the Seventh Circuit three years after Posner, has also used the mark more than three hundred times.

As to citation practices, we know that there is more to them than found in the *Bluebook* or other such manuals and that the authority a judge cites in an opinion can matter. In the same way that footnotes in scholarly books tell the sophisticated reader about the depth, level, and quality of research that an author has brought to the volume, citation practices reveal the citing judge's taste, values, and broader jurisprudential take on law. Judges singled out by name alone or by name and a quotation indicate that the opinion writer believes that the named judge has special standing and provides extra support for the point being made. Put differently, judges have reputations in a baseball card sort of way, making a Holmes more valuable than a Taney. The cards traded for and the judges cited reflect the citing judge's sense of judicial greatness.

If we look to Posner's own citation practices through 2014, a small group of judges get a disproportionate share of citations by name, giants all. Hand is cited 115 times (24 with quotations), Holmes 135 times (61 with quotations), and Friendly 47 times (16 with quotations). Posner's law clerks in their research are directed to note opinions by these judges. Hand is cited most often for his famous negligence formula (24 times), but he is also cited in the areas of criminal law (aiding and abetting and conspiracy mostly), copyright, trademark, patents, statutory interpretation, and monopoly. Friendly is cited most often on jurisdictional and standard-of-review issues, while Holmes is cited mostly for more general observations on law through quotations from his opinions, extrajudicial writings, and correspondence. Some favorites are that general propositions do not decide concrete cases,[113] that the only duty a contract imposes is to perform or pay damages,[114] and that the law is merely a prediction of what the courts will do.[115]

Posner also repeatedly cites some of the best-known English cases from the nineteenth century as part of explanations of various fundamental doctrines, such as *Raffles v. Wichelhaus*[116] (extrinsic ambiguity in contract law) nineteen times, *Gorris v. Scott*[117] (an injury resulting from the violation of a statute or other source of legal duty is actionable under tort law only if the statute was intended to avert the kind of injury that occurred) twelve times, *The Highwayman's Case*[118] (if opposing parties in a lawsuit are equally in the wrong and as a result neither has a colorable claim against the other, courts will not adjudicate their dispute) eight times, and *Burne v. Boadle*[119] (doctrine of res ipsa loquitur) six times. His citations give fresh currency to these cases, linking past and present. These cases make their points especially well; Posner writes, for example, that "as so often in tort law, an old case best illuminates the doctrine."[120]

He cites himself, though, more than any other judge, though not by name, recalling Holmes, who quipped that the primacy of authority moved from his own Supreme Court opinions, to his Massachusetts Supreme Court opinions, and finally to the opinions of his Supreme Court brethren.[121] Posner cites himself first if he has visited an issue before. Only if the US Supreme Court has precedent squarely on point will he cite that court first. Given the expansive nature of the Seventh Circuit's jurisdiction, these self-citations now touch nearly every area of the law. Posner rarely cites his own academic work, even when economic analysis is the issue, preferring to cite others, such as George Stigler, Ronald Coase, and Gary Becker.

Interpretation

He established his approach to statutory interpretation and its relationship to understanding language in his first years on the court and deepened that approach in the unfolding decades. His is the purposive style of interpretation rather than the rule-bound style that features literalism, plain meaning, and the canons of construction to understand what a statute means when the legislators have not thought ahead to changing circumstances or been as precise in their language as they could have been. This is called imaginative interpretation.[122] His starting point is not to fixate on words or clauses in question but to ask the broader question of the statute's purpose. Any judicial interpretation has to be consistent with that purpose. He recognizes the all-too-human aspect of legislating and in the process does away with the omniscient legislator and any idea that statutes are absolutely precise in their language and meaning. "Statutes," he writes, "are drafted in haste and sometimes carelessly, by busy legislators concerned with a particular problem but also concerned not to draft their statute so narrowly that it opens gaping loopholes."[123] With this in mind, legislative history loses its currency. More to the point, though, Posner in his premises asserts that judges in their heart of hearts know that "plain meaning" is not as simple as it sounds. They know that "the superficial clarity to which they are referring when they call the meaning of a statute 'plain' is treacherous footing for interpretation. They know that statutes are purposive utterances and that language is a slippery medium in which to encode a purpose."[124] This is not a new issue. It has been faced since Aristotle turned his attention to the problem, Posner tells us. Posner's insistence is on purpose and context. Resorting to definitions and dictionaries is no substitute for understanding the purpose of a statute, the context of a sentence, or even of a word. For him, rather than ask about the definition of a word, we need "to ask what is at stake in the definition."[125] We know that an appeal to plain meaning or to literalism cannot suffice with the simplest of examples, such as "KEEP OFF THE GRASS," which, read literally, would mean that even the groundskeeper would not be permitted onto the grass to cut it.[126]

He makes the point that his approach to interpretation has been recognized for at least 150 years and invokes Francis Lieber to support his position that "a text is merely a clue, though an essential one, to the meaning of a communication; that meaning is inferred from the text and its context rather than being 'in' the text in some simple sense."[127] Built into interpretation is the desire to avoid absurd results, as in the "KEEP OFF THE GRASS" example. As he did with his heart-of-hearts reference to judges knowing that plain meaning is far more complicated than they would otherwise let on, he states that literalists of statutory interpretation know full well that literal or strict construction, as he puts it, "misdescribes communication." Their interests, he explains, are "political rather than epistemological or hermeneutic," a way of cabining judicial interpretation. As he explains, "Perverse and absurd statutory interpretations are not to be adopted in the name of literalism; they merely show the limitations of literalism as a mode of interpretation."[128]

Using grammar and punctuation as a tool has limited usefulness for interpretation. It would be one thing if those who drafted legislation or contracts were grammarians, but they're not, so turning to a grammar text can hardly help.[129] The purposive, contextual approach to statutory interpretation of course is not limited to statutes; it applies to contracts and judicial opinions. Whatever the text, language works as a communicative tool only if "speaker and listener or reader share implicit contextual understandings rich enough to bridge the inevitable gaps in explicit communicating that economize on communication."[130] This approach leaps the literal approach, so that, as he explains, when you order a cup of coffee in a restaurant the waiter does not bring you coffee beans in a cup or a few drops of liquid coffee. Our assumptions break free of the literal.

Push for Economic Analysis

Posner wanted from the beginning to get the Seventh Circuit to accede to his views on economic analysis. Resistance to his push brought its own reaction from him, revealing the depth of Posner's commitment to bringing economic analysis into the law. For example, we best see the push, the resistance, and the reaction in *Roberts v. Sears, Roebuck and Company*,[131] a patent case early in Posner's tenure involving a humble quick-release socket wrench, for which Posner wrote the majority opinion and held that the patent was invalid because it failed the test of obviousness. Posner uses economic analysis to explain the principles of the obviousness test and explains that patents impose an economic drag because they confer a monopoly on the patented idea, which, "among its other effects, results in lower output of the monopolized product, and so reduces consumer welfare."[132] As a result, to keep from having patents exert an unnecessary drag on the economy, they should not be given for inventions that would have been made anyway, that is, without the patent, because such a patent would "confer no benefits that might offset the costs of monopoly." One reason to grant a monopoly is that the promise of the monopoly will induce inventors to devote the necessary time and resources for the invention, turning the question to whether the invention at issue is the kind that needed time and resources to develop. The socket wrench was not one of those inventions because prior patented inventions had led the socket wrench inventor to the door of his invention, so that if he didn't create the wrench, someone else would have. This is why the invention, distinguished by its obviousness, did not need patent protection and why the patent was invalid. In economic terms, "Patent protection would overcompensate the inventor in these circumstances and by so doing would draw both excessive resources into the making of minor improvements and impose unnecessary costs of monopoly on the community."[133]

The Seventh Circuit took up the case en banc and did not follow Posner's panel opinion and sent the case back to the trial judge on the patent issue. This frustrated Posner, as it was not clear to him what test the majority opinion had used for obviousness. It was too filled with generalities for him to be sure it followed his test (even if in a different verbal formulation), though in any event the majority opinion had not applied it to the facts at hand. He sensed a skittishness in the majority about his use of economic language, confronted the majority directly, and made his pitch for its use generally and in particular in patent cases turning on obviousness. "I know that many lawyers and judges find the language of economics repulsive. Yet the policies that have given shape to the patent statute are quintessentially economic, and the language of economics is therefore the natural language in which to articulate the test for obviousness."[134] It was not as though the majority had put forward a good alternative. Remarkable stuff. Here he was, new to the bench, lecturing his colleagues on their intellectual timidity. He was also frustrated that the en banc court wasn't willing to acknowledge that obviousness was an issue of law, declare the invention obvious, and be done with the case. The court did not have time for protracted litigation without merit, in Posner's opinion.[135]

The Hand Formula

Posner's principal doctrinal initiative in the decade (if not his entire time on the bench) was to apply the Hand Formula whenever he could in writing a majority opinion, which meant not just tort situations of the sort that spawned the theory but in all sorts of areas not usually associated with the implicit cost-benefit analysis of the formula. In *Carroll Towing*, Hand's famous admiralty case, a barge not properly secured had gotten loose from a pier and caused damage to some nearby boats, prompting Hand to consider the owner's duty in securing the barge as a function of three interrelated factors: (1) the likelihood that the barge would break its mooring, (2) the seriousness of any injuries or damage caused by the barge, and (3) what the burden to the barge owner would be to take sufficient precautions to avoid injury or loss. The distinctive feature of the opinion came, though, when Hand expressed his balancing of factors, his formula, algebraically as $B < PL$, where B is the burden of precautions, L the loss if there is an accident, and P the probability of an accident if the precautions are not taken. That Hand used the formula only eleven times and only from 1938 to 1947 suggests he did not think it a big deal. Not so for Posner.

The formula did what Posner so much wanted to do, translate the problem to be analyzed into economic terms. He put the formula to use twenty-four times through 2014 and nine times in his first judicial decade, if we can call it that, 1982–89. The decade showed a gradual progression from the introduction of the formula and then to its uses, first in an admiralty case and then in a wide variety of cases, most notably involving preliminary injunctions. In his first important use of the formula he made it the centerpiece of his negligence analysis in the admiralty case *United States Fidelity & Guaranty Co. v. Plovidba*,[136] in which the issue was whether a shipowner was negligent and therefore liable for the accidental death of a longshoreman who fell through an open hatch. He then in the preliminary injunction case *American Hospital Supply Corp. v. Hospital Products Ltd.*[137] turned to the Hand Formula as a way to understand the mistakes that a district judge might make in ruling on a preliminary injunction and to minimize the costliness of those mistakes. He used the Hand-inspired simple algebraic formula $P \times Hp > (1 - P) \times Hd$—which, when translated into words, states that the preliminary injunction should be granted "only if the harm to the plaintiff if the injunction is denied, multiplied by the probability that the denial would be an error (that the plaintiff, in other words, will win), exceeds the harm to the defendant if the injunction is granted, multiplied by the probability that granting the injunction would be an error. That probability is simply one minus the probability that the plaintiff will win at trial." It was offered as "a procedural counterpart to Hand's negligence formula" and not as a new standard. It was nothing more than the algebraic version of the analysis. "The formula is new," Posner wrote, but "the analysis it capsulizes is standard."[138]

Constitutional Torts

Posner from the beginning and through the decade inveighed against the trend of constitutionalizing claims that would otherwise be brought in state court against state, county, or municipal actors by bringing them under the federal umbrella of Section 1 of the Civil Rights Act of

1871, which imposes liability on anyone who, acting under color of state law, subjects, or causes to be subjected, a person to the deprivation of his or her federal civil rights. These rights implicate serious life or liberty interests. Allowing state court tort claims under the guise of the due process clause and 42 U.S.C. sec. 1983 should be resisted, he argued, lest unchecked expansion distort the meaning of the due process clause and in some cases impose on the federal courts oversight duties they were not equipped to take on. His push to curtail the expansion of Section 1983 rights (his second principal doctrinal innovation) took place under the watchful eye of the Supreme Court, so to speak, which affirmed his 1987 *DeShaney v. Winnebago County Department of Social Services* panel opinion,[139] though in the next decade the Court in *Sodal v. Cook County, Ill.*[140] reviewed Posner's panel opinion and found that he had gone too far in his campaign against 1983 expansion and reversed him, taking him to the woodshed to make its point.

There had been a lead-up to *DeShaney.* The question for Posner in staking out his theory on the scope of Section 1983 was whether the due process clause forbade state actors to take certain actions against some-one or whether the clause imposed obligations on state actors that cer-tain things not happen to someone. In the 1982 case *Bowers v. DeVito,*[141] that question was more concretely expressed as whether the state had an obligation to protect someone from a mental patient and previously convicted killer who upon release from a mental facility killed again. The claim was that the facility and its healthcare professionals had acted recklessly in releasing the killer.

The law was clear that people have a right not to be murdered by someone acting for the state, but that is not the same as the state not protecting someone from being murdered. As Posner puts it, "There is no constitutional right to be protected by the state against being murdered by criminals or madmen."[142] He writes, "It is monstrous if the state fails to protect its residents against such predators but it does not violate the due process clause of the Fourteenth Amendment or, we suppose, any other provision of the Constitution." The reason for what seems a callous result is that the Constitution "is a charter of negative liberties; it tells the state to let people alone; it does not require the federal government or the state to provide services, even so elementary a service as maintaining law and order." Put differently, if there is a complaint about what the state did not do, it is covered, if it is covered at all, by state tort law rather than by federal law.

The facts of *DeShaney* were heart-wrenching.[143] Four-year-old Joshua DeShaney was beaten into a vegetative state by his father against a backdrop of failed efforts by state of Wisconsin social workers to check up on him after reports of earlier child abuse. Lawyers for Joshua argued that the state had an affirmative obligation to protect him from his abusive father, especially in light of the "special relationship" between Joshua and the state once the state voluntarily assumed an obligation to protect him. Posner quickly dispatched the obligation-to-protect claim by looking to his "charter of negative liberties" as it had been adopted by the Seventh Circuit, writing that "the state does not have a duty enforceable by the federal courts to maintain a police force or a fire department, or to protect children from their parents." Political remedies exist for such failures, he explained, and of course states can provide remedies in their own courts. As for the "special relationship" wrinkle, he rejected the Third Circuit's conclusion in a recent case that once a state knows that a particular child may be abused, a special relationship arises that creates a constitutional obligation to protect the child from the abuse. There was nothing in either the language of the due process clause or in constitutional law generally to support such a conclusion. The law can create special relationships, as between inmates and jailers responsible for their care, for example, but the ties between the state and a child known to be at risk are too attenuated to create such a relationship. Moreover, Posner explained, creating such special relationships would make it more expensive for the state to provide protective services because litigation would follow failed efforts.

The conflict between the Third Circuit and the Seventh Circuit on the obligation to protect brought in the Supreme Court to settle the dispute. The Court through Chief Justice Rehnquist affirmed *DeShaney* and tracked Posner's analysis nearly point for point in concluding that the state of Wisconsin had no constitutional duty to protect young Joshua from his father after it received reports of possible abuse.[144] The Court also followed Posner's analysis in rejecting the Third Circuit's "special relationship" position. In the main, the Court borrowed nearly all of Posner's approach to this important issue of the scope of Section

1983 cases. That Rehnquist did not give credit to Posner for the "charter of negative liberties" phrase strikes a discordant note, raising the question why Rehnquist was chary in his acknowledgments.

Resistance

Posner between 1982 and 1989 was dissented against more often than any other judge in his circuit, sixty-one times, twenty-six more than his nearest rival. But the number of dissents, of course, does not tell us enough. We need to look to what his colleagues resisted in their dissenting opinions to get a better understanding of the differences between Posner and the rest of the Seventh Circuit.

Posner sometimes encountered resistance from other judges in substantive areas, sometimes in stylistic areas, and sometimes in a gray area between. Sometimes the tone of the commentary suggested that other judges wanted him to pull back. In *Vail v. Board of Educ. of Paris Union School Dist. No. 95*,[145] a public employment due process case in which Posner dissented, the concurring member of the panel defended the majority opinion and took Posner on for "reasoning from fundamental principles" in his dissent to conclude that the court did not have jurisdiction when adequate precedent suggested the opposite. Moreover, the majority had relied upon Supreme Court precedent, leaving no room for intermediate court appellate reconsideration of whether the higher court had gotten the issue right. "Whether it was correctly decided in some sort of ultimate jurisprudential or philosophical sense is not within my domain as an intermediate appellate court judge," the concurring judge wrote, "once I have decided that it was properly decided in the former sense. My brother Posner calls this approach to deciding cases 'putting the blame on the [Supreme] Court.' I call it adherence to *stare decisis* and to a superior authority." And Justice Potter Stewart, sitting by designation in retirement, strongly criticized Posner's majority opinion in *Marrese v. American Academy of Orthopaedic Surgeons*,[146] an antitrust case involving the denial of membership in a professional organization. Posner's opinion, said Stewart, takes on "difficult questions" concerning the doctrine of res judicata and the application of the Sherman Act and "forges new ground, despite the absence of a factual record in this case and despite the existence of contrary precedent in other Circuits."[147] Posner's majority opinion, according to Stewart, "formulates a completely unprecedented expansion of the res judicata doctrine" and arrives at a "novel analysis of the validity of the contempt citation" that enables the court to " 'express its views' on the merits of the antitrust question at issue in the case."[148] When that panel opinion was vacated and Posner rewrote it on narrower grounds, he omitted the parts that exercised Stewart.

Panel members on occasion resisted a Posner majority opinion they thought went beyond what was necessary for decision. In *Brunswick Corp. v. Riegel Textile Corp.*,[149] the district court had dismissed the complaint alleging patent fraud and monopolistic conduct in violation of Section 2 of the Sherman Act on the alternate grounds that the complaint failed to state an antitrust cause of action and that the suit was barred by the antitrust statute of limitations. Posner saw the appeal as the required occasion "to consider aspects of the relationship between patent and antitrust law," which he proceeds to do for several pages in intricate detail in the context of the goal of modern antitrust laws "to preserve the health of the competitive process."[150] For Judge Harlington Wood, though, the several pages of exegesis were so unnecessary that the best he could do was to concur with a separate statement. Since the cause of action was barred by the statute of limitations, for Judge Wood there was no reason for analysis on the patent and antitrust issues. "Therefore," he wrote, striking with bluntness, "although enlightening, I see no need for much of the antitrust-economic-patent discussion in Judge Posner's opinion."[151] Judge Swygert, on the other hand, boldly went where Judge Wood only intimated. In another antitrust case, *Jack Walters & Sons Corp. v. Morton Building, Inc.*,[152] Judge Swygert takes a typical example of Posner exploring the byways of the issues presented against the backdrop of an exegesis of antitrust law and potential problems lurking within the High Court's jurisprudence and warns that it needs to be identified as irrelevant to diminish its current and future influence. He is able to concur only in the judgment, not because Posner in the majority may be getting the law wrong in his excursions but because he believes that the excursions amount to dicta, "dicta that might tend to influence and prejudice decisions in cases yet unborn but which may come to this court for review. It could be argued that the discussion of matters other than those actually raised by this appeal has certain peripheral relevance, but such relevance, if it exists at all, is unnecessary for an understanding and treatment of this case. It is axiomatic, of course, that we should confine our discussion to the legal principles applicable to the case at hand. Shadows cast beyond the facts of a particular case tend to confuse the trial judges and haunt our own appellate court—inhibiting our freedom to decide future cases according to what we perceive to be the applicable law at that time."

That Posner's compass points to economic language and concepts rooted in economic analysis gets noticed and resisted by occasional panel members. In the prison case *Davenport v. DeRoberts*,[153] involving living conditions and issues such as whether five hours of exercise outside of a prisoner's cell is enough for prisoners kept in segregation for ninety or more consecutive days (the panel held that the trial judge was not clearly wrong in saying yes) and whether such prisoners are entitled to three showers per week (no, one will do—after all, many foreign countries do not put a premium on bathing), Posner in his majority opinion borrowed the convenient economic term of "disutility" and saw inflicting this disutility as one of the objectives of criminal punishment. Judge Cudahy in partial dissent disagreed with the majority conclusion that one shower per week is enough, thinking that the majority might be maligning the Japanese and their zeal for frequent bathing with a one-per-week justification based on the bathing habits found in some foreign countries, but what set his teeth on edge was the reference to the infliction of "disutility" as an accepted goal. "This sounds a bit ominous to me—assuming I understand it. On that shaky premise, I would also most respectfully disagree on this point."[154]

A prisoner litigation case ostensibly about the appointment of lawyers in civil cases brought by prisoners drew out Judge Cudahy's hostility not to specific applications of economic analysis but to a sensibility that looked first to this approach. The case of *Merritt v. Faulkner*[155] first came to the Seventh Circuit on the issue of whether the district judge had erred in not appointing a lawyer for the plaintiff in his prosecution of a claim, lost at trial, that prison officials were responsible for his blindness. The majority thought a lawyer should have been appointed, and it reversed the district court, over Posner's dissent, which argued that market forces rather than the courts should allocate representation. That the plaintiff had not been able to attract a lawyer's services with the usual contingency fee agreement for the type of injuries alleged reflected the weakness of the case, Posner argued. The case was returned to the district court, a lawyer was appointed, and eventually a settlement was reached that provided certain types of healthcare for the plaintiff. When the case returned to the Seventh Circuit for essentially unrelated issues, which the original panel decided in a per curiam opinion, Posner used his concurrence to explain what meritless prisoner cases generally exact from the judicial system and to assert again that market forces rather than judges should determine representation allocation. Cudahy in turn argued in his concurrence that the issue was fairness, not resource allocation, none of which seems particularly surprising or noteworthy—if not for Cudahy's 2000 article "Judge Posner through Dissenting Eyes,"[156] titularly described as a tribute, in which he proudly recounts several instances such as this one of his sniping at Posner's use of economic analysis.

A more significant objection to Posner's economic analysis comes in the previously discussed case *American Hosp. Supply Corp. v. Hospital Products Ltd.*,[157] which continued Posner's attempt on the issue of preliminary injunction to integrate a version of Hand's negligence formula into the analysis of whether a preliminary injunction should issue. That Posner uses the algebraic rather than the verbal formulation of the negligence formula dismayed Judge Swygert, who dissented, not because he disagreed with *Carrol Towing*, the occasion for Hand's articulated negligence formula, but because the negligence issue in *Carrol Towing* rested on the law side, while the issue of a preliminary injunction rests instead on the equity side, where judges necessarily need more flexibility than an algebraic formula allows, even if the values of the formula are not filled in and even if district judges are not compelled, as Posner acknowledges, to use the formula and be put in a "quantitative straitjacket." Swygert was nonetheless not convinced that anything other than a new dawn featuring the imposition of the Hand Formula on preliminary injunction analyses awaits. "District judges," he writes, "operate under enormous pressure to be decisive and precise. Much rides on their smallest decisions. Like a Homeric Siren the majority's formula offers a seductive but deceptive security. Moreover, the majority's formula invites members of the Bar to dust off their calculators and dress their arguments in quantitative clothing. The resulting spectacle will perhaps be entertaining, but I do not envy the district courts of this circuit and I am not proud of the task we have given them."[158]

Judge Flaum in 1986 in *Lawson Products v. Avnet*[159] set out to move away from the mathematical version of the sliding-scale approach linked to the Hand Formula Posner was trying to graft onto preliminary injunction jurisprudence. He sought to reestablish the traditional verbal formulation of the sliding-scale approach that featured the trial judge's discretion and the appellate court's deferential "abuse of discretion" standard of review. Not wanting his opinion to seem to be a severe rebuke, he needed to say that the formula approach was consistent with Seventh Circuit law while at the same time arguing that the approach had created confusion and that the verbal formulation of the sliding-scale analysis seemed easier and preferable. Echoing without citing Judge Swygert's dissent in *American Hospital*, Flaum noted that preliminary injunctions are equitable in nature and that judges can exercise discretion and cannot give precise answers, as using the formula approach suggests that they could. To suggest that, he wrote, would change the law of the circuit. Posner's pointed riposte to Flaum in *Villanova v. Abrams*[160] would have to wait six years.

Supreme Court Review

The Supreme Court has over the decades reviewed thirty-two cases covering a wide range of issues in which Posner contributed an opinion. He wrote the majority opinion in twenty-six cases. He was affirmed thirteen times and reversed ten times, though two of the reversals vindicated positions he had taken, and he was vacated three times. He concurred in two cases that were reversed. He dissented in four cases reviewed and had his dissents vindicated in three of them with reversals. He concurred in two cases reviewed and could be said to have his concurrences rejected when the Court reversed each time. The rates at which Posner's majority opinions have been affirmed or reversed are important measures, as something of a scorecard.

But going beyond affirmance and reversal rates (Posner's rate was on par with the Seventh Circuit's rate) and looking more closely at how the Supreme Court responded—or failed to respond—to Posner's approach to a case reveals the extent to which Posner's approaches to various cases fit within the mainstream. The Supreme Court, after all, defines what the mainstream is. Moreover, looking at those Posner opinions that were reviewed by the Supreme Court also helps portray the nature of his work on the Seventh Circuit. It is a goal of judicial biography after all to show a judge engaging with the law, with doctrinal analysis tracing a judge's cases on particular issues being the favored method. Broader exposure to a judge's cases provides a truer reflection of a judge's work, though, in that the work is done case by case as the cases come in. Some that come in, without regard to whether they qualify as important or as cases that would otherwise show up in doctrinal analyses, end up at the Supreme Court. Looking at them provides a type of cross-sectional jurisprudential approach to a judge's work. Learning about Posner's work on the Seventh Circuit this way emphasizes breadth rather than the depth that typical doctrinal analysis of a particular area produces. Breadth seems more fitting for a view of Posner as a judge at work.

Posner's majority opinions did not fare well in the 1980s. In the 1980s, the Court reviewed six and affirmed him only twice. Aside from *DeShaney*, discussed earlier, and its less than fully satisfying affirmance, the Court delivered a chastening affirmance in *Chicago Teachers Union, Local No. 1, AFT, AFL-CIO v. Hudson*[161] of Posner's majority opinion.[162] The Court agreed with Posner that the union's procedure was inadequate for resolving objections by nonunion employees regarding the proportionate share of union dues that they needed to contribute for the benefit of having the union act as their collective bargaining agent, but it cut back on Posner's attempt to broaden the scope of union activities that nonunion members did not have to support. The rule from *Abood v. Detroit Board of Education*[163] was that non-union members did not have to support through their dues the union's ideological causes not germane to the union's role as collective bargaining agent. Posner, though, determined that the scope of what nonunion employees did not have to pay for included not just political or ideological issues as described in *Abood* but any activities unrelated to the collective bargaining function. The Court did not want to reach the constitutional issues, though, and followed Judge Flaum's concurring panel opinion on the point and explicitly limited the question it was answering to the adequacy of the procedure in place to prevent compulsory subsidization of ideological activity by employees who object thereto without restricting the union's ability to require every employee to contribute to the cost of collective bargaining activities, thus implicitly rejecting Posner's proposed extension of *Abood*. This was not enough for Justice White, though, who in his concurrence noted his agreement with Judge Flaum and wrote that "[Posner's] remarks on the subject are therefore obvious dicta. Under our cases, they are also very questionable."

Posner did see his dissents in two cases vindicated by the Supreme Court. One was *Boyle v. United States*, in which the executor of an estate, claiming that his lawyer was responsible, sought a refund for a penalty assessed on the return because it was filed late.[164] The Court followed, but without giving him credit for it, the argument Posner had made in dissent, that if the purpose of the statute were to be followed— as it should be—it was clear that the taxpayer could not delegate his filing responsibility and, as happened here, blame a failure to file on someone else. The taxpayer must lose. And in the judicial immunity case *Forrester v. White*,[165] in which a fired probation officer sued the judge who had fired her under a sex-based civil rights discrimination theory, the Supreme Court went the other way and followed, if not adopted, Posner's dissent, which argued that in firing the probation officer the judge had acted in an administrative capacity and that while judicial immunity applied to a judge's judicial actions, it did not apply to a judge's administrative actions, making the judge fair game in the plaintiff's lawsuit. The Court crafted a functional test to distinguish between the two types of actions and in the process hardly paid attention to the detailed economic analysis Posner had set out to distinguish them, though the Court did elliptically quote Posner's dissent on the point that the need to protect officials comes up only if they would otherwise be seriously deflected from the effective performance of their duties, since "absolute immunity is strong medicine,"[166] a phrase later invoked often by circuit court judges considering the same issue.

The Court reversed Posner's majority opinion in *Newman-Green, Inc. v. Alfonzo-Larrain*,[167] a case testing the waters of an esoteric issue in civil procedure turning on whether an appellate court can retroactively dismiss a party in a case that has gone to final judgment when it is discovered that one of the parties does not qualify as a diverse party, thus depriving the district court of jurisdiction, this even though the case had completed its procedural journey to final judgment. Posner had explained that there was no authority to justify an appellate court to act retroactively to provide jurisdiction and thought that to do so would send a bad message to district judges in their ongoing battles to defend the jurisdictional fortress of the federal courts.[168] The Supreme Court thought that Posner's rigidity reflected an interest in "hypertechnical jurisdictional purity" and instead looked to practicalities in its reasoning. It even took Posner's observation (which had a nod to the poet Shelley) that, because "law is an instrument of governance rather than a hymn to intellectual beauty, some consideration must be given to practicalities" out of context and used it against him, magnifying the irony by describing—rightly so—the observation as "eloquently noted."[169]

The Court in *Marek v. Chesny*[170] also reversed Posner's majority panel opinion in a Section 1983 case on the issue of whether the reference to "costs" in Rule 68 of the Federal Rules of Civil Procedure on pretrial settlement offers includes attorney's fees. That rule states that if a timely pretrial offer of settlement is not accepted and "the judgment finally obtained by the offeree is not more favorable than the offer, the offeree must pay the costs incurred after the making of the offer." Posner had argued that it must include attorney's fees "to preserve its utility in an age of attorney-fee statutes." There were some but not nearly as many fee-shifting statutes when Rule 68 was drafted in 1939, Posner argued, making it likely that the drafters considered attorney's fees in the undefined category of costs. For him, the practical reason for including attorney's fees as part of costs is to encourage lawyers to take on Section 1983 litigation without the fear that a Rule 68 offer would work to their financial disadvantage in that fees would be determined by Rule 68 and not Section 1988, which allows for attorney's fees as part of costs. The Court dismissed Posner's reasoning as too market oriented, not even considering Posner's idea that not including attorney's fees in costs for Rule 68 would lead to fewer lawyers willing to take on Section 1983 cases. For the Court, since the drafters knew of fee-shifting statutes in detailing costs and had not included attorney's fees in Rule 68, that was proof that they should not be understood to be included.

Evaluations

The respected *Almanac of the Federal Judiciary* published its first evaluation of Posner in 1987. Lawyers noted Posner's brilliance and that he was reshaping practice in the Seventh Circuit before moving to both positive and negative comments about his performance at oral argument. "Several lawyers," we learn from the summary, "were especially outspoken in their criticisms of Posner's demeanor during arguments on issues about which he has strongly-held views. These lawyers used much the same language: arrogant, impatient, dogmatic, opinionated, dominates arguments, cross-examines lawyers as if they were 1-Ls in a Socratic exchange with a professor, etc." Lawyers going the other way thought him demanding but not rude or arrogant and thought he treated well-prepared lawyers courteously.

Books

THE FEDERAL COURTS: CRISIS AND REFORM (1985)

In the months before his nomination to the Seventh Circuit was confirmed and during his first two years on the bench Posner wrote several articles that touched on the federal court system. Between the time of his appointment and confirmation—the gestation period—he wrote one article on statutory interpretation and, when new to the bench, followed it with a second article extending the first. The high point of the two articles came in the conclusion to the second when he brought into focus the relationship between political orientation and modes of statutory interpretation—loose construction for liberals and strict construction for conservatives—and the nature of judicial activism. He delivered the bracing news that conservatives with their strict constructionism are also judicial activists. "I know of no principled, nonpolitical basis," he wrote, "for a court to adopt the view that Congress is legislating too much and ought therefore to be reined in by having its statutes construed strictly."[171] Strict constructionism is judicial activism "because it would cut down the power of the legislative branch."[172] His interest was in principled adjudication, he argued. As he saw it, the evaluation of a judge's work has little to do with whether the judge is activist or restrained. Rather, it turns on factors such as "self-discipline (implying among other things due submission to the authority of statutes, precedents, and other sources of law), knowledge of the law and thoroughness of research, a lucid writing style, a power of logical analysis, common sense, experience of law, a commitment to reason and relatedly to the avoidance of 'result-oriented' decisions in the narrow sense in which

I would like to see the term used, openness to colleagues' views, intelligence, hard work—all are qualities admired in the activist and the restrained alike; all are indeed the bedrock elements of judicial workmanship." Posner brought together these articles to form the core of *The Federal Courts*, published in 1985.[173] The articles are not just collected. There are revisions, subtractions, and additions. The section from the second statutory interpretation article firmly stating that strict constructionists are as activist as those applying loose construction, for example, does not make it into the book. Rather than say that both sides are activists, Posner hedges and explains that liberals think that Congress does not go far enough and want judges to do what legislators have not done, while conservatives think Congress has gone too far and want judges to rein in the work of legislators. The result is that "each school has developed interpretative techniques appropriate to its political ends."[174]

The book is divided into four parts. The first introduces the reader to the judicial system, describing the federal court system and its personnel. The second details the caseload crisis; discusses a bleak future of bloated, bland, and timid law clerk–written opinions; and offers palliatives such as raising filing fees to stem the tide of rising caseloads. The third "rethinks" the federal judicial process and makes bold suggestions for grappling with the caseload crisis, such as reshaping jurisdiction based on an economic rationale, with added considerations of judicial restraint as judges in hand-to-hand combat with the caseload crisis reimagine the branches of government in hopes of putting more on the shoulders of the other branches. It is also in the chapter on the judicial craft from the second section that we find Posner for the first of many times in his career writing about the failings of federal district courts, here described as "areas of recurrent deficiency," when it comes to policing federal jurisdiction, managing their cases, delegating work in their chambers, and making life more difficult than it should be for the appellate courts above them. The fourth takes a different tack and considers the federal courts in the contexts of statutory and constitutional law, of common-law adjudication, and of legal education and scholarship.

The book attracted several reviews. A common complaint was that it was really two books (parts 1–3 for one and part 4 for the other), with the reviewers interested only in the book about the core functions of the federal courts. Even the first three parts did not hang together well for some critics, with the result that the reader was put in search of a unifying theme among the parts and chapters. At the extreme of this criticism, one reviewer wrote that "perhaps the search for a unitary theme overstates the author's own objectives, which may simply have been to combine into a single volume his recent musings on the federal courts."[175] In sometimes harsh tones reviewers criticized Posner for advancing a conservative agenda. He found no takers for his suggestions on reshaping federal jurisdiction. One implied that Posner was using the book to promote his chances of getting to the Supreme Court. Others argued that Posner wanted to remove from the federal sphere both civil rights and habeas corpus litigation. And one reviewer wrote that "by challenging the notion that the federal courts are necessary to protect federal constitutional rights, Posner has challenged the foundations of contemporary legal consciousness."[176]

A detailed and sympathetic review came from Paul Bator for the *University of Chicago Law Review*, who brought not just a great understanding of the federal courts and the judicial function to the review but also personal knowledge of Posner himself that lights up the review. Bator had taught criminal law to Posner at Harvard, had supervised Posner's third-year thesis on habeas corpus, and had become a friend of Posner's following law school. Their paths also intersected later in Bator's career when he moved from Harvard to the University of Chicago. Bator wrote in effect that ours was something of a special blessing in being able to read the gifted Posner writing not just about the federal courts but on the craft of judging. His review, aside from ably assessing the book, is especially useful to us who are hoping to tease out the importance of personality to Posner's work and career. While longish, Bator's paragraph on the Posnerian manner strikes at parts of Posner we need to know about, assuming that Bator was sufficiently close to Posner to have formed these views. "The Posnerian manner," he writes,

is that of an interested, concerned, detached, (now and then) sardonic doctor. He has visited the house; he has, with prodigious intellectual energy and speed, plumbed and poked, listened and sniffed, measured and weighed, read and studied; and now he is delivering a candid report. The report is low-key, matter of fact, "scientific," pedagogical. It is assumed that it is interesting and worthwhile to find and report facts and to conjure up and test possible explanations. It is willing to contemplate—and finds pleasure in—explanations that confirm and those that defy the obvious. Skeptical and intellectually worldly, it nevertheless assumes that things can be (more or less) figured out and that it more or less makes sense to try to improve them. It is highly intelligent and sophisticated, but its intellectual preoccupations stay within a narrow range and are informed by a set compass. Doctor Posner is very much the plain-spoken, occasionally reductionist, American social scientist, not the philosopher or social theorist or moralist. He is never romantic or poetic. Even the suggestions most likely to outrage pious wisdom are flattened to *sound* as if they were the most self-evident thing in the world. . . . The text does not raise its voice or bully you. An occasional sarcasm punctuates the general no-nonsense atmosphere in which is conveyed a remarkable flow of intellectually sparkling common sense and uncommon sense and (only now and again) nonsense.[177]

Of course, it could be that Bator could not see Posner clearly even if he did know him well.

Judges and Lawyers

In what will become a theme through his time on the bench, Posner on the Seventh Circuit in his first decade was doing in practice what he had written about in *Federal Courts*—attempting with bluntness, sternness, and the occasional push to get judges and lawyers to meet his expectations for their contributions to the judicial process. It was a large part of his attempt to reshape how law works.

There's nothing subtle about Posner's treatment of district court judges when they do not perform as he thinks they should, especially when it affects the performance of the appellate court. Since the appellate court, with the rarest of exceptions, can review only final judgments of the district court (as found in Rule 58 of the Federal Rules of Civil Procedure), district judges have to make clear whether their orders are final judgments. Nothing less is acceptable. In one case in which the district judge's intent to dismiss a complaint was plain even though his judgment was less than precise, Posner set out his basic position on jurisdiction: "We repeat our plea that district courts head off spurious issues of appellate jurisdiction by complying with the letter of Rule 58."[178] In *Newman-Green* he takes to scolding, writing that "if we attempt to patch up the jurisdictional deficiencies in a case when the case comes up to us on appeal, the district courts will have less incentive to police their jurisdiction themselves. They are busy courts, and if they know *we* will clean up jurisdictional messes, we will see little attention to detail by them on questions of jurisdiction. It will seem easier to get on with other pressing matters and leave the esoteric jurisdictional points to the court of appeals. That would not be the disciplined regard for the limits of authority that we want to encourage in the courts of this circuit; and by subjecting litigants to proceedings before a judicial body that had no authority to act, it would impose a heavy expense on the public. It is not our office to create a (federal) lawsuit where none exists and in the process create our own authority by overruling our previous decisions."[179] The Supreme Court, as we saw in an earlier section, took a different view and reversed Posner—perhaps to cheers of judges and lawyers in the Seventh Circuit—and wrote, without specific regard to this quoted passage, that Posner's interest seemed to be in hypertechnical jurisdictional purity.

Other opinions look to the issues of judges doing their work and doing it promptly. He displays no patience for dawdling or lazy judges. Nor does Posner seem to have any interest in delicacy in bringing up promptness. In one case, for example, he noted that the judge "took his time"—it was eighteen months after the appellate court had vacated his judgment before he got around to entering his finding of facts and conclusions of law.[180] In another case the district judge appointed a special master to help him, in part because the judge found himself "confronted with an extremely congested calendar." The rules do allow for the appointment of special masters in exceptional circumstances, but Posner makes clear that the district judge had essentially abdicated his responsibility by having the special master prepare an opinion and then adopting that opinion as his own. Posner was writing, it seems, to warn district judges against using the special master rule as a crutch to help them with overcrowded dockets. This was not the rule's intent, nor was the intent to let lawyers appointed as special masters play judge.[181]

Turning the issue around, Posner has no sympathy for the complaint of one losing party that the district judge had gone beyond the testimony in the record by a statistical expert and conducted his own statistical analysis. The losing litigant apparently thought that the judge was to just sit there during trial. This prompted Posner to write that "judges, by the way, are not wallflowers or potted plants; and a district judge's effort to test the strength of a party's statistical evidence by determining how sensitive it is to the design of the sample—a standard method of evaluating statistical evidence—is rather to be commended than condemned."[182]

Turning to lawyers, he criticizes and even punishes them for not holding up their end in the collaborative process of judging. In various cases he criticizes lawyers for not stating in their briefs what state's law was applied in the trial court,[183] for not addressing the issue of jurisdiction,[184] for not plainly stating in a civil rights complaint that a state officer was being sued in both his professional and personal capacities,[185] for not stating in their briefs the applicable standard of review,[186] and for not determining before the statute of limitations runs whether personal jurisdiction can be gotten.[187] He grows frustrated with lawyers in arbitration cases who cannot seem to understand ("as we have said too many times to repeat again") that the only question a federal appellate court can answer is whether the arbitrator interpreted the contract, not whether the arbitrator erred in interpreting the contract.[188]

He wants to run a tight ship and toward this end admonishes one lawyer for exceeding the page limit for briefs[189] and sanctions another for not filing a brief on time, writing that "orders fixing the schedule for briefing an appeal must be obeyed if the business of the federal courts is to be conducted with appropriate dispatch, and we take such orders seriously."[190] He sanctions a lawyer for not adequately researching a complaint, ordering as part of the sanction that the lawyer herself rather than the client pay opposing counsel's attorney's fees.[191] He sanctions lawyers for presenting frivolous arguments.[192] Those submitting inadequate or subpar briefs are in for trouble. For one case in which the brief was "execrable," including an argument section of six extra-large-type pages without a single citation to authority, he warns that such handiwork can lead to the dismissal of an appeal.[193] In another case in which the briefs raise a serious question about the lawyer's minimum competence, he opts to send the briefs themselves and his opinion to the Illinois Registration and Disciplinary Commission.[194] The case for sanctions is plain, he writes in another case, not only because the arguments presented were frivolous but because the lawyer's briefs were "replete with misrepresentations; with syntactical, grammatical, and lexical errors; and with much sheer gobbledygook."[195]

ECONOMIC STRUCTURE OF TORT LAW (1987)

Beginning in 1978 Landes and Posner produced a series of articles on various aspects of tort law—such as negligence, strict liability, causation, products liability, and contributory negligence. They fleshed out their beliefs in the 1987 volume *The Economic Structure of Tort Law*, arguing that "the common law of torts is best explained as if the judges who created the law through decisions operating as precedents were trying to promote efficient resource allocation." The emphasis is on the positive of how the common law seeks efficiency rather than on the normative of whether such efficiency is a good result. In the ongoing debate they take the side that the purpose of tort law is to deter accidents rather than compensate victims. Wealth maximization is a goal but need not be defended since the academic exercise is to explain tort law's positive inner workings, a move that generally sidesteps the distracting issue of whether wealth maximization can be defended. This doesn't keep some reviewers from attacking Posner and Landes for a positive theory featuring the wealth maximization that the reviewers abhor. Reviewers confining themselves to the book's objectives praise the lucid exposition of the positive economic theory undergirding tort law while complaining about the book's "all-inclusive hypothesis."[196] The sharpest nonideological dig by a reviewer is to question originality and mention that "in fact, the book's conclusions do not diverge greatly from Judge Posner's treatment of tort law in his *Economic Analysis of Law*."[197]

Posner in fact had published the third edition of *Economic Analysis of Law* a year before *The Economic Structure of Tort Law*. This third edition caught the reviewing eyes of John Donohue III and Ian Ayers, perhaps because it added more than twenty-five sections and some 150 pages of new material.[198] They suggested that the new material, which they found alarming, had as its intended audience those in the Reagan administration selecting candidates for Supreme Court vacancies. But they pulled back on this suggestion because some of the new material, such as Posner's discussion of rape in economic terms, was so provocative—and so politically damaging to anyone including it—that it was clear that Posner was more interested in expressing his intellectual vision than in securing favor among conservative Republicans. There was much they wanted to bring to Posner's attention, though always in the context of acknowledging the greatness and even audacity of his project. They would do away with the chapter on the Fourth Amendment and the exclusionary rule that was added for the third edition, since its understanding of the value of suppressing evidence was far too crabbed. More troubling, though, were observations and arguments made in support of wealth maximization and against wealth redistribution. Pointing to these new arguments, such as the argument that the goal of wealth maximization argues against redistribution, they write that Posner felt sufficiently emboldened to make "possibly the most imperial pronouncement of the third edition," which is that "involuntary redistribution is a coerced transfer not justified by high market-transaction costs; it is, in efficiency terms, a form of theft."[199] They identify "three serious defects" in his wealth redistribution analysis: that he feels there is no problem, that law and social policy could not fix the problem even if there were one, and that "to the extent income inequality exists it tends to be efficient."[200] They go on to point to several flaws in Posner's empirical analyses on other topics, such as on the Truth in Lending Act, the adultery double standard, public lands, and the exclusionary rule, but the wealth redistribution critique is the slap that stings. For his part, Posner in the fourth edition, published in 1992, backed away from the wealth redistribution positions and thanked Donohue and Ayers "for the perceptive criticisms of the third edition in their review . . . from which I have tried to learn."[201]

LAW AND LITERATURE (1988)

Law and Literature[202] began its life as the essay "Law and Literature: A Relation Reargued," published in the *University of Virginia Law Review* in 1986.[203] It has the markings of a tour de force essay distinguished by Posner's learning and sensitive critical eye and a warm, modest, and earnest tone. Delightful to read, it positions Posner in the many bits of poetry he interprets as a literary critic not at all different from the literary critic he was in his thesis for Cleanth Brooks on Yeats's later poetry. He in fact turns to Yeats frequently—"Easter

1916," "Wild Swans at Coole," and "The Second Coming"—to make his points about literary interpretation and its limits as a tool for constitutional interpretation. His argument, as indicated by his title, is that law and literature, while perhaps overlapping at times, such as in the style of judicial opinions, are really of two separate spheres and require two entirely separate modes of interpretation. What can become unrestrained literary criticism simply has no application to interpretation in law, which necessarily proceeds with the constraints of authoritative texts. Law is subject matter rather than technique.

Posner believed that the essay did not complete the work that needed to be done. That work in part had him defending law and economics from criticisms by law and literature scholars. This defense led to a tone markedly different from the tone of the *Virginia Law Review* essay. In the third edition of *Law and Literature* Posner looked back and described the tone of the first edition as negative and defensive.[204] He is not wrong and might be treating himself too kindly when he also writes that the negative and defensive tone was gone by the book's second edition. Especially apparent in the first edition are both a relentlessness to the arguments and an impatience and even irritation when engaging with literary theories and literary theorists ill-suited for discussions about law.

Posner covers a wide playing field in *Law and Literature*. He engages in an extended analysis of revenge literature, provides accounts of law's reflection in literature, and in perhaps the most charged part of the book takes on contemporary literary critics writing about law and literature to argue that, when it comes to statutory interpretation in particular, law is fundamentally different from literature in reflecting the social force of its authors, such that it must be read practically and pragmatically to honor its purpose.

Many reviewers noted the book's tone, rightly so. But reviewers, perhaps revealing more about themselves in their criticisms than about Posner, launched an assault and marked Posner as an interloper of the worst sort, the politically conservative sort, and denounced his book as an attempt to arrest the movement in law school faculties toward interdisciplinary scholarship, a movement in which law and literature criticism was taking part. David Ray Papke titled his review "Problems with an Uninvited Guest: Richard Posner and the Law and Literature Movement."[205] Posner was described in various reviews as being uninformed and out of his depth. Papke noted that Posner read the great works of literature with the enthusiasm of a naive amateur, not the sophistication of someone who, like Papke, had a Ph.D. in literature. Moreover, Posner committed his cardinal error in uncoupling literature from politics, pursuing his preferred aesthetic approach to literature. His second error, even graver, was in siding in his readings with the powerful rather than the weak, thus marking himself as a representative of conservative rather than liberal politics. Postmodern literary theory can and should reshape the world, including the legal world, so the argument ran, and Posner was standing in the way—questioning as he did what postmodern literary criticism could offer the nuts-and-bolts world of law, in which for him decisions matter because they affect lives and must be supported by interpretations that persuade those involved. Even reviewers with estimable reputations, such as Stanley Fish, responded with a certain amount of foolishness to this point. Fish countered Posner's essential arguments—that law and literary criticism are designed to do different things and that the consequences that flow from them are different—with the assertion that "the actions of literary critics can have consequences as far reaching and practical as the decisions of any court ... and ... the difference between them [judicial pronouncements and edicts of literary critics] is the difference between differing spheres of and routes to consequentiality, not the difference between consequentiality and its opposite,"[206] an observation that by itself seems to support Posner's arguments that the reviewers are getting real life and reading literature mixed up.

There was something to the idea floated by one reviewer that it is not a coincidence that Posner wrote his book "at this moment in the history of legal academy." And that it is, as the reviewer put it, "part of a larger dispute over the terms and conditions of legal scholarship in an increasingly interdisciplinary era in which law and economics has established itself as a prominent (and often politically conservative) force."[207] Posner had written about the "right to dominate legal studies," as he put it in *Law and Literature*, in a 1981 article on the state of legal scholarship in which he bemoaned the decline of traditional doctrinal legal scholarship, which helped judges and lawyers, in favor of interdisciplinary scholarship, which seemed to be written only for other practitioners of such scholarship and could not, with the exception of a few fields such as law and economics, cognitive psychology, and feminist jurisprudence, pass the threshold test of relevance and practical impact.[208] Posner expanded on this position in three more "state of legal scholarship" articles over the decades.[209] The 1981 article on interdisciplinary legal scholarship did not make its way into *Law and Literature*, though, and instead was used in *The Federal Courts*.

Federal Courts Study Committee

Posner was appointed by Chief Justice Rehnquist in December 1988 to the fifteen-member Federal Courts Study Committee which Congress had authorized in response "to mounting public and professional concern with the federal courts' congestion, delay, expense, and expansion." Committee members included judges, legislators, academics, and lawyers. Consultants and advisers weighed in with areas fit for study and with analyses. The membership was divided among subcommittees on management and structure, workload, and state and federal relations. The committee expressly declared that it was concerned with institutional rather than substantive issues. The committee, put differently, was charged with recommendations for making the federal courts function better, not with reassessing case or statutory law. The final product was *The Report of the Federal Courts Study Committee* of two hundred pages published April 2, 1990, covering the waterfront of institutional issues and two one-thousand-page volumes published July 1, 1990, of working papers from the subcommittees relied upon by the full committee.

Posner chaired the Subcommittee on the Role of the Federal Courts and Their Relation to the States, one of the three subcommittees assembled to study the problems set out by Congress. Working with him were three committee members, including Rex Lee, former solicitor general and at the time the president of Brigham Young University. Posner had also recruited Larry Kramer, future dean of the Stanford Law School, whom he had known from the University of Chicago Law School, where he was then teaching, to serve as the subcommittee's reporter.

Posner and Kramer wrote the subcommittee's report, coming in at 645 typescript pages, which comprehensively considered the caseload problems of the federal courts and outlined specific recommendations in a number of areas. While the report did not recommend

Posner's economic analysis proposals for reshaping federal jurisdiction that he had made in *The Federal Court: Crisis and Reform*, it did recommend eliminating diversity jurisdiction with only the rarest of exceptions. Among other recommendations, the report recommended vesting exclusive jurisdiction over all civil tax cases in a single court of limited jurisdiction, creating a new Article I adjudication structure for disability claims, repealing the Federal Employers' Liability Act in favor of federal or state worker compensation systems, establishing a $10,000 minimum for federal tort claims, repealing the Jones Act and modifying the Longshore and Harbor Workers' Compensation Act to cover seamen, and broadening pendent jurisdiction. The full committee adopted all these positive recommendations in its final report and also followed the subcommittee's recommendation against the creation of a specialized Article III court of administrative appeals with exclusive jurisdiction over orders of federal administrative agencies.

Supreme Court Consideration

Posner was often mentioned as a short-list candidate to be nominated by Ronald Reagan to the Supreme Court. The *Wall Street Journal* in particular pushed for his nomination. In a June 29, 1987, editorial on possible nominees for the president's second appointment to the Court (Scalia having been the first), the paper drew particular attention first to Robert Bork and then to Posner before listing other possibilities, such as Frank Easterbrook, Laurence Silberman, and Ralph Winter.

Posner at first made it seem that he had no interest in being named to the Supreme Court. He had written Henry Friendly, for example, that he never thought about the possibility of advancement.[210] In a recent interview, though, Posner acknowledged that he wanted in the mid-1980s to be named to the Court, qualifying his declaration of ambition by saying that any judge newly appointed to the circuit court would want to be promoted.[211] Either way, Posner had no chance of getting nominated to the Supreme Court. He has said that he was never contacted by anyone about being considered, and a handful of inner-circle advisers to President Reagan said in interviews that Posner never made the short list of about a dozen possibilities. However, Posner's article from the 1970s in which baby selling was brought up as part of a cold economic analysis of adoption had nothing to do with not making the short list. As one of President Reagan's closest advisers explained, the president wanted an originalist. Another, when asked about the irony that Hand, Friendly, and now Posner had been passed over for the Supreme Court despite being the preeminent appellate judges of their respective generations, he chuckled and said that the giants preceding Posner never made it to the Supreme Court for the same reason that Posner was not going to make it—that they thought for themselves; an appointing president instead wants them to think the way he thinks.[212]

4

Law Assaulted and Pragmatism Asserted (1990–1999)

AT THE BEGINNING OF the 1990s Posner described off the bench what had been going on with him on the bench in the 1980s with a progress report of sorts, one that complemented what he was reporting on in his opinions. Some of what he was describing was known from articles in the late 1980s, the two most important of which were on law as an autonomous discipline and on what he called the jurisprudence of skepticism. But when these articles and others were brought together and reworked in 1990's *The Problems of Jurisprudence*, to be joined by a new essay concluding the book, "A Pragmatist Manifesto," powerfully and provocatively titled to ensure that it was noticed,[1] Posner presented the full scope of his thinking.

"Law as an Autonomous Discipline,"[2] written to commemorate the one hundredth anniversary of the *Harvard Law Review*, did anything but pay homage to the formalist theory of law for which the Law School had been famous and which had been in full bloom when Posner was there in 1959–62. The essay challenged the core idea that formalism—that is, following the legal reasoning of precedent and relying on it to answer all questions—was enough for what law needed to do in our modern, complex world. That world, Posner argued, requires judges in difficult cases to use other tools—other disciplines—and determine what economists, statisticians, and social scientists can add to the law. Law is no longer autonomous; it is interdisciplinary. He soon followed this declaration with another, drawn from his experience as a judge, in "The Jurisprudence of Skepticism" that judges needed to maintain a healthy skepticism about both formalism's ability to answer all questions and illusions of certainty that it might inspire. He wrote that his "skepticism is a mood or attitude—a disposition to scoff at pretensions to certainty, to question claims (even my own) to the possession of powerful methodologies founded on professional expertise, and to disbelieve in absolutes and unobservable entities—rather than a theory."[3] The essay "A Pragmatist Manifesto" concluding *The Problems of Jurisprudence* completed the judicial progress report and described Posner looking pragmatically in each case for the right answer. He wanted law done differently. He wanted judicial analysis (and academic scholarship as well) to be "bold, scientific, and descriptive." He wanted out from the status quo. What was going on around him was "unoriginal, unempirical, conventional, and unworldly, overwhelmingly verbal and argumentative (indeed, verbose and polemical), narrowly focused on doctrinal questions, mesmerized by the latest Supreme Court decisions, and preoccupied with minute and ephemeral distinctions."[4] Oddly, the point of the concluding chapter was generally lost on reviewers. As if to prove Posner's point that jurisprudential philosophy and law rarely if ever intersect, reviewers raised no questions about the arrival of Posner's book after he had settled in on the bench. Moreover, reviewers did not look into Posner's approach to judging and his turn to pragmatism. No one saw the connection between his insistence on interpretation that was fair-minded and contextual, as opposed to ideological (as in originalism), and his belief that pragmatism produced the best results.

Posner also gave a more personal take on judging in his correspondence. After explaining that there is a judicial game, which like other games has rules, and that there is a science game, in which lining up theory with observation is the key rule, he writes, "I would like to nudge the judicial game a little in the direction of the science game. That's my jurisprudence in a nutshell."[5] He states explicitly what readers of his opinions usually suspected, that his "goal is to make the opinion as faithful as possible a reproduction of the thinking process that produced the result." He confirms as well that he goes against Lear's dictum that nothing comes of nothing. "On the question of the Great Opinion," he writes to law professor Larry Kramer, "I do think I often take nothing cases and make them into something. Most of my cases would be nothing cases in the hands of other judges. And once in a while I try to explore an area—law of the case, statute of frauds, jurisdiction to enforce arbitration awards, nude dancing (my area of particular expertise), functionality in trademark law, strict liability, etc. But I do feel strongly, and maybe wrongly, that a judge shouldn't attempt to do serious scholarship. That's for the academy." The usual restraint of his dissenting opinions has an easy explanation. He writes to Daniel Farber, then a law professor at the University of Minnesota, "I try to minimize comment about the majority opinion when I am dissenting. I like the dissent to stand by itself. I *never*, when writing a majority opinion, so much as allude to a dissent or concurrence. I might restate the arguments in the dissent or concurrence and answer them, but I would never *attribute* them to another opinion in the case—again in the service of making my opinion appear self-contained." To an outsider such as Martha Nussbaum he explains the judicial sensibility and the need to keep some distance from the case. "Judges," he writes, "do not have the time or the emotional resilience to become empathetically involved with the parties to litigation. They are like doctors. You can't be a doctor, year after year, without developing a certain callousness, a hide; and it is the same with judges. A judge may sentence a hundred persons a year. I vote on more than 200 cases a year. One can't function in such a job without a considerable measure of detachment from the turmoil, the desperation, of the litigants. It's different with jurors—for them it is usually a once in a lifetime job." In another letter to her he expands on the idea, writing that "some measure of *callousness* is an occupational requirement for a judge." And in a third letter he explains that "indifference to the inner lives of litigants is an aspect of the classic liberal policy of limiting the power of the state. It is not that people don't have inner lives, but that the state has no business with those lives. The only conformity it seeks is external. Mercy is too *personal* an emotion to occupy an altogether secure role in the liberal theory of the state, so its being pushed to the margin (the pardon power) may make good political sense. Behaviorism may not be a good philosophy of mind but it may be a good political theory of punishment."

Personality Revisited

Posner in the decade was charging ahead, with no personality change in sight from the 1970s, when his correspondence revealed a no-mercy, take-no-prisoners approach to interacting with others. It is unfortunate that Posner's correspondence for his first years on the bench was lost due to a secretarial oversight.[6]

When the correspondence picks up again in the 1990s blunt criticism is still the order of the day. He remains a stickler, purist, and defender of nontrendy usage. He finds fault with one colleague using "unpack" and says that a moratorium should be placed on its use. He finds "privileged perspective," "interpretive turn," and "dialogic turn" hackneyed phrases. "Over time," he says, is "a vile phrase, as Polonius would have said." He does not like "the awful legalism 'facially neutral'" and quips, "leave facials for the beauty parlor." As a purist, he says, he insists on "forbid to" rather than "forbid from." When an academic colleague uses the phrase "see their mysterious inner world," he sees through it and declares it oxymoronic. "The inner world," he writes, "is invisible to outsiders—that's what makes it mysterious." He corrects a Nobel Prize winner's use of the term "hoi polloi." The prize winner has added the definite article to the phrase, prompting Posner to tease, since the prize winner is a good friend, "so 'the hoi polloi' implies a lack of acquaintance with Greek grammar—a lack associated with 'hoi polloi.'"

He is as interested in tone as in usage. He warns one colleague that his paper is "too adversary and dismissive." To another he writes, "There are too many adjectives and adverbs (many of them empty, like 'literally' and 'indubitably'), generating all too often a shrill, strident, and embattled tone." To another he writes that "there is an occasional hectoring, dogmatic, schoolmasterish tone," the result of phrases such as 'as false as it is common,' 'it is wholly implausible,' 'a bizarre claim,' 'the least that might be said,' etc." The "obtrusive, self-regarding, self-consciously 'cute' style" that one colleague has chosen, he writes, obtrudes, which is disappointing because this colleague writes very well when he wants to but instead often chooses a style that features "irritating and wiseguy (= egotistical) characteristics."

And he is tough, even harsh when editing or critiquing substantively. Writing on a subject without knowing enough about it provokes a rebuke, as when he writes to Martha Nussbaum that hearing about economics and economists is not the same as knowing about and understanding both. Her criticism of Chicago-style economics disturbs him "because your acquaintance with economics seems so distinctly second-hand." It is mainly, he points out, derived from conversations with economists "who are either hostile to economics tout court or hostile, whether on methodological or political grounds, to the type of economics that Gary Becker and I and others—those whose work you criticize—practice." He draws a bright line when Nussbaum tries to argue for the advantages of rent-controlled apartments, in the face of having learned in an earlier letter from Posner that, while it might seem counterintuitive to her, the academic literature supports his position that rent control retards the creation of affordable housing. "Not to seem too impertinent," he writes, "it seems to me that your views of rent control stem from ignorance of a large economic literature about it." Her argument that modern American factory workers resemble factory workers in mid-nineteenth-century England receives a sharp response. "Do you actually know any factory workers?" he asks and explains that "our factory workers receive high wages ($10–$20 an hour)—higher than most workers in the service sector—and they work in much safer and pleasanter surroundings than their nineteenth-century counterparts. The oppressed of modern America are not found working in factories; for the most part they are people without jobs." To her argument that Americans feel inferior because they have no culture and know only economics, movies, and Wagner, he responds: "Leave out economics and Wagner, and it's still wrong. I don't think you know what country and century you're living in."

Not that Nussbaum is the only person who provides occasions for sharp criticism. He goes after his colleague Richard Epstein in 1992 in an extraordinary letter when Epstein falls in with the law and economics crowd but insists on moving himself to the front ranks. He cuts Epstein to the quick on his claim of preeminence. What might have been especially galling to Posner is that Epstein, who had been for years at odds with law and economics, had delivered a paper at a conference and used the occasion as a combination of a coming-out party and coup. Posner had been at the conference and had only partially responded to Epstein's paper when queried by the moderator. Not so in his letter. After engaging in a lengthy analysis of its particulars, Posner in the letter points out that, even though Epstein had covered what Posner describes as "well-trodden ground," the paper refers only to Ronald Coase as a previous treader of that ground, no one else. "Now, all of a sudden you have changed your tune [about law and economics], which is fine, but one might have expected some glimmering of recognition of those who composed the new one." He then takes on the idea that all by himself Epstein had "found his way to Ronald Coase," the seminal law and economics scholar. That of course is possible, he writes, "though I find it hard to accept the suggestion you made at the conference that the only significance of my work and Bill's [Landes] was to *confuse* you by its legal errors (what legal errors) and thus postpone your acceptance of the economic approach." He writes first that "all of us have had the experience of thinking up an idea on our own and then finding it somewhere in the literature already. When that happens we have to acknowledge that someone beat us to the punch, and then we go on from there." He then praises Epstein for making important contributions to the positive economic analysis of the common law before delivering the knockout blow. "So even if you're not quite the prodigal son returning to the fold, your accession to the ranks of the law and economics movement and corresponding defection from the ranks of the corrective-justice buffs are extraordinarily welcome. But the suggestion that you have *created* the first sound positive economic approach to the common law—that the arc of lightning between Ronald and you does not touch the earth on which us lesser mortals crawl about making our pathetic mistakes—is not easy to swallow."

Sometimes amid his criticism Posner takes a step back and describes his belief in the importance of criticism. Occasionally he gets himself into trouble by coming across in a harsher tone than he intended. He realizes this when the correspondent with whom he has been harsh complains. Regarding his comments on a paper by Larry Lessig, whom he much admires, he begins his follow-up letter by writing, "I infer from the last paragraph of your fax of yesterday that my comments seemed harsh, and rereading my letter I can see how I indeed might have conveyed an impression of fear and rage. That was unintentional. I meant what I said about your paper being very impressive." Like everyone else, he likes to be praised, but he finds value in criticism, though he does note that a curious thing about praise is that "it's enjoyed even when it is not believed." When Nussbaum tells him that she has been commissioned to review *Sex and Reason* for the *New Republic*, he writes, "I am delighted that you will review my book. Of course you must not pull any punches. Nothing you say will damage our friendship. I often disagree with and occasionally am hurt (in my feelings, not in anything more tangible) by criticism, but I do not allow myself to take it personally. I have never *not* been on speaking terms with anyone, etc. I am not tempestuous."

He believes that it is important for writers to always want to get criticism. He firmly points this out to a correspondent after she writes that at her age (in her forties) she is entitled to comfortable circumstances and, implicitly, deferential criticism. He is not sympathetic to this attitude. "I think that as we get older and more established," he writes, "the *last* thing we should want is comfort, deference, and honor; we should want—we should insist upon—challenge and criticism, the rougher the better; for one of the great dangers of achieving eminence is that people are afraid to criticize you and then you end up inhabiting a fool's paradise. It is a danger for both judges and philosophers, two occupations in which there is a strong sycophantic streak and undue respect (based on fundamental intellectual insecurity) for authority." To another correspondent he puts the matter bluntly: "You want criticism rather than comfort and praise," he writes. "As Blake said, damn braces; bless relaxes."

We see him nonetheless sensitive to certain kinds of perceived criticism. Sometimes he gives up a point only grudgingly. He thanks someone faulting a chapter in one of his books for not distinguishing properly between a general and specific point and says that he will amend the chapter. He proceeds, however, in the balance of the paragraph to argue, using the language in the correspondent's own letter, that the correspondent is wrong. To a scholar ostensibly arguing that the law and economics movement has not come to terms with the idea that the difference between legal analysis as practiced by judges and economic analysis is just nomenclature and that legal analysis has dominated because it is more efficient, he responds by pointing out, with chapter and verse, so to speak, that he had made all of the points contained in the article in his *Economic Analysis of Law*. There was nothing new in what the scholar had written.

He flares up when he, along with Princeton economist Orley Ashenfelter, wants to establish a new peer-reviewed journal in economics and gets back from Cambridge University Press a letter not quite understanding what he and Ashenfelter outlined in their proposal and who they are. Irritated, he writes, "I have no doubt that the Cambridge University Press has numerous high hurdles that must be o'erleapt before a new journal is approved. But Professor Ashenfelter and I are not, at this stage, looking for approval. We are looking for bids—which may be as tentative as you like, but which will enable us to decide which presses we want to go further with. Why do you want our C.V.s at this stage? Don't you know who I am? Haven't you ever heard of Orley Ashenfelter, a very well known Princeton economist who is the editor of the American Economic Review, which has a circulation of 80,000?" Ultimately, Ashenfelter and Posner brought the journal *American Law and Economics Review* to Oxford University Press and Posner served as a co-editor with Ashenfelter from 1998 to 2005.

Nor does he take well to having been accused of not following the borrowing rules at the University of Chicago Library. The letters from the dean of the Law School indicate that Posner had ignored recall notices and failed to return so many books on time that the library would need to suspend his borrowing privileges. He responds by suggesting that the majority of overdue books were noted as not returned out of error on the library's part and that, given the high number of books he borrows annually, late returns naturally happen. If this is not the case, he writes, "I would have preferred to have learned about it in a less peremptory minatory form." Jab delivered, he in the closing line writes that he will do everything he can to prevent the problem's recurrence. A year later, when another university official sends him a rebuke for additional recall notices, he takes a different tack. "I would like," he writes, "to invite consideration of the following hypothesis: that the number of overdue recall notices a borrower receives is a linear function of the number of books he borrows. . . . If you have information indicating that I have a higher *percentage* of overdue recall notices (that is, a higher ratio of such notices to number of books borrowed), rather than a higher *absolute* number of such notices—a meaningless statistic (implying that the optimal user of the library is an academic who, since he does no research, borrows no books)—I shall be properly abashed.

But not otherwise." The administrator, seemingly knowledgeable about both economics and statistics, takes issue with the point about the linear function of recall notices but says it is beside the point. Users do not get free passes on recall notices even if their recall notices came in at a lower rate relative to the number of books they have borrowed. The administrator then commits to looking into Posner's claim that the recall notices were clerical errors on the library's part. Not willing to let it go, Posner in his response returns to the point that a high-energy academic such as himself gets penalized because the rebuke letters go out based on the absolute number of unreturned books, not on the number relative to the number of books taken out. Thus, the borrower who fails to return the only book he took out in a year gets a better result (no rebuke letter) than the borrower who takes out one hundred books and fails to respond to five recall notices.

Judicial Greatness Judged

Posner on three occasions in the first half of the decade inquired into the issue of how great judges distinguish themselves, considering the lives, careers, and judicial performance of Cardozo,[7] Hand,[8] and Holmes.[9] On a fourth occasion he took on the genre of judicial biography but had little to say on the topic of judicial greatness. He confined himself instead to a canvass of judicial biography and its inherent failings before making the case that judicial biographers should give up looking for the "essential self" of their subjects and instead focus on how courts and judges work, topics best handled not by ideological or biographical approaches but by a combination of social scientific, jurisprudential, and statistical approaches.[10]

His interest in Cardozo is more with reputation than with the typical interests of a judicial biographer. He wanted to take a subject such as Cardozo with a generally acknowledged reputation as a good if not great judge and sort out what the reputation might be based on, though on the way to describing and then using his analytical tools Posner does trace the outlines of Cardozo's personal, professional, and judicial lives. His is an evaluative study of the sort we need more of, he argues. In part he applies statistical analysis (if it can be used for baseball players, he muses, why not for judges) based most notably on judicial opinion and law review citation counts and patterns and then, having established Cardozo's high rank, brings both literary analysis and substantive legal analysis to Cardozo's opinions, looking deeply into his most famous opinions, *Palzgraf v. Long Island R. Co.*[11] and *McPherson v. Buick Motor Co.*[12] He credits Cardozo's gift for the memorable phrase and an effective prose style as well as his penchant for pragmatism to explain why Cardozo is still with us, so to speak.

Most of the reviewers thought the subject and approach sensible and worthwhile, while some questioned the analytical premise of counting citations. Some reviewers questioned the purpose of the study, with one writing that the book's exercise in what the reviewer calls reputology "represents the ultimate in academic solipsism."[13] Some reviewers slyly referred to Posner's own reputation (for one reviewer eminent and for another formidable), while one featured Posner's reputation in the context of Cardozo's as his theme, declaring in his opening sentences, "A book often tells you as much about its author as it does about its subject. No better proof for this proposition can be found than Richard Posner's *Cardozo: A Study in Reputation.*"[14] In two stringent pages at the end of the review he draws biographical and professional links between the two judges. On the positive side he argues that two of the essential reasons Cardozo was well regarded—Cardozo's antiformalist pragmatism and his rhetorical eloquence—apply as well to Posner. But on the negative side he gets deeply personal and argues that while Cardozo had an attractive persona that he used much to his advantage and that undergirds our reverence for him, "Posner has no such favorable persona,"[15] an assertion he supports in a footnote to articles in *American Lawyer* and the *National Law Journal* and stray references to Posner's alleged lack of leadership skills, his intellectual aggressiveness and arrogance, and his inability to let intellectual inferiors feel comfortable. He quotes Posner's observation that among the great judges of Cardozo's time Cardozo "is perhaps the most neutral, the most even, the most at home in the legal profession, the most comfortable insider: the most *professional* judge," before quipping that "this surely does not describe the aggressive, doctrinaire Richard Posner of the early 1980s."[16]

Posner took Holmes on in 1992 with an edited collection of his selected judicial and extrajudicial writing, *The Essential Holmes.* Posner provided a lengthy introduction charting the different aspects

of Holmes's life and emphasizing the importance of Holmes's governing philosophies rooted in skepticism, pragmatism, and the writing
life. He argues, as he had with Cardozo, that Holmes's vivid prose
style marked by memorable language has added to his shelf life. The
introduction, noted in one review as worth the price of admission and
as elegant in another,[17] places Holmes in the context of American politics and philosophy, describes his philosophical approach to life and
law and its influence on his judicial opinions, and culminates with
Posner's assertion that Holmes's "distinction as a lawyer, judge, and
legal theorist lies precisely in the infusion of literary skills and philosophical insight into his legal work." Reviewers agreed that Posner had
done the law a service in bringing out his selection of Holmes's writing. Two reviewers noted the connection between Posner the judge
and Holmes. One mentioned in passing that Holmes had written in
his famous "Path of the Law" essay that "for the rational study of the
law the black-letter man may be the man of the present, but the man
of the future is the man of statistics and the master of economics" and
connected Holmes's future man of the law with Posner: "Judge Posner
is one of those men of the future."

The second review noting Posner's connection to Holmes—ironically
not published in a law journal but in *Ethics*—recognized that Posner's
book was important in part because it tells us something about Posner.
The book "is a paean by an influential modern scholar and judge to his
intellectual mentor." And perhaps more to the point, "Posner's wonderful introduction should make clear the close affinity that Posner sees
between Holmes's and Posner's own career."[18] The review recited biographical similarities (both were first scholars with important books
written while young, with Posner's *Economic Analysis of Law* recalling
Holmes's effort in *The Common Law*) and similarities in their preferences for pragmatism, economics, and the social sciences. Lastly, each
judge's reputation suffered because, as Posner put it about Holmes, he
had "no natural constituency among lawyers and others interested in
legal and public policy." The reviewer could have added that each judge
has been criticized for cold and detached judicial opinions. Posner's
book, the reviewer suggests, is meant in part to remedy the problem
that Holmes, as Posner sees it, "while respected, is not deeply appreciated or loved in the way that he should be."[19]

Looking to Posner's archival correspondence, we see that he explains his interest in Holmes in ways that we do not find in his published writing. Posner considers Holmes a great figure in the law. "You force me," he writes to Stanford Law School professor Tom Grey, "to admit that my evaluation of Holmes as 'the greatest' judge is highly questionable. Let us define 'jurist' to mean any participant in the legal enterprise from Justinian to Nader—practicing lawyer, law professor, judge, Attorney General, whomever. Then I contend that Holmes is the greatest jurist, at least of modern times, because the sum of his ideas, metaphors, decisions, dissents, and other contributions exceeds the sum of contributions of any other jurist of modern times." Posner, to be sure, sees something special in Holmes. Referring to *The Essential Holmes*, he declares, "I am an uncritical, fawning worshiper of Holmes, despite the pretense of detachment in the introduction." Why G. Edward White, another Holmes scholar, cannot see Holmes as Posner sees him baffles him. He writes to White after reading a draft of White's article "Holmes as Correspondent" and wonders "how . . . you resist concluding that Holmes was a *wonderful* man—a hero—a great American—the premier figure in the history of law, I don't understand." To Nussbaum he speculates on the answer. He explains that the "one thing that hobbles White when he writes about Holmes is that he is *so* very unlike Holmes that he cannot crawl inside him, which is what you want in a biographer. I feel, probably unwarrantedly, that *I* can crawl inside him."

Posner's 1994 review of Gerald Gunther's judicial biography of Learned Hand was Posner's next occasion to consider judicial greatness. While offering effusive praise for aspects of Gunther's approach, he criticizes Gunther for not writing enough about Hand the judge. Gunther for him provides little information about Hand's day-to-day work on the bench and his relationships with those he worked with, including lawyers, and he all but ignores Hand's judicial output except for his constitutional law opinions. Gunther's interest was in Hand's personal life, and the result was an "old-fashioned narrative history" of Hand's life, well done and a significant contribution to the genre of judicial biography, but deeply flawed nonetheless.

As detailed and as illuminating as Posner's review is, it can be read as an essay on why Hand is a great judge and on what greatness is in judging, though he acknowledges that it is difficult to judge judicial greatness. He describes three ways to evaluate it. One is through a judge's creativity. Another is through a judge's prose style, which can make expressions of familiar propositions memorable and in the process give added momentum to a principle to spur greater comprehension and even to stimulate new thought about the proposition once considered familiar. The third is through the greatness of a judge's opinions. This is where Posner finds Hand's greatness. As he puts it, "the very pith and marrow of Hand's achievements" are to be found in his shelf of opinions.[20] Posner tells us that judicial opinions are not great because they happen to become classics. For greatness to be a function of the substance of a judge's opinions, those opinions must contribute to the development of legal rules and principles. This explains Posner's irritation that Gunther does not mention Hand's famous formula for assessing negligence.

On the Bench

Bar

On the bench, Posner's notices of lawyers who performed below professional standards continued apace in the 1990s. A lawyer comes close to being sanctioned for asking to be excused from oral argument, which Posner considers to be akin to client abandonment.[21] Lawyers are sanctioned for filing frivolous appeals.[22] He admonishes counsel for accusing, without evidence, another lawyer of unethical behavior, behavior unethical by itself,[23] and for signing a pleading known to be false. In this last instance the offending lawyer was from out of state, and the court opted to send its opinion to the lawyer's home state bar disciplinary authority.[24] Government lawyers come in for a whipping. A lawyer from the Illinois Attorney General's Office is upbraided for deliberately withholding nonprivileged information from an opponent to help a state official avoid "being brought to justice for violating a prisoner's federal rights."[25] Lax lawyers who fail to cite pertinent authority are reminded that the court is not obliged to do a party's research.[26] Lawyers are rebuked for failing to cite pertinent authority and thereby forfeiting arguments, especially when as in one case a party fails to cite controlling precedent even though to prevail the case not cited would need to be overruled.[27] Lawyers are reminded "that they are not obliged to make futile arguments on behalf of their clients,"[28] and in what appears to be a developing theme, lawyers are called on their outrageous arguments, as in one criminal case in which a defense lawyer's argument about the onset of the police state "carries advocacy to new heights of hyperbole."[29] A lawyer's argument in another case prompts the reaction: "That is the kind of argument that makes lawyers figures of fun to the law community."[30]

There is some fun to be had at the expense of lawyers. In one case in which a mentally unbalanced defendant was suspicious about his lawyers, we get the parenthetical "Nothing unusual about that!"[31] What might be seen as Posner's negative view of lawyers is counterbalanced by praise in one case. He commends counsel "for the exceptional quality of their briefs and argument," and concludes, "We have not hesitated to criticize counsel who fall below minimum professional standards for lawyers practicing in their court; equally, counsel whose performance exceeds those standards by a generous margin deserve our public recognition and thanks."[32]

He also provides strong defense of lawyers' right to earn fees in the face of a district judge wielding a paring knife with too much enthusiasm in a fee petition case.[33] Pity the lawyer, though, who essentially dinged an estate he was representing for $75,000 of nonwork. He had to pay all the money back and was barred from seeking further fees in the case.[34] No thanks go out to lawyers who do not carry their burden for visual evidence when needed. He complains that the lawyers did not include photographs in a case involving a book's cover art.[35] And in a railroad employee disability case turning on what it means for the employee to "spot cars," which requires an understanding of how the rail yard operates, he complains that "the parties have not favored us with maps or photographs or even dimensions."[36] The message is that lawyers are prone to think that all lawyering is done with words. Posner writes that "appellate lawyering is an oververbalized activity. There is, as we have remarked before, little appreciation of the power of images even in cases, such as trademark cases, in which visual impressions have controlling legal significance."[37] He ends snappily: "The appellate lawyer's adage might be, a word is worth a thousand pictures. 'Tain't so."

District Judges

Lawyers were not alone in Posner's admonishments. Several judges were found to be underperforming. Posner beseeches them—and not for the first time—"to obviate disputes over appellate jurisdiction by paying careful attention to the requirements of the rules governing orders and judgments."[38] District judges should write usable opinions for the benefit of the appellate court, not like the district judge who was silent on valuation in a contract case, the principal issue, and did not analyze the presented evidence regarding that valuation.[39] Dawdlers were reminded when cases were returned to them to get on with it, such as the judge who let a preliminary injunction matter drag on for twenty months.[40] In two cases, giving directions to district judges did not sit well. In a fee application case, the district judge had ignored the appellate court's directive to consider market rates for the lawyering under review. In sending the matter to the district court a second time—with the issue now four years old—Posner tells the district judge that "judicial mandates must be obeyed, and litigation must have an end."[41] In the second case a judge had been reversed on a sentencing issue and expressed in the resentencing hearing his displeasure at the appellate court's decision. He did not like to do resentencings and did not like the sentencing guidelines that had tripped him up in the first place. This led the appellate court to have the defendant resentenced by a different judge, with Posner noting that "a civilized society insists that the forms of justice, of which judicial detachment, impartiality, and equanimity are central, be visibly maintained in its courts."[42] In another case surprising comments came from a district judge at sentencing, who in pronouncing the sentence felt compelled to say to the defendant, "You're a strange man. In fact you're a flake." This prompted Posner to write, "We are not a ceremonious people, but there are occasions on which solemnity remains the proper mood and criminal sentencing is one of them."[43]

Hand Formula

Posner in the 1990s continued his aggressive attempt to shape the law by using the Hand Formula whenever possible. He wanted, for example, to expand the application of the Hand Formula to include Fourth

Amendment (search and seizure) analyses and probable cause assessments in criminal cases, with the result that a district judge's probable cause determination should, when reviewed, be given greater deference with the use of the "clearly erroneous" standard rather than the preferred "substantial basis" test.[44] But because his argument appeared in a concurring opinion, it had no precedential value. He used the Hand Formula in a probable cause case again in *Villanova v. Abrams*,[45] though this time the issue was whether probable cause existed for psychiatrists to civilly commit the plaintiff for twenty-four hours. He expresses the test of a reasonable commitment, points to the similarity between these terms and the mathematical terms of Hand's formula for negligence, and notes that the resemblance is not an accident. He writes that "the test of negligence at common law and of an unlawful search or seizure [which a civil commitment surely is] challenged under the Fourth Amendment is the same: unreasonableness in the circumstances." He's back with an application of the formula in the admiralty case *Brotherhood Shipping Co., Ltd. v. St. Paul Fire & Marine Ins. Co.*[46] and notes both that the Seventh Circuit has endorsed the formula as the proper admiralty standard in *United States Fidelity & Guaranty Co. v. Plovidba*[47] (though not mentioning that this was his case) and that the case had been cited approvingly by other courts in admiralty cases, listing them. He next invokes the formula in *Vande Zande v. State of Wisconsin Department of Administration*,[48] an Americans with Disabilities Act case turning on an employer's obligation to reasonably accommodate a paraplegic employee's disability. After noting that reasonable care is not synonymous with maximum care, he looks to negligence law for the recognition that the cost of increased care is to be factored into a reasonableness analysis, writing that "similar reasoning could be used to flesh out the meaning of the word 'reasonable' in the term 'reasonable accommodations.'" Without such limitations, employers would have "potentially unlimited financial obligations to 43 million disabled persons," an obligation that in effect will have imposed "an indirect tax potentially greater than the national debt." "We do not find," he concludes, "an intention to bring about such a radical result in either the language of the Act or its history."[49]

Economic analysis seems to be everywhere. In an analysis of T-shirts in two different markets, for example, he helps spread the language of economic analysis and comments that, in technical economic terms, what is at issue goes by the name of cross-elasticity of demand.[50] And in a bankruptcy case, he explains the high priority postpetition debt receives in the distribution of a debtor's estate by saying the purpose of the rule is to keep the debtor afloat as long as possible, adding that "in economic terms, the prioritizing of postpetition debts enables the debtor (or trustee) to ignore sunk costs—treat bygones as bygones—and continue operating as long as the debtor's business is yielding a net economic benefit."[51] He uses economic analysis to explain rules and doctrines, such as the scope of the tort employment doctrine[52] and the rule on the issue of attorney's fees in class action cases.[53] And of course he uses economic analysis to approach a problem, as in one case involving public officer immunity, suggesting that it be abolished and replaced with the imposition of respondeat superior liability—making the employer (master) responsible for employee (servant) torts incurred while on the job—this even though the Supreme Court had a dozen years earlier rejected that idea.[54]

The economic analysis language Posner wanted to make readers more comfortable with raises an important point about the extent to which judges can get their ideas into the pages of the *Federal Reporter*. The unwritten rule, which had not always been followed by Posner's brethren in his first decade on the bench, is that other panel members defer to the style and language that the judge writing the majority opinion wants to use. Bruce Selya of the First Circuit, who has a fondness for sprinkling his opinions with obscure words, has said that in his very first case he used some obscure words and got a stern note from a panel member insisting that he delete the exotic vocabulary. Selya did not want to and went to the third panel member, who happened to be the distinguished judge Carl McGowan of the District of Columbia Circuit Court of Appeals, who was sitting by designation. McGowan told the complaining panel member that writing the majority opinion carries with it the prerogative to choose the style and language that the writer wants and that the other panel members must defer to these choices, in the same way that panel members would defer to the stylistic choices the complaining member made in his future opinions.[55] Panel members can bring substantive concerns to the majority opinion writer and seek modification to ward off either dissents or concurring opinions, but on matters of style the judge writing the majority opinion gets an unencumbered berth. This explains Posner's ability to both use economic language in his opinions and to make the implicit suggestion that such terms are not so scary and should be pointing the way for other judges to take up more economic analysis.

Chief Judge

By 1993 Posner, at fifty-four, met the statutory requirements relating to age, seniority, and length of service and became the chief judge of the Seventh Circuit, succeeding William Bauer, whose seven-year term had run. The job is primarily administrative, but the chief judge can make choices on a variety of issues, such as whether judges from elsewhere in the federal judiciary can sit on the Seventh Circuit by designation as visiting judges. The chief is always the presiding judge, which gives him the power to assign the writing of opinions if he is in the majority. The chief judge also attends a semiannual meeting of the Judicial Council, chaired by the chief justice of the Supreme Court. Posner found the Judicial Council meetings "on the whole boring, presided over by Rehnquist (a very able and genial person, by the way, though tortured by a terrible back) with barely concealed boredom." There were, though, some impressive chief judges from other circuits at the meetings, "some even with first-rate academic credentials." In 1997 he complains to Michael Boudin of the First Circuit that the last conference meeting was "a bore to end bores."

Posner described the concerns of chief judges in their respective circuits as "rather parochial—how to light a fire under a slow judge, etc." He advised Ralph Winter of the Second Circuit that he should delegate as much as he could of the administrative work, "which can be tedious." On the delegation issue, he jokes with Guido Calabresi that he had told Jon Newman, the outgoing chief judge of the Second Circuit, "that I don't do a tenth of what the chief judge of the Second Circuit does, that I have delegated the other nine-tenths, and so he will doubtless write me off—justly—as a judicial *flaneur*." He jokes to Bruce Selya of the First Circuit that he is enjoying the job of chief judge, "although," he writes, "I feel stupider since I became chief judge—administrative duties are bad for the brain." His routine correspondence was so heavy that he took to using a signature stamp.

The chief judge has under him not just his circuit but all the district courts within the circuit. The chief judge becomes the face of the circuit and plays an important role in promoting morale within the circuit, its smooth operation, and a good relationship between the district courts and the circuit court. Needing to better know his circuit, Posner prepared for becoming chief judge by visiting, as he put it to Martha Nussbaum, "out-of-town judges in their local lairs." "These visits," he continued, "are great hits—it is easy to create a good impression throughout an organization simply by visiting parts of it no one has thought worth visiting before." He also put together a chief judge's manual for his circuit that he had sent as well to the Federal Judicial Center and to the Administrative Office of the U.S. Courts.

He cared about collegiality on the Seventh Circuit. When colleague Harlington Wood sent him a Ninth Circuit opinion in a capital case, *Thompson v. Calderon*,[56] in which Stephen Reinhardt had written a concurring opinion going after Alex Kozinski, Posner felt compelled to write to Reinhardt to criticize him for abusing his colleague. He was shocked by the tone of the dissent. "I don't think I've ever read a more intemperate opinion," he wrote. "I don't understand how you can congratulate your court on its 'collegiality' while in the same breath abusing a colleague in the way that you do." Judges in their opinions, he argues, should "strive to preserve dignity and restraint, at least in the rhetoric of their opinion, and to avoid what can only be interpreted as vituperative personal abuse of a colleague." In his note back to Harlington Wood about this "truly shocking document," he writes, "May we never have one like it in our circuit."

Resistance

Posner, with forty-four in the 1990s, drew the most dissents on the Seventh Circuit to his majority opinions, though the number alone does not convey the nature and depth of the resistance from some of Posner's colleagues to his push for economic analysis. Judge Flaum in the 1990s was again a bulwark against jurisprudential changes proposed by Posner. It had been Flaum who had steered the Seventh Circuit away from the mathematical formulation of the Hand Formula in preliminary injunction cases and back to its verbal counterpart. At the beginning of the decade, in the earlier discussed Fourth Amendment search case of *United States v. McKinney*,[57] Flaum went out of his way in his panel opinion to rebut the suggestion of Posner's concurring opinion that the standard of review to be applied in reviewing the magistrate's probable cause conclusion in issuing a warrant should be the "clearly erroneous" standard rather than the "substantial basis" standard. Flaum countered by explaining that the Supreme Court had not, contrary to Posner's assertion, backed away from the "substantial evidence" standard, adding with flair, "[w]e must wait an explicit order from our superiors before scuttling the Fourth Amendment."[58] The steady trend Posner had discerned moving in the direction of greater deference to the trial judge's decision received equally sharp words, with Flaum writing that "the 'steady trend' the concurrence cites as limiting appellate review of fact-related issues in the name of judicial economy is, we assert, neither steady nor a trend."[59] The goals Posner was seeking of simplicity, uniformity, and minimizing the number of legal formulas that judges apply were not for Flaum goals in themselves.

Not willing to give up the fight, Posner pointedly told his colleagues two years later in *Villanova v. Abrams* that they had got it wrong. He recognized that on the question of preliminary injunctions the district court's exercise of discretion remained paramount—but not without delivering a salvo restating the virtues of the Hand Formula. If only his colleagues did not give the formula such a crabbed reading, he wrote, it would be clear that its analytic approach, while not a panacea for the difficulties of judicial decision-making, "has value in expressing rules compactly, in clarifying complex relationships, in identifying parallels between diverse legal doctrines, and in directing attention to relevant variables that might otherwise be overlooked."[60]

Resistance of a different sort came from his colleague Kenneth Ripple, who complained about Posner's use of dicta. In the equal protection case of *Milner v. Apfel*,[61] the question whether persons who were acquitted of criminal offenses by reason of insanity but civilly committed at public expense should be denied Social Security benefits was easily answered. Since no suspect classification such as race or gender was at issue, the legislation suspending the Social Security benefits only had to have a rational purpose, such as Congress's obligation to spend wisely. That had been the rational basis found by the courts to justify legislation suspending benefits to committed guilty but criminally insane persons and it applied to acquitted but insane and committed persons also. In the long dicta section faulted by Ripple, Posner explored the idea of moral luck and the idea that legislatures can legislate with regard to morality rather than being restricted to demonstrable harms, or what John Stuart Mill called "other-regarding acts." As Posner saw it, "legislatures are permitted to treat criminals worse than they treat the law-abiding without having to establish a functional justification for the difference in treatment." The problem for Ripple was that there was no reason for the majority opinion to go beyond the simple rational basis analysis and consider morality, especially since "our common law tradition reflects no well-established tradition to support the proposition that it is morally or constitutionally acceptable to punish those who are not responsible for their actions."[62]

Supreme Court Review

The Supreme Court reviewed eight Seventh Circuit cases in which Posner had written the majority opinion. It affirmed four, reversed two, and vacated two. The Court also reviewed and reversed one case in which Posner had written a dissenting opinion, affirmed another case in which he had dissented, and reversed a case in which Posner had written a concurring opinion.

Zafiro v. United States,[63] exploring the issue of when a severance should be granted in a multiple-defendant case in which various defendants make claims of mutually antagonistic defenses, was the Posner opinion that received the warmest welcome from the Supreme Court. The key to the issue generally for him was that judges should not need to sort through possible differences between mutually antagonistic defenses and mere finger pointing, with the former justifying severances and the latter not. Rather than stay with this canonical formulation, and mentioning that Holmes had warned "that to rest upon a formula is a slumber that prolonged means death," Posner in his panel opinion wanted to "dig beneath the formulas."[64] His test, set out "as an original matter," was that "persons charged in connection with the same crime should be tried separately only if there is a serious risk that a joint trial would prevent the jury from making a reliable judgment about the guilt or innocence of one or more of the defendants."[65] Beginning with Posner's premise that questions about mutual antagonism illuminate what the courts are trying to discern, the Supreme Court then set out a new rule on severance that paralleled Posner's.[66] The only bit missing from the Court's embrace of Posner's analysis was his explanation of the default position and the benefits of joint trials. He used the language of economic analysis and noted that "joint trials, in this as in many other cases, reduce not only the direct costs of litigation, but also error costs."[67] That type of economic analysis and language did not make its way into the Supreme Court opinion.

The Court in *American Hospital Association v. N.L.R.B.*,[68] a case about the number of bargaining units that a National Labor Relations Board rule called for in acute care hospitals, affirmed Posner's opinion and also tracked his approach.[69] Perhaps because it was not necessary to the opinion or perhaps because the Court wanted to stay away from implicit value judgments, it did not mention Posner's explanation that the fight between labor and management on the number of bargaining units was an expression of the self-interested approaches that each side took. Labor wanted more units because it would be more homogeneous and easier to whip into line on labor issues, while management wanted more necessarily heterogeneous units for exactly the opposite reason, to weaken the resistance of the union. The Court avoided these economic truths of how the sausage is made.

In two other affirmed cases Posner essentially struck out, as his opinions were affirmed on grounds different from those advanced in Posner's majority opinion. Both were Section 1983 cases. In *Albright v. Oliver*,[70] a substantive due process case with false arrest roots and claims of malicious prosecution, the Court brushed aside Posner's analysis, which concluded that the nominal liberty and other deprivations at issue were not enough to involve "the heavy weaponry of constitutional litigation."[71] The Court decided that the case had been incorrectly analyzed at the Seventh Circuit and that it was the Fourth Amendment, not the substantive due process clause, under which the plaintiff's claim needed to be analyzed. In *Heck v. Humphrey*,[72] a prisoner had made a Section 1983 claim that called into question the constitutionality of his underlying conviction but in Posner's view had not exhausted his state remedies as he otherwise needed to if his suit was to be understood as a habeas corpus petition seeking his release. That the suit should be dismissed for failure to exhaust state remedies was not the issue for the Supreme

Court, though. It swept away the analysis of Posner's majority opinion[73] and held that the plaintiff's suit was not cognizable under Section
1983 because the predicate that the plaintiff's underlying criminal conviction had been reversed on appeal had not been met. End of story.

Posner had mixed results in the two cases in which he was reversed.
Bracy v. Gramley turned on its specific facts about judicial corruption in
Chicago and a habeas corpus petitioner's claim that he should be able
to conduct discovery to obtain evidence that the judge in his case, who
was later convicted of accepting bribes from criminal defendants, was
biased, entitling him to a new trial.[74] The Seventh Circuit had agreed
with the trial court, which had denied the petition,[75] but the Supreme
Court, while agreeing with the Seventh Circuit that the petitioner
might never be able to turn up the evidence he needed to carry the day,
concluded that the petitioner had nonetheless met the "good cause"
standard to have a go at it and reversed the panel opinion. In contrast to
this instance of a higher court drawing different factual conclusions, a
unanimous Court in *Sodal v. Cook County, Ill.*[76] reversed and laid waste
to Posner's majority en banc opinion,[77] as mentioned earlier. Posner
had taken a bold position not this time on the due process clause as
a charter of negative liberties but instead on the Fourth Amendment
prohibition against unreasonable search and seizure as the underlying
right protected by the clause in a case involving the seizure and removal
of plaintiff's mobile home by county deputy sheriffs. Posner had argued
that it was the plaintiff's privacy interests rather than his possessory
property interests that were at issue and that in fact there was no property seizure and that any violations of those privacy interests were not
sufficient to turn a housing court matter into a constitutional case. A
unanimous Court, though, eviscerated Posner's majority en banc opinion[78] and all but stated its displeasure at the Seventh Circuit's approach
to the section 1983 cases.[79] "We fail to see," Justice White wrote for
the Court, "how being unceremoniously dispossessed of one's home
in the manner alleged to have occurred here can be viewed as anything
but a seizure invoking the protection of the Fourth Amendment."[80]
The Court continued its theme of incredulousness on the predicate
reasonableness of the seizure. It described the Seventh Circuit's Fourth
Amendment holding "novel" and had "difficulty" with a passage from
Posner's opinion discussing nominal Fourth Amendment application

and no invasion of privacy. Elsewhere the Court noted that the lower court's efforts on the protections of the Fourth Amendment are "both interesting and creative."[81] Posner's opinion had argued that the Fourth Amendment protects privacy but not property. As part of its firm, empathic point-by-point rejection of the Posner majority opinion's attempt to redraw Fourth Amendment boundaries, the Court remained unconvinced and noted that it saw "no justification for departing from our prior cases"[82]

Posner's dissents in three Seventh Circuit cases reviewed by the Supreme Court did not, on the whole, perform well. In the first, the Court affirmed the case of *International Union, United Auto., Aerospace and Agriculture Implement Workers of America v. Johnson Controls, Inc.*,[83] which concerned a manufacturer's policy barring all women, except those whose infertility was medically documented, from jobs involving actual or potential lead exposure. Posner had dissented when the case was decided en banc by the Seventh Circuit,[84] but the Court did nothing other than note his dissent, which had argued that the record before the court was too sparse and that a trial was needed for the factual record. In the second case, the LSD mixture case *Chapman v. United States*,[85] in which the Court held that the weight of the medium fit within the "substance or mixture" rule for determining the weight of the drug for sentencing purposes, the majority did not mention Posner's dissent, though Justice Stevens in his dissent quoted a long paragraph of Posner's explaining the absurdity and inequity that results when the blotter paper weight is added to the weight of the LSD for sentencing purposes.[86] The Court in the third case, *Farey v. Sanderfoot*,[87] did, however, follow Posner's dissent in reversing the Seventh Circuit on a loophole in the Bankruptcy Code that the debtor and ex-husband had used to escape the lien his ex-wife put on the marital home.[88] The case features the near metaphysical issue of whether the right to avoid the lien arose at the same time of the divorce settlement in which title to the formerly jointly marital home passed to the ex-husband. Other circuits when presented with the issue had come out as Posner had, for different reasons, but the Supreme Court thought Posner's reasoning was the better way to get to the result of denying the ex-husband his claim to lien avoidance because that reading followed the purpose of the statute at issue. Purpose trumped what might be called lawyerly arguments.

Evaluations

The *Almanac of the Federal Judiciary* evaluated Posner in its 1992 and 1997 editions. Lawyers seemed awed by his intellectual powers but objected to the way he presented himself at oral argument. They didn't mind the challenging hypotheticals he posed but drew the line at intellectual arrogance. One lawyer believed Posner treated lawyers with disdain. At the same time, several lawyers in the evaluation commented on changes from earlier years. "He doesn't seem to be as interested," one lawyer reported, "in driving you into the ground as he used to be." Another lawyer said that Posner was now more positive and "now almost life affirming." "He's written some decisions," the lawyer continued, "you would never ascribe to him five—or even three years ago." The sharp edge of law and economics also seemed to be in retreat. "He's not as stridently doctrinaire as he was when he took the bench, but he's still committed to his economic theories," one lawyer noted. Another added that "he still uses economic analysis, but in a much more narrow way. He's much more into a pragmatic analysis, which goes well beyond simple cost-benefit analysis. He's much more now into empowering judges to come up with solutions to problems."

Some new complaints popped up in the *Almanac of the Federal Judiciary* to go with assessments of excellence. Some lawyers noted that Posner's intellect was not tempered by litigation or trial court judging experience. "He did not have experience at the district court level," one lawyer pointed out, "and that's a problem" because he had no appreciation for the nature of lawyering. Lawyers complained that he treated them like pawns in a game or as the famous Professor Kingsfield treated his students in *The Paper Chase*. "He peppers you with questions without care for what the answer is," one lawyer objected, while another said that Posner did "not have time for weak arguments, or silly arguments, or attorneys who aren't prepared." The evaluation noted that "a significant minority" of the lawyers surveyed believed that Posner's opinions were not as instructive as they should be and that they represented a "sort of stream of consciousness with the law from his point of view, which is from an economic perspective." "He seems to have an interest in making law with his opinions."

The lawyers quoted in the *Almanac of the Federal Judiciary* were not the only lawyers evaluating him. The Chicago Council of Lawyers, which was formed "out of a concern by a wide variety of lawyers that other local bar associations were unwilling to criticize current judges and were too parochial in their interests," also weighed in with a study of the Seventh Circuit and its individual judges.[89] The study, conducted in the public interest and with the belief that the judiciary should know what lawyers practicing in their circuit think of them, all but exhorts Seventh Circuit judges to listen to the bar's collective pain. That the study has this tone—and coming as a second means to complain following the *Almanac to the Federal Judiciary*—makes it seem at times as though the bar was on the verge of revolt. In the section of the study assessing the court generally, sharp complaints were lodged over the court's composition; over a preoccupation with procedural rules, described as being designed only for the convenience of the judges; over jurisdictional rules; and over a tendency to too quickly sanction lawyers for rule noncompliance.

Turning to Posner individually, the Council's evaluation of Posner's performance at oral argument recognized that Posner applied the highest standards and represented a "great professional challenge" to those appearing before him, making a good performance before him a mark of high achievement. The evaluation noted that Posner's questions "are nearly always insightful and often suggest that he is looking at a case differently than the lawyers." Lawyers reported that "he understands their cases better than they do." Nonetheless, some lawyers were critical of Posner's performance at argument. He did not seem concerned with the point of view of the lawyers and sometimes used oral argument to explore at the expense of the lawyer's argument those issues of interest to him. He was too willing to point out that the briefs had not been helpful. He was arrogant "to the point of being offensive" but had softened over the years. The final summary is that "although he is not overtly rude or hostile at oral argument, it is reported that he remains somewhat condescending toward advocates."

The Council evaluation harshly criticized Posner for his treatment of the bar. It complained that he too often and without a sufficiently developed record sanctioned lawyers and that he was too willing to embarrass them publicly with descriptions of inadequate performance. He was too rigid and too strict in enforcing the Circuit's procedural rules. The evaluation also criticized his eagerness to pounce on waiver and jurisdictional issues. Presented with these criticisms, Posner responded in a letter to the Council that takes a hard line on waiver and jurisdiction. "But once a ground is properly before the court," he wrote, "I aim in disposing of it to give the reader a full and candid explanation for the reasons of my disposition. If candor requires me to acknowledge disagreement with precedent, or puzzlement at the parties' failure to explore a particular line of analysis, or distress at the lawyers' incompetence or belief that proper disposition hinges on an issue not recognized by the parties, I say so; and that is why my opinions strike some lawyers as being outside the professional groove. I say outright what other judges prefer to keep under their hat."

The Council evaluation also criticized Posner for excessive dicta and use of his opinions as occasions for digressions on the application of general principles to law. He did not show sufficient respect for "precedent, history, and the proper limits on appellate judging." His opinions were too long, not sufficiently structured, and sometimes "more difficult to follow than they ought to be." His opinions displayed a "stream of consciousness approach to legal reasoning," and he underestimated the confusion his opinions caused.

Cited

Posner leads circuit judges in citation counts. During the 1990–99 period, Posner was cited by name 269 times by circuit judges outside the Seventh Circuit. These references to "Judge Posner" do not include the 346 times during the decade in which Posner was named parenthetically in a citation, as in "(Posner, J.)" following the case citation. He had also been cited by name 86 times by judges outside the Seventh Circuit in the 1982–89 period. These "Judge Posner" occasions in the 1990–99 period tell us something about both Posner and those who cite him. Judges cite him by name to add weight, authority, and a certain distinction to their opinions. More specifically, they use Posner to help them explain particular issues, to take advantage of a well-struck phrase, for the insight of his observation, for the nature of the analysis he has conducted, for his willingness to cut to the heart of issues, and for his boldness in seeing an issue afresh. They often make their admiration for his work known. Strikingly, the references rarely invoke the economic analysis that Posner so pushes in his opinions. There are dozens of citations to his *Economic Analysis of Law* in circuit court case law over the years, suggesting Posner's influence as an academic, but when judges turn to Posner, it is for reasons separate from the economic analysis he puts in his opinions. They cite him by name for what they have in common with him—for his responses to the workaday issues that circuit judges run into.

Clerks

Posner's law clerks from the 1990s in emails and interviews give unique information and assessments that only insiders can provide.[90] One clerk explained that when he worked for Posner all research for his opinions was done in book form: "we would assemble library carts of books with Post-its in them, and then wheel the carts into his office with a memo explaining what the books were meant to show." The clerks used Westlaw and Lexis-Nexis, of course, but did not give him their research in electronic form. That came in the next decade.

One clerk recalled that "the most salient feature of Dick's process was that he would draft his opinions the night after the oral argument (or maybe within two nights); and those drafts would look just like the finished opinions, but no authorities cited for anything—just '[citations]' every place where he wanted them. It then fell to the clerk to go find authority to support what he had said." Usually this wasn't difficult, because the propositions for which he wanted support were straightforward. But sometimes the clerk would become convinced that Posner had the facts or law wrong, and would send back a memo to that effect. A few times a year a typical clerk would convince Posner to change the rationale or outcome of a case in this way, and that was always a source of surprise and satisfaction. One clerk used to refer to changes in the rationale as field goals, and to changes in the outcome as touchdowns.

This clerk noted that Posner "had an amazing ability to remember what he had said in his prior opinions (amazing because there were so many of them). Sometimes he would make one of those statements, in a draft opinion followed by '[citations],' and you would dig for hours trying without luck to find authority to support the claim. You would dutifully report the failure to him, and he would assure you that he had said something like it before, and perhaps mention some facts from the case where he had done it. Sure enough, the case would turn up, and he had indeed said something like it before—and that was the citation he had sought."

Posner stressed analysis first in his opinion writing. As a clerk put it, it was not of a "bottom up" character. "On the legal side he writes his analysis first, then looks for legal support afterwards; he doesn't go read all the authorities and then build to a conclusion. Likewise, on the factual side he tells the story of the case as it strikes him, emphasizing the facts that he finds significant, which may not be the ones the parties thought were important. Possibly the most important job of the Posner clerk was to scour the record of the case to make sure Dick got the facts right; but even that checking often won't catch the choices of emphasis that will infuriate the losing party."

Posner in person was relentlessly mild, kind, and good-humored, several law clerks reported. One clerk with a detailed assessment noted that

> there was something a little odd, almost unearthly, about his cerebral nature, his bird-like quality, his almost drifting style of motion, his high, sing-song voice; so it always seemed a little funny or jarring to hear about his engagement in ordinary things, like enjoying rock music or B movies. Every day of work for him was a pleasure. He must have often thought that I (like any of his clerks) was clueless much of the time—for we certainly were—but he was always too generous to give any indication of it. Of course that's largely because he didn't care; he barely needed us except as a way to save himself some time. I sometimes felt that he hired us as court jesters: our job was to help him stay amused and to tell him when we thought he was wrong, because occasionally we might be right about that. Despite his brilliance, and the high opinion of himself that he no doubt enjoys (or maybe because of that), he never minded being told that he was screwing up. He would be happy to listen to the reason, and once in a while would decide that you were right.

Law clerks on the oral argument issue reported that Posner would sometimes get annoyed by lawyers. "I remember him," one clerk recalled,

coming back from one of those and saying that debating with one of the lawyers was like arguing with a rhinoceros. I've also seen him get a little hot at faculty lunches at the University of Chicago when he's arguing with someone who is displaying some intellectual vice that offends him—some sort of formalism. There's an aggressive contempt that sometime surfaces in those cases. He'll tell his adversary that what he's saying is fraudulent or is bullshit, and in a tone that is not much fun to receive. The worst fate a lawyer could have was to appear in front of Dick and Frank [Easterbrook] together—at least if the lawyer was anything other than sharp and well-prepared. (For a sufficiently skilled lawyer the experience might turn out to be a treat in the end, though no doubt scary while it was happening.) They would inevitably perceive problems in the case right away (they often would have chatted about the case in advance), and would egg each other on in tearing the lawyer apart, sometimes chortling at each other's jests (in fairness, Frank did most of the chortling). It was sometimes entertaining for the spectator in an awful sort of way. Dick and Frank love to torture a lawyer with hypotheticals to test whatever claims he is making—the law professor's habit.

Turning to the way Easterbrook and Posner performed at oral argument, one clerk said that he had seen Posner devastate lawyers, but that "there was always something impersonal about it. In Frank's case there was a different edge. When I speak with people who have never met Dick but have read his writings, they sometimes imagined that in person he must be a brute; in fact I think they imagine him as someone more like Frank."

Another clerk noted that Posner

expected more of the government's lawyers (as he once was one) and was frequently disappointed. He expected more out of lawyers at large firms and was sometimes disappointed. He was frustrated when the lawyer was more of a litigator and not a substantive law expert.

One of my favorite lines is when he would characterize a lawyer's answer as "mere words" when in fact he wanted a "real reason." He wanted to ask lawyers the hard questions and was frequently annoyed when he knew a lawyer's case better than the lawyer. He could come across as difficult and mean in oral argument. That is a mistaken impression. Rather, he demands professional excellence and he wants lawyers to address the hard questions. He is not tolerant when they do not. With that said, his approach is much different than Judge Easterbrook's. At times, I really thought Judge Easterbrook's goal was to embarrass and humiliate the lawyer. That is never Dick's goal. Dick's goal is to have a dialogue to reach the correct answer.

On this point, lawyers providing assessments for the *Almanac of the Federal Judiciary* saw Easterbrook's performances at oral argument and the contrasts between him and Posner much the way that the clerks did. Lawyers in the 1992 edition praised Easterbrook's intelligence, knowledge of the record, and tough questioning that can at times embarrass a lawyer, one lawyer noting that Easterbrook "hones in on the weakness in a case and drives it in" and that he "often chuckles and passes notes to other judges." Comments in the 1997 edition grew more pervasively negative and more caustic. More than half of the lawyers interviewed complained about Easterbrook's demeanor. There were complaints that he made comments at the expense of the lawyers arguing, that "he will sometimes tilt back his head, laugh and look at his law clerks and encourage them to laugh at what the lawyer has said." Lawyers noted that he was abrasive, rude, condescending, and flip, though lawyers in the minority described his demeanor as generally good but sometimes domineering.

Articles on Influence and Citations

Posner's citation numbers were in the second half of the decade beginning to attract attention. The Chicago Bar Council survey included an appendix prepared by Larry Lessig of citation counts that showed Posner to be the leader by far on the Seventh Circuit. An article that Lessig wrote with William Landes and Michael Solimine explored citation analysis as a proxy for influence and, considering a number of factors, ranked Posner the leader among all sitting circuit judges.[91] The study considered the difference between the number of times a judge is cited in his own circuit and the number of times judges outside his circuit cited him, with the idea that the latter is a greater reflection of influence.

His opinions also led in a different, nonjudicial, category. He was the leader by far in the number of opinions appearing in a selection of some three hundred casebooks used in law schools from June 1999 to May 2000.[92] Posner had 118 opinions used, while his closest competitor, Frank Easterbrook, had 56. Of the 118 opinions, 26 were in contracts, 12 in torts, and 10 each in antitrust and remedies. Turning from the courts to the academy, we find Posner again at the head of the pack. Fred Shapiro in his article "The Most-Cited Legal Scholars" determined that Posner was the leader by far in the database of legal studies.[93] He had through the end of the 1990s been cited nearly eight thousand times. His nearest competitor, Ronald Dworkin, had been cited approximately forty-five hundred times.

Books and Articles

Major Social Issues

Between 1992 and 1995 Posner published three books—each a major effort—on social issues: *Sex and Reason, Private Choices and Public Health: The AIDS Epidemic in an Economic Perspective*, and *Aging and Old Age*.[94] (In 1996 he complemented *Sex and Reason* with *A Guide to America's Sex Laws,* which he wrote with Katharine Silbaugh.)[95] The books, beyond their respective examinations of social issues—old age, sex, and AIDS—shared three other characteristics. They were original, as opposed to collections of previously published essays reworked for book publication; they used the economic analysis pioneered by Gary Becker in his treatise on the family and applied it to the subjects at hand; and they were all synoptic. The books on AIDS and sex shared a relentless tone and argument reminiscent of *Economic Analysis of Law.* The old-age study, though, dips into the personal, both with many references to Posner's favorite poet, Yeats, on old age and with discussions of old-age-associated problems as they presented themselves in his mother, father-in-law, and one of his grandfathers.

At the core of his book on AIDS, cowritten with economist Tomas J. Philipson, is the argument that economic analysis does a better job than epidemiology in projecting the extent of the AIDS epidemic. The epidemiological approach, which predicted that ultimately everyone would have the disease, did not consider what is at the core of the economic analysis—volition and rational choice. Posner and Philipson present a model of how rational actors make choices and show its application to risky sex choices, leading to the perhaps counterintuitive implication that government intervention and public involvement waste money and are unnecessary.

Posner uses economic analysis to consider sex as a subject by itself and as a socially regulated activity. He begins *Sex and Reason* with a history of sexuality. Later chapters tackle a theory of sex and biology, sex and rationality, the history of sexuality from the perspective of economics, and the optimal regulation of sexuality. He covers all of this with economic analysis that considers its subject to be no different from any other to which it can be applied. He tackles the questions of marriage and sex, the control of pregnancy, homosexuality, sexual abuse of adults, sexual abuse of children, adoption and artificial insemination, and pornography. His leanings are functional, secular and utilitarian, libertarian in the sense of John Stuart Mill, and perhaps contractual, since he would not mind jettisoning marriage in favor of contractual cohabitation. He's interdisciplinary in his approach but applies economic analysis as the most useful tool. His economic analysis, though, features sociobiology, which he acknowledges is controversial. He uses economics, he says, because it is "the acid bath" that peels away "layers of ignorance, ideology, superstition and prejudice."[96] His is a sexual world of "incentives, opportunities, constraints, and social function."[97]

In addition to economics, he uses in *Aging and Old Age* evolutionary biology, cognitive psychology, philosophy, and literature, though "economics wields the baton of [his] multidisciplinary orchestra."[98] Featured in the economic analysis are Becker's theory of human capital and its emphasis on the investments we make in ourselves and the theory of time-consistency of preferences, often called the problem of "multiple selves." Economic analysis, he argues, does a better job than any other discipline in helping us understand aging as an attitudinal and behavioral phenomenon and in solving policy problems. He considers as background the nature of aging and old age as social, biological, and economic phenomena before applying his economics-charged model to a variety of problems, including mandatory retirement, euthanasia and physician-assisted suicide, the Employment Retirement Income Security Act, the Age Discrimination in Employment Act, and the Social Security Act. The analyses produce the conclusions that ERISA has not been needed and has not done what it promised, that ADEA has been ineffectual and works perversely against the interests of older workers, that the move to abolish mandatory retirement is misguided, that the Social Security system withstands scrutiny as a fair contract between the young and the old, and that carefully regulated physician-assisted suicide is desirable.

Posner's interest in old age and death in his correspondence in the 1990s complements what he was writing academically on the subjects, especially about the death of his parents. His mother's death is a recurring topic. He tells Nussbaum that "when my mother died at 89 two years ago, having been completely senile for several years, I, age 51 then, felt no grief," though he did feel a slight anxiety for his father, who, as it turned out, "recovered quickly enough from *his* grief." The passing of Nussbaum's own mother presents the issue again. Posner asks Nussbaum if she remembers T. S. Eliot's comment about Hamlet, that his upset at his mother seemed excessive in relation to its object, and says, "I have the same reaction to your upset at your mother's death. I hope that does not seem brutal." The same inability to empathize comes up again in their correspondence with a reference to a mutual colleague who is sad at losing his mother. This makes no sense to Posner since the mutual colleague had disliked her. "I will exhibit my emotional simplicity (if not insensitivity)," he writes, "by asking why [our mutual colleague] is sad about his mother, since he dislikes her so much. Shock, fearful coming of age, full of premonitions, etc., but why sad?" And when a mutual acquaintance dies at the age of eighty, Posner writes that he liked her "but I find it hard to understand the depth of emotion occasioned by her death. It seems that when a person dies at 80 the survivors should accept it with equanimity. We could use more of the stoic virtues."

He explains why he did not seem more sympathetic to the news of Nussbaum's mother's death, writing, "I was characteristically insensitive in not realizing that your mother's death would be a heavy blow to you. My own mother as I mentioned died at almost 90 after years of senility, and I had not seen her in the last year and a half of her life as she no longer recognized me, and it is an odd feeling not to be known to one's own mother. Of course I did not hold this against her; nevertheless in these circumstances her death could not be felt as a loss; obviously your situation is different." When Nussbaum writes that her late mother was a wonderful mother, he is at a loss to understand. He asks, "what *was* wonderful about your mother? I don't think there was anything wonderful about mine although I loved her very much when I was a child and indeed until I was about 20."

He becomes almost feisty in rejecting Nussbaum's suggestions that he does not mean what he says about his mother. First he pushes back. "It is not true that I think of my mother 'with great affection,'" he writes. "She was fearfully senile for a number of years before her death and this horror effaced most of my recollections of her in her prime." Then he continues with what seems to be the key issue—he did not choose his parents. "Then too," he writes, "she wasn't really my type of person and I prefer to choose my intimates than have them chosen for me, although I make an exception for my children and their wives." He concludes his thought with some wicked humor. "My friend Joe Epstein in his 'Aristides' column for the *American Scholar* wrote recently about how much he misses his mother, who died recently in her eighties and on the evidence of his column was in no wise exceptional and indeed rather a *yenta*—and my reaction to the column was that of a eunuch being told about the delights of sex." And to cinch the idea, he writes to Nussbaum that when it came to his parents, he did not "have a strong family feeling."

Writing similarly, when a correspondent suggests that there is something terrible in the death of a parent, he responds that it probably depends on the age of the parent and the age of the child. When a nonintimate correspondent reports on the death of his father, Posner responds with stiff-upper-lip exhortation. "I am very sorry to hear that your father died," he writes. "I know it must be a great loss to you, but of course it is something we must all go through sooner or later. Please accept my condolences." Even with a longtime correspondent with whom he felt close, he struggles to find the right tone in a condolence letter, mixing well-expressed sympathy with a self-reference. "Please accept my condolences," he writes. "I had heard that your wife had amyotrophic lateral sclerosis, but did not realize that it had progressed so rapidly; perhaps that was a blessing; and one cannot feel entirely sorry for someone spared the ravages of old age (of which I am especially conscious at the moment, because I am preparing a series of lectures on the subject). But it is a terrible loss for you, for which I am very sorry." He gets it right, though, when a mentor with whom he was close lost a child and his note expresses sympathy not undermined by broader observation. "Charlene [Posner's wife] and I offer you and [your wife] our most sincere condolences; as parents, we can glimpse, at least, the magnitude of loss and the depth of your shock and sorrow." And when an older faculty member loses a spouse, Posner sends a note of eloquent, genuine sympathy, reading, "I do not possess the words adequate to such a sad occasion, but I do want to tell you, however artlessly, how much my heart goes out to you. Of all the recent deaths this is the most unjust because of [your wife's] youth, goodness, and vitality. If I had a faith this would test it, but I don't. I can't improve on Edgar's dictum that 'man must endure his going hence even as his coming hither.'"

OVERCOMING LAW

Posner over the first half of the decade wrote nineteen articles and book reviews that he brought together, adding two articles from 1989, a handful of new essays, and a lengthy introduction to make *Overcoming Law*, his 1995 collection.[99] In the introduction he explains with bold language that the "law" of his title refers to "a professional totem signifying all that is pretentious, uninformed, prejudiced, and spurious in legal tradition."[100] Economic analysis, he explains, is but one of the keys to legal theory. The others are pragmatism and liberalism. He also sums up one of the book's major goals, which is "to nudge the judicial game a little closer to the science game."[101] His preface, though, might have been the most important part of the book. As summarized there, his argument "is that a taste for fact, a respect for social science, an eclectic curiosity, a desire to be practical, a belief in individualism, and an openness to new perspectives—all interrelated characteristics of a certain kind of pragmatism, alternatively of a certain kind of economics and a certain kind of liberalism—can make legal theory an effective instrument for understanding and improving law, and social institutions generally; for demonstrating the inadequacies of existing legal thought and for putting something better in its place."[102]

The subjects range widely and include, to mention some but not all, medieval Iceland, Hagel, Richard Rorty's politics, the legal profession, legal reasoning, pragmatism, economic analysis, affirmative action, law and literature, and Ronald Coase.[103] In two essays he also continues criticisms of, respectively, legal scholarship and the work and work habits of judges. This last essay continues his complaints in 1985's *Federal Courts* about judges not writing their own opinions but goes further, premising his approach to the work lives of judges on the idea, rarely encountered in print, that judges are ordinary people and treating them as such in his analysis. His essay on legal scholarship bemoans the decline of traditional doctrinal scholarship in the face of the academy's preoccupation with theory and with "law and" subjects that add little which judges can use in their work. The academy's political drift to the left and its laxer publication standards coupled with an ever-increasing law review market mean that the academy is a world of its own and with fewer connections to the profession and the judiciary.

The reviews were highly favorable, with many pointing to the extraordinary range of the subjects, though some thought it was too much of a collection. One review, for example, though describing it as "a very good book indeed," noted that Posner seemed to labor to bring the various essays together thematically and that "the book is in many ways a potpourri."[104] Another reviewer wrote that "the book is incorrigibly eclectic, even more than most edited collections of discrete essays."[105]

THE PROBLEMATICS OF MORAL AND LEGAL THEORY (1999)

In *The Problematics of Moral and Legal Theory*, Posner brought together and reworked four lectures on legal theory, moral theory, and the legal profession. The title of his Holmes lectures at Harvard became the title of the book version of the articles.[106] The book's theme, not a new one for him, is "the demystification of law and in particular the freeing of it from moral theory."[107] *The Problematics of Moral and Legal Theory* completed a trilogy on what he described as "the major normative issues that beset the modern judge, moralist, and policymaker."[108] There was no doubt as to where Posner stood in advocating pragmatism over moral philosophy as a judicial tool. He defined how a pragmatist judge works by contrasting his definition with the definition Dworkin had given. For Dworkin, "The pragmatist thinks judges should always do the best they can for the future, in the circumstances, unchecked by any need to respect or secure consistency in principle with what other officials have done or will do."[109] Posner tweaks Dworkin's definition a bit to get it right. He thinks that "pragmatist judges always try to do the best they can do for the present and the future, unchecked by any felt *duty* to secure consistency in principle with what other officials have done in the past."[110]

Posner takes a sharp-stick-in-the-eye approach to arguing that moral philosophy, law, and judging do not mix. Moral philosophy does not and cannot, he argues, help judges work through their hard cases. For help they need to turn, as he had begun arguing in *The Problem of Jurisprudence* and *Overcoming Law* earlier in the decade, to the social sciences. He claims that "moral philosophy has nothing to offer judges or legal scholars so far as either adjudication or the formulation of jurisprudence or legal doctrines is concerned," but also "that it has very little to offer anyone engaged in a normative enterprise, quite without regard to law."[111] Turning the argument to academic philosophers, he asserts that there is simply no reason to think that academic philosophers have anything to add to the tools that judges use to decide cases. "There isn't even evidence or reason," he writes, "to believe that academic moralists have superior moral insight when compared with other people."[112] "The intellectual gifts moral philosophers exhibit need not, and in their normative work usually do not, generate a positive social product."[113] The academy is complicit in the failings of academic philosophers. The academy wastes resources on academic philosophers that it could better use with social scientists, who give judges information that they can use.[114]

In comments that reflect the responses of critics generally, those invited by the *Harvard Law Review* to respond to Posner's Holmes lectures answered with a vengeance, often making their attacks personal. Fellow circuit judge John Noonan, of the Ninth Circuit, was the only one of the group to compliment Posner. He was impressed by Posner's candor, courage, and clarity of expression. Of the dissenters, Dworkin set the tone of his caustic response with his title, "Darwin's Bulldog," while Charles Fried characterized the lectures as a "display of dyspepsia" and a "diatribe against moral and political philosophy." Anthony Kronman thought that Posner's general approach was "awash in cynicism" and seemed "despairing from start to finish." Martha Nussbaum argued that Posner was defending "an implausibly mechanistic picture of human personality" and that the enterprise as a whole was an "occasion for sadness." In his reply, which Posner included in the book versions of his lectures, Posner fought back, conceding the need for amplification and correction in several particulars but even more confident of his position after having read the criticisms.

Reviewers complained primarily about the nature of Posner's pragmatism and his rejection of the contributions that moral philosophy and by extension academic moral philosophers could make to the law and to life. They were not content with Posner's explanation that socially shared values rather than moral values, as vague and as slippery as they can be, help form the foundation on which judges make decisions. In hard cases, Posner had claimed, judges can get no help from moral philosophy. "Pragmatism will not tell us what is best," he argued, "but, provided there is a fair degree of value consensus among the judges, as I think there is, it can help judges seek the best results unhampered by philosophical doubts."[115] One reviewer, Daniel Farber, recognized two points overlooked by others. Farber perceives something in Posner approaching the sensibility of a provocateur, as suggested by his title, "Shocking the Conscience." He describes Posner as being drawn by his desire to be hardheaded "into occasional insensitivity toward certain moral values."[116] And Farber alone of the reviewers looks to Posner's work on the bench to evaluate the book and with regard to moral values is able to write that "Posner's work as a judge shows that he himself is not insensitive to these values," though "they seem oddly shortchanged in his theoretical account."[117]

LAW AND LEGAL THEORY IN THE UK AND USA

Posner produced other writing in the decade that advanced his arguments for pragmatism and against moral and legal philosophy. His *Law and Legal Theory in the UK and the USA*, a short book expanding his Clarendon lectures at Oxford, gave him a chance to tell his British audience that it could well learn from the American example of using social sciences in the law and that there is no payoff to philosophical speculation relating to law. In the first lecture, which takes Dworkin on once again, Posner addresses the question Dworkin poses, "What is law?" He says that the question should not be asked "because it only confuses matters."[118] Pragmatism presumably falls outside what is contemplated by "What is law?"

A Major Political Issue

Posner in 1999 published *An Affair of State* about the 1998–99 Clinton impeachment crisis, closing out his list of books in the decade. It would prove to be a very different kind of book.[119] The crisis seemed to bring together much of what he was interested in and had in fact been writing about, though to date strictly academically. It featured factual complexity and legal issues of all sorts, ranging from criminal and constitutional law to the law of impeachment itself. There were also issues of jurisprudence, private and public morality, and political theory, to say nothing of political and cultural sociological factors underlying the behavior of what he termed the "moralistic Right" and the "academic Left." To be understood and properly appreciated, the complex set of facts and the overlay of issues needed ("cries out for") "the sort of synoptic, compendious treatment" he had given to sex and old age in earlier books, though without the economic analysis that drove *Sex and Reason* and *Aging and Old Age*.

He sets the stage with a narrative of President Clinton's conduct leading up to the impeachment and an assessment of its criminality before detailing and assessing the prosecution and defense; the history, scope, and form of impeachment; the issues of public and private morality in play; whether President Clinton should have been impeached, and if impeached convicted; the role of the "intelligentsia," by which he means highly educated people, mainly academics and journalists, who write books and articles on important social and political matters; and the lessons we can learn from the impeachment crisis. For convenience he draws up a balance sheet to determine whether we are better or worse off for the impeachment crisis experience. He had three goals for the book. One was to give a "freshness and immediacy" to the account and analysis by writing apace with the unfolding of the events themselves and delivering the manuscript to the publisher, Harvard University

Press, just four days after the Senate voted to acquit President Clinton. Key to this goal was a nonpartisan approach. The second was to create what he describes as "distinguished contemporary history," citing as predecessors in the genre Tacitus, Thucydides, and Suetonius. The third goal was to use the account and analysis of the crisis as an empirical test in the realm of law and philosophy against which pragmatism as he has been espousing it could be judged. His pragmatic approach on the one hand could be judged against competing formalistic, philosophical, and historical approaches, and on the other hand the competing theory of constitutional and moral theory as applied to the impeachment crisis could be assessed.

Though Posner described the book as scholarly, it was stylistically very different from his previously published scholarly books and articles. Here he wrote with the voice, language, and reader engagement found in his judicial opinions. The approach, like that which we find in his judicial opinions, is more conversational. As he does in his opinions, Posner in *An Affair of State* often uses literary and historical allusions, with Shakespeare, as is true in Posner's opinions, showing up most often. He uses the same indicators of reader engagement as in his opinions, with phrases indicating that a conversation is taking place: "we now have to consider," "remember that," "suppose that," and "we must remember." He also engages in the same type of spinning, of thinking through related ideas implicated by his analysis, prefaced with "it might be argued" or a phrase with similar meaning. He is also in the book, as he does in his opinions, always explaining the better approach, the one pragmatism counsels. There is reason to think that Posner thought of the materials he consulted, such as the Starr Report, as similar to the materials he consults for his judicial opinions, as when he describes the impeachment trial as "an enormously distended appellate argument, with the Starr Report taking the place of the trial court's decision, the usual springboard for an appeal" and says that his own book is the next layer of review of what both Congress and the Supreme Court had done.[120] As he does in his opinions, he considers assertions, objections, and concerns in thinking through the issues.

In Posner's evaluation, only the press in its coverage of the crisis does well. Everyone else gets a failing grade. The Supreme Court gets one for not killing the independent counsel law in *Morrison v. Olsen*[121] in 1988 when it had the chance and for letting the crisis develop when it should have appreciated the political dimensions of the problem in the Paula Jones case, *Clinton v. Jones*,[122] which the Court let proceed. On the *Jones* opinion, he notes that the Court did not seem to understand what was going on and what was at stake. What's missing from the Court's opinion, he writes, "is an intellectual suppleness, a practicality, and a realism that judges and lawyers ought to have in a society in which disputes of high political moment are routinely submitted to courts for resolution."[123] He faults the lawyers on both sides in the impeachment trial, Clinton's lawyers for being too facile with the truth, if not worse, and Congress's lawyers—themselves—for being in over their heads. Academics and commentators are criticized for losing their objectivity and going beyond their expertise in their opinions and, in the case of liberal academics, signing letters to the editor on the nature of impeachment. "It is tempting to conclude (though overgeneralization is a danger here)," he writes, "that the left intelligentsia lacks a moral core, while the right intelligentsia has a morbidly exaggerated fear of moral laxity."[124] And as for Clinton himself, Posner's concludes that he disgraced the presidency and likely committed a number of felonies, which, if he were not the president and had been prosecuted in federal court, would have exposed him to thirty to thirty-seven months of prison time under the sentencing guidelines. But for him pragmatism counsels that it matters that Clinton was the president, certainly as it affects how we understand the impeachment provisions of the Constitution. But after making the argument that the president should be given a wider berth on the constitutional front, on the ultimate issue Posner hedges, writing that "about all that can be said is that a moral rigorist would be inclined to think that the President committed impeachable offenses, while a pragmatist would lean, although perhaps only slightly, the other way."[125] In a 2002 C-SPAN interview he delivered a somewhat different conclusion. "My conclusion," he said, "was that there was very little doubt that President Clinton had committed serious offenses of the sort that could have gotten him prosecuted. But on the other hand, I didn't think it was possible to really make a judgment on impeachability, because there just are not sufficient guideposts in the Constitution or in political theory, so I actually thought that his misconduct was serious, and I thought it probably was a good idea that it got a very public airing, but I don't think it would have been good for the Senate to convict him and remove him from office. So I was pretty content with the result."

Posner had begun the decade with a progress report on his approach to judging and continued throughout the decade to put into practice the pragmatism he had described as best suited for judges interested in both the present and the future. At the end of the decade with his book on the Clinton impeachment crisis Posner showed that he was moving away from the smaller pond of scholarly writing and was interested in writing about—with analysis, exposition, and commentary—subjects with pressing national import. The country needed, he seemed to be declaring throughout the decade, his one-of-a-kind voice and intellectual approach. He had arrived.

5

Public Intellectual (2000–2009)

THE DECADE OF THE aughts saw Posner moving onto the national stage, not that he had been known only in academic circles prior to 2000. He had, after all, been talked about in the mid-1980s as a possible Supreme Court nominee. But with the new decade he became better known. His book on the Clinton impeachment, published in 1999, had gotten significant attention leading into 2000, selling twenty-five thousand hardcover copies and being listed by the *New York Times* as one of the best books of the year. At the end of 1999 Posner was regularly written about in the press when he was asked to act as a mediator in the Microsoft antitrust litigation that was making front-page news daily. That same year he got into—was drawn into—a charged dispute with Ronald Dworkin in the *New York Review of Books*, one of the nation's leading intellectual journals. In 2001 his book on the election crisis of 2000 made a splash with its analysis of the Supreme Court's decision in *Bush v. Gore*, and also that year the *New Yorker* profiled him. During the decade he seemed to be everywhere, adapting to changes in the publishing world with blogging and online magazine contributions and almost continually asserting himself, with a torrent of fifteen books, not counting updated editions of earlier books or edited volumes, many of which were on subjects of national interest, such as the 2000 presidential election, national security and terrorism, and the financial collapse of 2008. All of this was set against a background of a decade's worth of judging on the Seventh Circuit.

Microsoft Mediator

The highly publicized antitrust case between Microsoft and the government had at the end of 1999 all but wrapped up in Judge Jackson's courtroom following several months of trial. Judge Jackson had assembled his proposed findings of fact but wanted to give the parties an opportunity to settle the case and avoid the uncertainty that would come with the remedies he would fashion upon its completion. Because he believed only Posner had sufficient stature to get the attention of the parties, he asked if he would mediate and Posner agreed, throwing himself into the mediation while continuing with his otherwise full schedule on the circuit court.

Posner's archive file on the mediation, while thin, reveals much about Posner and his approach to the antitrust problem, the litigation, and the parties.[1] The file contains notes for the agenda of the first meeting that presented his overview of the mediation; a flurry of letters and emails in the beginning of March 2000 about the fourteenth and hopefully final draft of an agreement (though more were to come), which Bill Gates had signed; and a thirty-page memo to himself analyzing the case. He explained to the parties at their first meeting how he planned to approach the mediation and offered as part of his contribution complete confidentiality and a willingness to accommodate the schedules of the parties, including weekends. He prepared an algebraic settlement model, shared with the parties, that considered the plaintiffs' minimum demand, the defendant's maximum offer, and a settlement range. His depth of involvement, beyond the memo he wrote to himself, is reflected by the number of his meetings with the parties (more than a dozen) and by references to long conversations at this critical moment with Joel Klein of the Justice Department and with Gates. Posner spoke often with Gates, sometimes in extended phone calls. Ken Auletta, whose compelling narrative in *World War 3.0* of both the litigation as a whole and of the Posner mediation interval, for which he was able to interview representatives from Microsoft, the government, and the state attorneys general, marks Posner and Gates talking on the telephone in four conversations for a total of more than eleven hours.[2]

Posner's thirty-page memo to himself represents a complete factual and legal analysis of the case, complete with assessments of the testimony of all the witnesses, and informed speculations about how the case would fare with a variety of appellate panels on the D.C. Circuit. Its opening pages set out his fundamental mediation operating principles: that he saw the case presenting the contrast between a pragmatic and principled approach and that he saw the dynamics of the case as a sort of investment decision that considered Microsoft's huge potential liability, which could be traded for a smaller present liability, depending on settlement terms. Law's relevance, he wrote, was only a factor as it related to the business decision that Microsoft had to make. He reminded himself of Holmes's observation that law is just a prediction of what courts will do in a particular circumstance. He also reminds himself of the dangers that the lawyers who had lost at trial presented in possibly opposing settlement for reasons other than the client's best interests.

He had dozens of questions for Gates about his internal "Internet Tidal Wave" memo from May 26, 1995, which had been introduced into evidence and which starkly if not defiantly set out Microsoft's position on its approach to competition. He also wrote out questions going to whether Gates was bringing a pragmatic approach to the litigation. One question designed to prompt Gates to see the litigation differently asked whether he would refuse to settle if he thought the terms unfair, even if he were certain that he would do worse in the courts. Made more precise, the question asked whether he was looking at the litigation in the pragmatic way he would if he instead had a big investment in a Third World country with a corrupt judiciary.

Letters and emails show a skilled manager and writer. Posner conveys what the other party is complaining about and then offers to help the party he's talking with to deal with the complaint. For example, in a March 3, 2000, letter to Klein he reports that Gates had told him in their last conversation that Gates believed that the government had an obligation to come up with a list of demands that would be definitive and form the basis for the last push in negotiations which would follow acceptance of the fourteenth draft. Posner then tells Klein that he wants to help him with the list as a way of making sure Klein puts on the list all the items that matter to him but at the same time leave room for compromise. He again says that he thinks that both the content and the tone of the list are important. He also advises Klein on how he might want to handle the attorneys general, suggesting that they as a group prepare a single list of items.

His skills are on display in a key moment. A problem arose when Posner, acting on what he graciously suggested later was a misunderstanding, called into question the government's good faith in negotiating. Doubts had been raised for Posner because the government seemed to be changing its position on the key issue of vacating the trial court's findings of fact. It was now against vacating the findings and said that its position was nonnegotiable. This nonnegotiable demand plus the government's other nonnegotiable demand that Microsoft be forced to disclose certain technical operating system information seemed to convince Posner about the government's true intentions in the negotiations.

But thinking that he may have gone too far, he tried to mollify the government, first by explaining that he may have misunderstood the government's position on the findings of fact and then by trying to repair any possible affront Klein might have taken with respect to good faith by telling Klein how highly he thought of him and that he has told Microsoft that he thinks Klein is a lawyer of the highest integrity and is negotiating in good faith. Moreover, he has told Microsoft that he does not think that Klein is particularly interested in money and that he is not using his representation of the government as a stepping-stone to a highly paid law firm job representing Microsoft's competitors. Posner has done this, he explains, not as a negotiating ploy but because he believes it. He even strokes Klein by telling him that he has trusted him from the beginning of the mediation and that he felt a greater rapport with him than with anyone else. He writes that he is of course neutral in the mediation but that he is permitted to have personal favorites and that, if he ever had a legal problem, he would entrust it to Klein because he has complete confidence in his ability and integrity. The letter to Klein kept the negotiations on track, for a week at least, until all hope was lost and Posner declared an impasse and sent the case back to Judge Jackson.

Ronald Dworkin

Posner's book on the Clinton impeachment was the occasion for Dworkin's attack on Posner. It was delivered in a review in the *New*

York Review of Books that also considered Posner's *The Problematics of Moral and Legal Theory*.[3] Dworkin shot at all possible targets. That Posner was a conservative, appointed to the bench by Ronald Reagan, was one. Law and economics as taught in law schools was another. He even found fault with Posner's work as an academic on the basis that he had retreated from his commitment to wealth maximization as the cornerstone of economic analysis of law. Going to what would likely trouble Posner the most, he then questioned whether Posner had violated judicial ethics by writing about a case that was still going on and which his views as a judge might have an influence on. The rest is a point-by-point rebuttal of the assessments Posner had made that were critical of liberal law professors who had become engaged in the impeachment fight with a signed letter running in the *New York Times*. He brings in Posner's book on the problematics of legal theory and its criticism of both moral and legal philosophy and its practitioners as proof of Posner's bias. He accuses Posner of "anti-intellectual furies" against these philosophers and takes on Posner's declaration that he had written the Clinton book to illustrate "the thesis of *Problematics* that moral theory is useless and that facts are everything." The books, Dworkin ripostes, actually disprove that thesis.[4] These books, he argues, taken together with other of Posner's recent books demonstrate his self-destructive anger at moral philosophy and philosophers.[5]

Posner felt compelled to respond, he wrote, not because he had a habit of complaining about negative reviews but because Dworkin's review was "so unmistakably a personal attack that [he] would be poor-spirited not to respond."[6] He responded first in the pages of the *Review* and then in an article in the *Northwestern Law Review* that reprinted much of the *Review* matter but also added some new material. He defended writing the book despite being a sitting judge because the events were far removed from him as a judge and because his assessment was based on nothing other than the record compiled and used by Congress, as opposed to whatever evidence would be used if the impeachment affair spilled over into the criminal courts. He also went through an item-by-item defense of his various assessments of the facts and his position on moral and legal philosophers and on pragmatism as a superior way of solving problems.

The extent to which each combatant took the attack and then the response personally is an open question. Posner had in 1991 and 1992 attended at New York University a colloquium on Philosophy, Law, and Political Theory that Dworkin ran with academic philosopher Thomas Nagel. Describing the 1992 event, he wrote to a friend that the event was great, that one of the participants skewered him very nicely on some philosophical points, and that Dworkin was "super."[7] He also in 2001 attended the London version of the colloquium that Dworkin ran with Stephen Guest at University College London. These events led Posner in a 2007 tribute to Dworkin to describe him as an ideal intellectual host. He wrote that he had "the privilege and pleasure of presenting large swatches of book manuscripts three times at the colloquium. Not only the insights that Dworkin generously shares with the speakers on those occasions, the discussions that he orchestrates, and the improvements in my books that have resulted, but also the courtesy with which he delivers his penetrating criticisms, make these occasions memorable and wipe out the smart of our combats."[8] In that same tribute Posner noted that their intellectual relationship "was essentially one of antagonism, even antipathy."[9] Their intellectual relationship seems not to have been connected to their personal relationship.

BREAKING THE DEADLOCK (2001)

Posner took to the election controversy as he had to the impeachment crisis, by writing a book about it and using the same synoptic approach and generally the same style, though the extensive statistical analyses and the detailed constitutional law analyses dampened some of the spark of the impeachment crisis book. He ranged widely in discussions of constitutional law, political theory and political science, racial politics, the nature of the Supreme Court, and technology as it related to voting machines and elections. He also needed statistical analysis to sort through the votes from Florida. The purpose of the book was also the same as that of the impeachment book—to show the superiority of pragmatism over other approaches in solving the political and legal issues. He had at first written an academic article on the election controversy filled with statistical analyses and drier analyses of the Supreme Court opinion in *Bush v. Gore*,[10] but upon finding a receptive audience for the article even before it was published, he expanded it into a book.[11] His goal in the book, beyond trumpeting pragmatism's virtues, is to make sense of the controversy with narrative, explication, and analysis, with a few suggestions for reform added at the end. His conclusions are that it is unlikely that a recount would have declared Gore the winner, that the Supreme Court's opinion was a professionally respectable job delivering a kind of rough justice animated by the need to provide political stability, and that the sky will not fall if the public acknowledges that the Supreme Court is a political court by its very nature.

Posner's academic article did not include the best bits of the election controversy book—his attack on public intellectuals generally and academic lawyers specifically, suggesting, based on his enthusiasm in faulting the offenders, that this was the real reason he wrote the book. As he had with public intellectuals and academics in the impeachment crisis, Posner thought that the commentary of the public intellectuals and academic lawyers "lacked serious doses of competence and disinterestedness."[12] The problem was worse in the election controversy, he argues, because the academic lawyers in particular played a bigger role this time around. The academic lawyers were partisan, a sin by itself, and they were not knowledgeable about what they were speaking and writing about, suggesting that they did more harm than good. Academic lawyers in their reviews were of course offended, but beyond near complete disparagement of his take on public intellectuals and academic lawyers, reviewers tended to take from the book what they had taken from the election controversy itself. They saw the controversy from the lens of their partisanship and faulted or approved of Posner accordingly, with only a few reviewers noting what they described as Posner's neutrality or Olympian detachment in his narrative and analyses. His pragmatism, which here he defines as "adjudication guided by a comparison of the consequences of alternative resolutions of the case rather than by an algorithm intended to lead the judges by a logical or otherwise formal process to One Correct Decision, utilizing only canonical materials of judicial decision making,"[13] was generally rejected in the reviews, with one reviewer calling his approach to judging antidemocratic and noting that Posner's approach is what Learned Hand had in mind when he described rule "by a bevy of Platonic Guardians."[14] It was a complaint he would run into again in his 2003 book *Law, Pragmatism, and Democracy*.

New Yorker Profile

For its profile the *New Yorker* took the magazine's usual approach for its million-odd readers. Reporter Larissa MacFarquhar followed Posner around for a few days, engaging in directed conversation, talking with friends and people familiar with his work, and summarizing his career to date. The role of mediator in the Microsoft litigation is mentioned in the profile, but Posner does not answer any questions about it or volunteer any information. Aside from his observation that he has the same personality as his cat in being "cold, furtive, callous, snobbish, selfish, playful, but with a streak of cruelty,"[15] the two most interesting bits of declaration involve his parents and his work as a judge. His comments here are in line with his more expansive treatments of the topics in his correspondence. On his parents' deaths, Posner said that they had not affected him at all. He also told MacFarquhar about not thinking of himself as having been fully socialized into law, that when it comes to being socialized into the law he thinks of himself as an imperfectly housebroken pet. "I still have difficulty understanding—and this is something that most people get over in their first two weeks of law school—lawyers spouting things that they don't believe. If someone is obviously guilty, why do they have to have all this rigmarole?"[16] In a 2014 interview, Posner was asked about his candor in the *New Yorker* profile and answered that Larissa MacFarquhar was very skillful at extracting unguarded comments from him.[17]

Public Intellectuals

Public Intellectuals: A Study of Decline[18] examines public intellectuals and the marketplace for their ideas and is related in purpose to Posner's examination of moral and legal theorists in *The Problematics of Moral and Legal Theory*. The book's genesis, he explains, was his dismay at the role and performance of public intellectuals in the impeachment crisis, which he had noted but did not have a chance to explore. Here he does, bringing economic analysis and sociology to bear on what he describes in the book's final sentence as an "odd and interesting market."[19] For the balance of the book, though, the market is characterized as riddled with defects, principally because it is a market "with little in the way of gatekeeping consumer intermediaries."[20] He uses—to cite just two examples—Dworkin's *New York Review of Books* attack on him as an example of an academic as public intellectual run amok and repeats his criticism of the many academics who compromised their credibility in the letter-signing episode of the Clinton impeachment crisis by irresponsibly injecting themselves into the crisis without competence in the constitutional fields at issue or the disinterestedness needed to justify their imposition of themselves on the public.

The modern university for Posner has much to do with the decline of public intellectuals because of its relentless movement toward specialization or, as he calls it, "compartmentalization of competence."[21] The real problem is with the compartmentalized academics who do not realize the shortness of their reach and extend themselves out as public intellectuals in areas beyond their competence. This phenomenon prompts Posner to write that "a successful academic may be able to use his success to reach the general public on matters about which he is an idiot."[22] Then, pushing the knife into the stereotypical academic public intellectual he is skewering, he adds imperially that "it doesn't help that successful people tend to exaggerate their versatility; abnormal self-confidence is a frequent cause and almost invariable effect of great success."[23]

Public intellectuals have performed poorly, he argues, if measured against the accuracy of predictions they make and what he calls the "truth value" of what they write. Put differently, they make whopping mistakes and, worse, they are not held accountable for those mistakes or for the failure to persuade. He provides examples from various fields of how off the mark some academics have been in their function as public intellectuals, with economist Lester Thurow his favorite whipping boy. Without the checks on accuracy and competence that the academic publication process featuring peer review provides, public intellectual work by academics becomes just hack work. The market, the argument runs, needs to be improved, primarily through accountability. Archiving and posting a public intellectual's work so that it can be checked for the accuracy of its predictions, for example, is one of Posner's proposals.

Little of Posner's analysis, complaints, and proposals, though, could compete with the attention that his ranking of public intellectuals got. He devised a big list of public intellectuals, cut the list down to 586, and then ran checks based on the Lexis-Nexis data and citation counts for the academics of the group to come up with a top one hundred. Henry Kissinger topped the list, while Posner himself came in at 70. The book was widely reviewed and Posner was the subject of much attention, though in a minor or muted way, as in appearing on C-SPAN's *Booknotes* for an hourlong interview April 15, 2002.

Most reviewers did not like the book. Many complained about the arbitrariness of his list and gave examples of people unfairly included or left out. There were complaints, as from the *New York Times*, that the book was slapdash and sloppy.[24] On occasion reviewers looked beyond the book and raised probing questions. One reviewer, after noting what the *Times* had written, wrote that the book should raise in Posner's mind "a most serious question about whether his amazingly copious productivity has now reached a point of declining returns."[25] The eminent academic philosopher Thomas Nagel in the *Times Literary Supplement* raised a question about Posner's appetite. He wrote that Posner's success as a legal academic and his success on the bench did not seem to be enough for him and that this was why he wrote what Nagel described as "a stream of fluidly written, informative and intellectually undemanding books on law, politics and society."[26]

Posner in his archival correspondence wrote often about both academic philosophers and public intellectuals and about academics generally. To Martha Nussbaum, a philosophy professor with public intellectual aspirations, he repeatedly expresses his doubts about the suitability of academics generally and philosophers in particular for the role of public intellectual. He tells Nussbaum that she has a claim to it if anyone does, but as a general matter "it is possible that the *public* intellectual, left or right, is a vanishing species, as specialization continues its inexorable advance." "I just don't think our modern cloistered academic philosophers, in this age of specialization and complexity, are likely to have much influence," he writes in another letter. "I think the problem for philosophers," he writes in yet another letter, "is that in an age of specialization it is difficult for a philosopher to learn enough about a field to write about it in a way persuasive to insiders."

He questions, for example, the competence of philosophers to opine on political issues. "I have the highest professional and personal regard for Richard Rorty," he writes, "but he obviously is unsuited to intervene in public controversies except to challenge fallacious philosophical arguments. He knows a lot, but what he knows is the work of other ivory towerists." The contrast for him is with economists. "I am too much a materialist to think that a philosopher can have much influence on the world," he tells her. "An economist can, by telling politicians and businessmen how to accomplish their ends more effectively. As I keep saying, if an economist or someone else who is in a position to influence things uses bad philosophical arguments, then you're the person (or one of the persons) who can refute them. But beyond that I don't see much role for a philosopher in the public realm."

He is tough on academic philosophers. "Most philosophers," he writes, "are academic time-servers, drones." In different letters he writes that "philosophers today are tenured bourgeois," that "being steeped in moral philosophy doesn't make one a better person," and that he does not think "that the average member of a philosophy department, or even the average specialist in moral or political philosophy within a philosophy department, is more admirable than the average member of any other department—including the economics department."

There is also a related sense of contempt for academic intellectuals. Part of it comes from his perception of their smugness and claim to higher moral ground. "I just don't think that culture makes people better," he writes to Nussbaum. He grants, though, that "university people are more interesting than other people," cutting back on the comment with the observation that "they also live, on average, more disordered personal lives." To help make his argument against them, he points to Nussbaum's anecdotes that the results of the 1994 election had many intellectuals thinking of emigrating and says that "the people in [her] 'set'—the donnish people—are contemptuous of ordinary Americans." The reports of emigration threats confirm for him his "sense of a vast and unhealthy gulf between ordinary people and academic people." They are upset with the election, he argues alternatively, because it "confirms their marginality."

His commentary on academics in the wild as he witnesses them reflects both his own values and his personality. All the types are here, and more. In his comments he is interested in intelligence, personality, manners, and variations of weaknesses, flaws, and foibles.

A law school colleague is "genuinely nice and very smart, though I think he is intellectually timid and unenergetic, and as a result his output is rather meager and not exciting." One colleague "is a very intelligent and charming person and I think an excellent academic administrator, though not a scholar or creative thinker, but I may be wrong. [He] is somewhat narcissistic, highly emotional (which makes life very hard for an administrator—I mean on his insides), and a name dropper, but those are minor defects." Another faculty member "is nice and very smart, but also very self-absorbed." He writes that he was very impressed by a famous economist he had met, "especially by his expository skills, which are extraordinary. But I was particularly impressed by the lucidity of his mind."

One academic legal philosopher very much impressed him, though he goes on to write that "of course he is a poor public speaker, and indeed quite inarticulate even in a small group, but one gets intermittent glimpses of the powerful analytic machinery beneath. The complete lack of vanity and dogmatism, in a man of his years and success, is the most remarkable feature in a personal encounter." He reports that he met and liked another philosopher—a world-class philosopher—enormously. "Maybe he's a skillful con man," he writes, "but he struck me as extraordinarily modest, simple, friendly, and low key, utterly lacking in side without being *pretentiously* humble." One colleague was distinguished by "extreme recessiveness." Another is an "extremely competitive person." One Chicago colleague is "certainly ambitious, but that cannot be rated a fault. He has a vaguely cold and supercilious exterior; of the inner man I cannot speak because I do not know. But I do have trouble seeing him actually marrying an outdoors girl [as was the rumor], as he is very definitely the hot-house intellectual plant." Another faculty member is "a fearful type" and "can be quite intimidating." Debriefing after a University of Chicago event, he writes that he is not much impressed with a philosophy department faculty member at Chicago who struck him, as he had before, "as a timid small-bore type."

He describes a University of Chicago colleague in another department as reminding him "of the serpent in the Garden of Eden—big smile, wonderful manners, but a sly, watchful look on a small pale head." He writes that an Ivy League university president struck him "as an incredibly polished and effective manager. I was very impressed by the ease and graciousness of his wife and himself." One young faculty member "does not have the polish, the diplomatic skills, that most good lawyers and law professors have. He has a 'superior' air, which didn't bother me but which would rub some people, including some students, the wrong way."

Reporting about the goings-on at a conference, he describes a leading legal historian at another school as "very good on paper but almost inarticulate and even rather dumb-looking in person. I like [him], but he does have rather a lackluster affect, if that's the word." A member of the economics faculty "is a very imaginative, intelligent, and productive economist, although his conversation is not measured. Some people say stupid things because they use conversation to try out their ideas." One well-known feminist legal scholar "is not open to conflicting ideas. She is Ms. Idee Fixe or maybe Idees Fixes." Of one conference attendee he notes that "her comment on [the presented paper] was of the order of what she had been reading in the newspaper the last few weeks." Recounting a party he had gone to at a rival law school, he writes that one professor was "madly incomprehensible," while another was "loquacious and meandering—no advertisement for his law school."

He meets Saul Bellow, who taught for many years in the University of Chicago's Committee on Social Thought, and declares that he "does not give the impression of being a very nice person," adding that he "has a face like a shark's and radiates coldness."

Everywhere

Posner seemed to be everywhere almost from the beginning of the decade. He was writing for both online news and commentary sites and for a wider variety of national magazines and newspapers. For *Slate* in 2001 he exchanged letters with Peter Singer on animal rights and had a dialogue with Alan Dershowitz on the 2000 election. For *Atlantic Monthly* he contributed articles on universities as businesses, on plagiarism, and on national security and terrorism. His essay on plagiarism sparked the interest of Pantheon Books, which brought out in 2007 Posner's slender (if even that) but learned and entertaining *The Little Book of Plagiarism* on the subject, urging tolerance on the supposed offense. His pieces for *Atlantic Monthly* on national security and terrorism in 2001 were followed by several articles on the subjects in newspapers such as the *Boston Globe, Washington Post, New York Times, Chicago Tribune,* and *Wall Street Journal.* He participated in debates around the country with Geoffrey Stone and David Cole, respectively, on First Amendment and national security issues. He also engaged in online debates first with Stone in *Legal Affairs* and then with Philip Heyman in the *New Republic Online* on the same topics. In print there was an exchange with David Cole in the *New York Review of Books* on national security and privacy. He appeared on the *Charlie Rose* television interview show four times discussing national security and the economy.

His travel schedule for the decade certainly makes it seem that he was everywhere. The available years of the aughts (2003–9) for Posner's financial disclosure report filed each year with the Administrative Office of the U.S. Courts show that he indeed traveled quite a bit. He took on average fifteen trips per year and was away traveling on average thirty-five days per year. His peak year was 2006, with twenty-seven trips and fifty-nine days of travel. Primarily he traveled domestically to attend conferences and workshops, to debate, and to lecture, though there was some travel to Europe: Lund, Sweden; Lake Como, Italy (twice); and Rome, Italy.

He also blogged. He blogged for *Slate* for a week as part of its Diary series and gleefully described in his five postings a frenetic schedule of speaking events, court hearings, teaching, and writing. He was a guest blogger for Brian Leiter and for Larry Lessig on their respective blogs. He started the Becker-Posner Blog with Gary Becker in December 2004, which ran until Becker's death in 2014. The blog wrestled with a wide variety of topics looked at with the lens of economic analysis. The first two years of the blog were published by the University of Chicago Press in 2009 as *Uncommon Sense: Economic Insights from Marriage to Terrorism*.[27] Its 125 entries and comments are divided into eight parts, reflecting the blog's range: Sex and Population, Property Rights, Universities, Incentives, Jobs and Employment, Environment and Disasters, Crime and Punishment and Terrorism, and The World. In February 2009, immediately following the publication of his *A Failure of Capitalism* on the financial crisis, he began a blog for *Atlantic Monthly* online to continue the saga and his analysis, running into 2010.

He reviewed books often for newspapers and magazines. Most but not all were books about law and legal figures. He wrote sixty thousand words of reviews for the *New Republic* in the aughts. Posner also contributed five stand-alone opinion pieces (nearly twenty thousand words worth) to the *New Republic*. Some of the articles previewed important positions he was taking as the issues were presenting themselves or, in the case of the essay on Keynes, how he had come to change his mind on a cornerstone of what had been his economic view of the world. His piece on the Supreme Court and gun control, which closely examined the *Heller* case, is where he first lambasts Justice Scalia for his majority opinion, a decision he noted in a 2014 interview as one of the two worst Supreme Court decisions.[28] He had begun this opinion piece writing habit in 1987 with "What Am I? A Potted Plant," his *New Republic* dissection and rejection of strict constructionism.[29]

National Security and Terrorism

Serendipity had a role in the six books Posner wrote in the decade on national security and terrorism. He had reviewed Alan Dershowitz's book *Why Terrorism Works: Understanding the Threat, Responding to the Challenge* for the *New Republic* in 2002 and in particular praised it for recognizing what doctrinaire liberals could not—that the "scope of our civil liberties is not given in stone, but instead represents the point of balance between public safety and personal liberty."[30] Then also in 2002 Posner was asked to review Margaret Atwood's dystopian novel *Oryx and Crake* for the *New Republic*,[31] and with this review his interest in the phenomenon of catastrophes was sparked. This led to his 2004 book on the subject, *Catastrophe: Risk and Response*.[32] Then the *New York Times* asked him to review the 9/11 Commission's report. The six books then followed.

The books as a group share a tone reflected in what they represent: Posner's response when asked to look at the worlds of national security and terrorism, usually through documents, and to analyze and report on what he finds. The difference in tone and related approach between these books and Posner's book on the impeachment crisis is that with the latter Posner with an engaging tone works to show that he is worth listening to, while with the former he simply assumes that his opinion has been called for and didactically delivers analyses and assessments without the need to justify the reader's engagement. He assumes in these books that we have asked for his opinion, which is exactly what the *New York Times* did when it approached him to report on the work of the 9/11 Commission in a book review.

Catastrophe looked at the phenomenon from the economic analysis perspective and presented a taxonomy of four categories of catastrophes, which included natural catastrophes (pandemics and asteroid collisions, for example), scientific misadventures (such as a rogue particle accelerator), the unintended consequences of human activity (as in global warming), and deliberate events (such as bioterrorism or cyberterrorism). The solutions to these catastrophic threats—to the extent that there can be solutions—come from using probabilistic theory, an approach made far more difficult because we have so little experience in conjuring up minute probabilities. He uses a cost-benefit analysis to show that we need to think about catastrophes because the harm factor is so great—extinction of the planet in some scenarios—that we would be reckless not to consider the cost of what can be done to prevent the harm.

The probability analysis of *Catastrophe* became the foundation for his approaches to national security and terrorism issues in the five remaining books of the group, of which a selection—*Preventing Surprise Attacks: Intelligence Reform in the Wake of 9/11;*[33] *Uncertain Shield: The U.S. Intelligence System in the Throes of Reform;*[34] and *Countering Terrorism: Blurred Focus, Halting Steps*[35]—Posner thought of as a trilogy, though unplanned, on the reform of the nation's intelligence system following the terrorist attacks of 9/11. Of the remaining two books, *Remaking Domestic Intelligence*[36] also looks at national intelligence, while *Not a Suicide Pact: The Constitution in a Time of National Emergency* considers the tension between civil liberties and national security in times of national emergencies but also discusses national intelligence.[37]

In *Preventing Surprise Attacks*, which had begun its life as Posner's *New York Times* review of the 9/11 Commission report, Posner was able to meet with several leading figures in the intelligence community, such as former CIA director George Tenet and FBI director Robert Mueller, and have them critique his analyses. His biggest complaint with the 9/11 Commission was that its members, being mostly lawyers, were not well suited for the task at hand, a problem compounded by their lack of interest in and ignorance of previous efforts at reorganization of the intelligence community. More to the point, the Commission in its proposed reforms was offering the wrong kind of solution—structural—to a problem its own narrative had indicated was managerial. Cost-benefit analysis, though, drives Posner's analysis of disasters and preventing surprise attacks. "In the language of cost-benefit analysis, the benefits of avoiding a disaster must, before they can be compared to the costs of prevention, be discounted (multiplied) by the probability that the disaster will actually occur if no additional measures are taken to prevent it. The lower the perceived probability of attack, and the less harm the attack will do if it occurs, and the higher the costs of preventive measures, including the cost created by false alarms, the less likely it is that the measures will be taken."[38]

Published the next year, *Not a Suicide Pact*, indicating that the Constitution should not be turned against us for absurd results, continued Posner's interest in probabilities and the interest he had demonstrated on the bench for years in applying the Hand Formula. Rooted as it is in probabilities, the Hand Formula looms over (though not acknowledged) not just reorganizational questions for the intelligence community but also over the civil liberties questions he explores in *Not a Suicide Pact*. There's also a significant strain of pragmatism affecting the analysis that presents itself in Posner trying to remind the audience (perhaps perceiving it to be made of ACLU lawyers) that terrorism is a real threat and that our understanding of constitutional rights has to prioritize national security before individual liberties lest there be no nation as we know it in which those liberties would need to be honored. When Posner returns to national intelligence issues in *Remaking Domestic Intelligence*, it is with organization in mind.[39] His conclusion is that the United States needs to create a domestic intelligence service outside the FBI, along the lines of Britain's MI5 or Canada's Canadian Security Intelligence Service.

Economic Crisis

Posner's 2008 *A Failure of Capitalism*,[40] by which he meant not the idea of capitalism in the abstract but its workaday infrastructure, including regulation, sought to sort out the economic crisis of 2008 by looking at both the cause of the crisis and government's response to it. He marked the crisis, unlike many who continued to call it a recession, as a depression. The book, beyond taking the reader on a tour of economic mismanagement and bad judgment, says a great deal about Posner and his emphasis in the aughts on becoming more of a public intellectual. It shares with *An Affair of State* a near contemporaneousness in its composition, with Posner writing, as he likes to say, in medias res. Here, though, *A Failure of Capitalism* grew out of entries on the economy from his blog with Gary Becker, with Posner promising to continue with unfolding events with a blog he has set up with *Atlantic Monthly* that would begin running a week after the book's publication. But unlike *An Affair of State, A Failure of Capitalism* does not use footnotes and does not take a synoptic approach to unravel the roots of the economic crisis. He pares his prose back stylistically and moves ahead steadily and quickly with exposition, first with an introductory round and then with a round of greater detail and analysis. His prose, rather than seeking to engage the reader in the way that *An Affair of State* did, reads more like a memorandum to the president on the financial crisis. He sees that his talents, skills, and the work he did in his books *Catastrophe* and *Preventing Surprise Attacks* arm him for the task at hand. "There is a need," he writes, "for concise, constructive, jargon- and acronym-free, non-technical, unsensational, light-on-anecdote, analytical examination of the major facets of the biggest U.S. economic disaster in my lifetime and that of most people living today."[41] This his book will deliver.

He finds blameworthy actors at every turn, though, somewhat surprisingly, as hard as he is on economists for not predicting the crisis and for misunderstanding it, he gives them something of a pass. Chairman Ben Bernanke of the Federal Reserve Bank gets no such pass and is repeatedly faulted for inexcusable failures. He failed by providing excessive optimism, which distorted the markets getting us into the problem, by waiting too long to act, and then by devising an ineffective strategy to improve the nation's economic health. Businessmen are not the villains of the piece. They instead took advantage, as they should, of cheap money and great demand in the housing market because of regulation failures and were shortsighted only in not recognizing that their success would sink the ship they were cruising on. The government is faulted for interest rates that were so low as to create bubble conditions, not on their own but in connection with home buyers naturally seeking to take advantage of offered credit (why not, it was a rising market) though without enough savings to maintain adequate spending once economic contractions began.

Posner is willing to think afresh about problems and even to abandon long-held positions, positions that in some cases went to the core of his approach to economics. *A Failure of Capitalism* provides perhaps the most dramatic evidence of Posner's willingness to rethink his positions to find a better solution. He, to the gasping surprise of many, praises Keynes often in *A Failure of Capitalism* and premises his assessment of the government's recovery efforts by holding them up against what the Keynesian approach calls for. If the public cannot spend enough because of inadequate savings and lost wages, the government has to do it. Keynes's understanding of the psychology of spending seemed geared to the specific problems the stagnating, credit-bound economy needed fixed.

Critics noted that Posner had abandoned his much-thumbed free-market playbook and was now looking to Keynes for answers. True believers in free markets and no government intervention did not seem interested, though, in why it was that one of their great advocates had changed teams. For them, Posner was just wrong. As they saw it, loose mortgage lending practices generally and Fannie Mae and Freddie Mac specifically caused the crisis.

Honored

The middle of the decade saw Posner begin to receive a number of honors, though his first honor came in 2002, when he won the Ames Prize ($10,000) from the Harvard Law School faculty, given out every five years for the most distinguished work of legal scholarship over a five-year period, for the fifth edition (1998) of *Economic Analysis of Law*. Then in 2005 his name was connected to federal appellate judges who had in their respective generations been recognized as preeminent. In May 2005 he received the Learned Hand Medal for Excellence in Federal Jurisprudence from the Federal Bar Council, and in October 2005, in what must have been an interesting ceremony, Posner received, along with Ronald Dworkin, the Henry Friendly Medal, presented by the American Law Institute. They were jointly honored for their prolific and profound contributions to legal thought in the spirit of the late Henry Friendly. Michael Boudin, the chair of the Henry J. Friendly Award Committee, noted that Posner's "greatest long-term contribution has been his role in helping to develop and make widely known the law and economics school of legal analysis which has had a striking impact on teaching and scholarly writing in the nation's law schools."

Also in 2005, with his twenty-fifth anniversary on the Seventh Circuit approaching, Posner was honored by the *New York University Annual Survey of American Law*, which dedicated its 2005 issue to him. The journal ran short tributes from federal judge Pierre Leval, who had been a year behind Posner at Harvard Law School; Robert Ferguson of Columbia University, who had taught in the English department at the University of Chicago before moving to Columbia University and knew Posner as a friend and fellow reading group member; among others.[42] The tributes were filled with praise, admiration, and affection, as might be expected from the genre, though Ferguson's tribute, based on years of knowing him well, seems to be especially heartfelt and thoughtful. He wrote of Posner that "the quiet demeanor and good humor of the man never changes. He not only knows who he is at every moment, he knows without ever losing the most intense interest and sympathy in explaining what is taking place around him." He then writes that "it would be a mistake to characterize this intense interest as simple curiosity. In Judge Posner, it takes the form, rather, of what I will call dispassionate affection for the things of this world. The affection is 'dispassionate' because it quite readily skewers the many foibles it sees, some quite close to him. It remains affection, nonetheless, in that it always engages in possibilities. Its chief virtue lies in its ability to see well beyond itself in its desire to fashion a better answer to the problems before it."[43]

And lastly in 2005, Posner was the inaugural recipient of Harvard University's Thomas C. Schelling Award and its prize of $25,000, presented annually to an individual "whose remarkable intellectual work has had a transformative impact on public policy."

In 2007 both the *Harvard Law Review* and the *University of Chicago Law Review* dedicated issues to him featuring articles by prominent legal academics. The theme of Posner's use of economic analysis on the bench dominates both issues.

THE ECONOMIC STRUCTURE OF INTELLECTUAL PROPERTY LAW

The decade saw Posner with an increasing interest in intellectual property. It was displayed on Posner's scholarly side with his 2003 *The Economic Structure of Intellectual Property Law*,[44] written with

William Landes. It argued that economic analysis, as the great simplifier of law, had much to offer in understanding intellectual property law and its four major fields of trademarks, trade secrets, patents, and copyrights. Put differently, though Landes and Posner do not discuss the article, the book seeks to show that distinguished law and economics advocate George Priest had been wrong in 1986 when he had written that "economists can tell lawyers ultimately very little about how to enforce or interpret the law of intellectual property."[45] Economic analysis, for example, helps explain trademark law by looking to its effect in lowering search costs for consumers, making it easier for fans of particular products to find them, and in inducing quality control on manufacturers to be sure that consumers seeking out their product are not disappointed in their expectations based on prior experience with the product. Economic analysis also helps explain what the Supreme Court did not consider when it gave constitutional approval to an added extension of the Copyright Act of 1976—that a better, though not easily feasible, alternative is to have copyrights that can be renewed indefinitely. Moreover, only economic analysis helps cut through the incentive-versus-access tension. Social cost is minimized for older works because they are not likely to be renewed, increasing the store of public domain works. For newer works a wider definition of "fair use" would provide the social benefit of greater access. The book made other arguments based on empirical studies, such as that the Federal Circuit's monopoly on patent appeals was contributing to the problem of too many patents by siding with patentees at a higher rate than their regional circuit court predecessors. Posner followed *The Economic Structure of Intellectual Property* with a number of articles in the decade, many reacting to the Supreme Court's decision in *Eldred v. Ashcroft*[46] extending copyright duration terms.

Essay Collections

Posner in *Frontiers of Legal Theory* continues from previous books his argument against law as an autonomous discipline, going as far as to appropriate the term "legal theory" and give it a gloss to suit his purposes. He uses the term to describe theories outside law that make up what he describes as a scientific conception of law. His interest is in other disciplines, outside or at the frontier of law, including economics, sociology, and psychology. And as much as the title potentially misleads, the table of contents also misleads with its five sections, thirteen chapters, and 440 pages of text disguising the fact that the chapters represent the reworking of twenty-two previously published reviews and essays. The struggle is to cut and paste and rework the previously published material to make it work in its new form. The five sections set out the landscape and its points of interest in essays tracing historical aspects of economic analysis; law's interrelationship with history; psychology in law as it appears in behavioral law and economics; epistemology in law, primary in the field of evidence; and empiricism in law as represented by the interest in and usefulness of citation count studies of courts and judges. One reviewer complained not only that the book was "inherently spotty" and that the chapters seemed disjointed but that it recycled too many responsive conference papers that did not give enough context for the reader to appreciate the arguments.[47] The book was not widely reviewed.

Posner was true to his word in the title to *Law, Pragmatism, and Democracy*, in which he clarifies (or restates) his position on pragmatic judging, making it a part of what he calls "everyday pragmatism." He distinguishes it from pragmatism as understood by philosophers such as John Dewey and defends his everyday pragmatism against critics who argue either that it looks too much to immediate consequences or that, because it gives judges more discretion and power than with other approaches, it is antidemocratic and makes judges more like Plato's guardians than Congress believed Article III judges should be. He looks to Chief Justice John Marshall's pragmatism to see pragmatism done right, and he goes back in separate chapters to the Clinton impeachment and the 2000 election to show, as he had in earlier books, that pragmatism was not to be found in the Clinton case and that the opinion in the 2000 election case represents a defensible exercise in pragmatism. The pragmatism he argues for, he explains in response to the antidemocratic arguments, is consistent with the idea of an elite— rather than participatory—democracy that America has and should have. An elite democracy "accepts people as they are, does not think it feasible or desirable to try to change them into public-spirited and well informed citizens [of an idealized participatory democracy] and regards representative democracy as a pragmatic method of controlling, and providing for an orderly succession of, the officials who (not the people) are the real rulers of the nation."[48] The efficacy of this judicial pragmatism is the book's principal theme. In the introduction he by way of definition explains that "the pragmatic judge aims at the decision that is most reasonable, all things considered, where 'all things' include both case-specific and systemic consequences."[49] "Everyday pragmatism is the mindset denoted by the popular usage of the word 'pragmatic,' meaning practical and businesslike, 'no-nonsense,' disdainful of abstract theory and intellectual pretension, contemptuous of moralizers and utopian dreams."[50] The distinguished political philosopher Richard Rorty in his otherwise favorable review tried nonetheless to identify just what it was that troubled him about Posner's vision of democracy. What he called Posner's realism and cynicism "are healthy antidotes to leftist fantasies of an electorate modeled on a university seminar," but his disdain for "utopian dreamers" went too far and missed great American figures, such as Lincoln, who could be described as among that group. American democracy might well be, as he puts it, "a matter of pragmatic compromise between interest groups," but it is often more than that.[51]

Other Books

In 2009 Posner published a second edition of *The Federal Courts*[52] and a third edition of *Law and Literature,* which he described as not quite a treatise on the subject but "the closest that the law and literature movement has come to producing one.[53] In addition, Posner's scholarly work on economic analysis continued in the decade. There was a second edition of *Antitrust Law,*[54] and the sixth and seventh editions of *Economic Analysis of Law.* There was also a series of books published by Edward Elgar that had started in the 1990s with the three volumes of *Law and Economics* (coedited with Francesco Parisi), and which continued beyond the decade of the aughts, all of which were collections of Posner's economic articles on various subjects, edited by Parisi alone, or collections he co-edited with Parisi of articles by others on different subjects, including the Coase Theorem.[55]

On the Bench

Economic Analysis Applied or Encouraged

Posner in the 2000-2009 decade pushed the Hand Formula further to the frontier in his application of it. He turns to it in what might be the unlikeliest of cases, a child abduction claim brought under the International Child Abduction Remedies Act, which implements the Hague Convention on the Civil Aspects of International Child Abduction.[56] An American parent wanted to hold on to her visiting children in the United States even though they usually resided with their plaintiff father in Belgium under the terms of a custody order. This would otherwise qualify her as an abductor under the Act and the plaintiff father would win and the children would be returned to him. An exception to the Act states, however, that the children need not be returned if returning them presented them with a grave risk of physical or psychological harm. The lower court had not given any weight to the affidavits submitted by the defendant mother detailing physical and verbal abuse (leading to the appearance of some of the foulest language seen in any Posner opinion), which for Posner seemed to miss the point. The risk described by the Convention needed to be assessed, and the best way to assess it was to consider the odds of both risk and harm, with the seriousness of harm also factored in. He sets out his statement of the rule, that "the gravity of a risk involves not only the probability of harm, but also the magnitude of the harm if the probability materializes," citing Hand's *Carroll Towing* case, wherein the Hand Formula is set out.[57] The children were not returned to Belgium.

More conventionally—but still with a twist—he applies the Hand Formula to a negligence case from Indiana. The twist in the case was that the plaintiff had brought his tort claim under Indiana's products liability law, which allows for a claim if the design defect at issue was the result of negligence in the design. Put differently, it became negligence by any other name. Negligence, after all, is where the Hand Formula lives. This made it easier to apply the formula in this case in which a load fell on the plaintiff from an allegedly defective crane and to recognize the factual question as to the cost of changes the manufacturer could have made to guard against the risk.[58]

And as he had in prior decades, Posner in the decade continued to acclimate his audience to economic terminology as part of an attempt to further integrate his approach into the mainstream. For example, he introduces the economic analysis term "complementary products" in an antitrust case involving a tying agreement, explaining that in economic terms "raising the price of a product reduces the demand for its complements. (If the price of nails rises, the demand for hammers will fall.)"[59] He also does this with an explanation of the common fund doctrine, which considers what happens when someone spends money in legal fees and obtains a judgment that confers a benefit on someone else. "The theory," he explains, "is that a beneficiary of another's legal efforts should contribute to the cost of those efforts; otherwise they would not have been taken." Further explaining, he writes that "in economic terms, the successful plaintiff in such a case confers (if he is not compensated) 'external' (to his pocketbook) benefits, which he has no incentive to do unless he is compensated and they therefore are internalized to him."[60] In a last example, he also uses economic analysis to explain the anachronistic (but useful for analogy purposes) doctrine of charitable tort immunity, which states that a charitable organization is not liable under tort law. "In economic terminology, the immunity is a method of externalizing costs (shifting them to others' shoulders—tort victims') in order to encourage the externalization of benefits (the conferral of benefits on others) by reducing the costs of the enterprise."[61]

Moving from an emphasis on terminology and explanation to just the explanatory power of economic analysis, he turns to economic analysis in a series of trademark and copyright cases involving the maker of Beanie Babies, a move that might be expected in light of his 2003 *The Economic Structure of Intellectual Property Law*, written with William Landes, and its theme that economic analysis has more power to explain intellectual property law than it has been given credit for. In a case involving a collectors' guide to the lovable Beanie Babies, he explores "fair use" in explicit economic analysis terms. He looks to the purpose of the doctrine through this lens rather than relying on statutory definition case law, in part because the case law is not illuminating but mostly because looking at the purpose of the doctrine reveals its fit to the facts at hand, to conclude that such a guide does not infringe on the copyright enjoyed by the Beanie Baby manufacturer.[62] In a trademark case asking questions about a personal name used as a mark, in this instance a beanbag-stuffed camel named Niles manufactured by a Beanie Baby competitor, Posner, in examining the rule that personal names cannot be trademarked without proof of secondary meaning, looks to the purpose of the rule and considers consumer welfare and the promotion of competition to show that the personal name "Niles" enjoys protection despite not having secondary meaning.[63] He also uses economic analysis to explore the secondary market concept in the context of the antidilution statute. He explicitly goes beyond the case law to economic analysis because that case law has not dealt with the rationale for the antidilution statute. This, of course, is what economic analysis does for him.[64]

Resistance

Posner just barely led the decade in dissents filed against him, with twenty-nine, one more than Easterbrook. There was also less open resistance to Posner's opinions in this decade. Principal resistance came from Judge Evans, who in 2004's *Guchshenkov v. Ashcroft*[65] resisted not only the notion that immigration judges are not performing very well but also the majority opinion's explicit criticisms of the immigration judge's performance. Posner had described the immigration judge's opinion as perfunctory and badly reasoned. He wrote specifically of the opinion and of immigration opinions generally that the judge's "analysis fell far below the minimum required to support an administrative decision. It is one more indication of systemic failure by the judicial officers of the immigration service to provide reasoned analysis for the denial of applications for asylum. We are mindful that immigration judges, and the members of the Board of Immigration Appeals, have heavy caseloads. The same is true, however, of the federal district judges, and we have never heard it argued that busy judges should be excused from having to deliver reasoned judgments because they are too busy to think." Judge Evans, on the other hand, looked at caseload statistics for immigration judges and their working conditions and took a more sympathetic view. He could not countenance the many criticisms in this case and the many others that had recently appeared in Seventh Circuit opinions describing inadequate analysis, ignored evidence, lapsed logic, errors, and an unwillingness to listen. He concluded that, all in all, the immigration judges were doing a fairly good job.

Supreme Court Review

The Supreme Court during 2000–2009 reviewed eight Posner majority opinions and affirmed six and reversed two. The best-known case of the decade to be affirmed was the sentencing guideline case *United States v. Booker*,[66] in which Posner followed the Supreme Court's recently decided *Blakely v. Washington*[67] case to its logical conclusion to reason that sentencing increases based on a judge's factual determinations pursuant to the guidelines violated a defendant's Sixth Amendment right to have a jury instead make such factual determinations. The Court agreed with the analysis, bringing a dramatic change to the application of the sentencing guidelines, and went well beyond the Seventh Circuit opinion to handle as only it could the procedures to be followed by the effect of *Booker*. The Court in *Crawford v. Marion County Election Board*[68] affirmed his majority opinion in the election voting case challenging Indiana's law requiring government-issued photo identification to vote and essentially followed his analysis that turned on the lack of evidence of disenfranchisement.[69] And the Court in *City of Indianapolis v. Edmond*[70] also followed Posner's basic analysis in a roadblock case in which the roadblocks had been set up not for specific problems, such as to find drunk drivers, but for all-purpose crime detection,[71] though absent from the Court's analysis was the cost-benefit analysis Posner had set out in his opinion balancing the benefits of a random system of searches or seizures such as vehicle stops against the costs, which look to the harm caused to property or the privacy of the people whose vehicles were stopped. In the equal protection case *Village of Willowbrook v. Olech*,[72] the Court affirmed but on a different theory. In a clash between a homeowner and a town in which the allegation was that the town was seeking an easement from the homeowner that was greater than the easements the town had sought from other homeowners, Posner wrote that the homeowner's allegation, which included a component of ill will, was enough to state a claim under the equal protection clause.[73] The Court, however, followed a different theory and reasoned that it did not need to consider ill will and held that in this type of "class of one" litigation the "irrational and wholly" arbitrary element of the complaint was sufficient to state a claim for relief under traditional equal protection analysis. Both Posner and the Court agreed in the bankruptcy case *Raleigh v. Illinois Dept. of Revenue*[74] that the burden of proof was not on the state but on the debtor as a corporation's officer liable for a state tax on a plane purchase. Posner took a more basic and simpler approach because putting the burden on the debtor follows the general approach of tax law in which, as the Supreme Court had held in 1935, "payment precedes defense, and the burden of proof, normally on the claimant, is shifted to the taxpayer."[75] The Court did not follow Posner's simpler approach and arrived at the same conclusion on the burden of proof falling on the debtor, but only after a far more intricate statutory analysis.

When the issue in the First Amendment case *Thomas v. Chicago Park District*[76] was the alleged vagueness of the municipal park ordinance regulating the use of Chicago city parks for events attracting more than fifty persons, the Court through Justice Scalia and Posner came to the same result but for different reasons. Scalia summarily dispatched the challenge to the ordinance's ambiguity by saying that the grounds given by the ordinance for its regulation regime "are reasonably specific and objective" and do not cross into the forbidden zone of regulations applied on a whim. In contrast, Posner had considered the hot-button language of the ordinance—words such as "material" and "misrepresentation"—and prefaced the specific analysis with an explanation that language is general and that "a challenge to the wording as distinct from the application of a regulation invites semantic nitpicking and judicial usurpation of the legislative drafting function in an effort to avert, without creating loopholes, dangers at best hypothetical and at worst chimerical."[77]

Of the two cases of his in which he was reversed, Posner likely did not mind at all being reversed in *Chambers v. United States*,[78] though the reversal in *Hein v. Freedom from Religion Foundation*[79] probably did not go over so well given the way that Justice Alito, writing for the Court, treated his Seventh Circuit majority opinion.[80] In *Chambers,* the issue was whether the defendant's conviction under Illinois law for escape qualified as a violent felony under the sentencing guidelines.

Other circuits had concluded that failing to report to prison or walking away from a halfway house could be distinguished from jail or prison breaks, with only the latter qualifying as a violent felony. That distinction could not be applied in the Seventh Circuit, though, because the circuit had only recently held that all conduct under the Illinois statute qualified as a violent felony, even the defendant's conduct in being convicted of the statute's "failing to report to a penal institution" section. Unable to overrule circuit precedent and forced to hold against the defendant, Posner suggested that the court in the future could get itself out of the prior precedent jam and join the other circuits if it had information that helped judges with the connection between violence and the type of conduct involved. "It is an embarrassment to the law when judges base decisions of consequence on conjectures, in this case a conjecture as to the possible danger of physical injury posed by criminals who fail to show up to begin serving their sentences or return from furloughs or to halfway houses."[81] Perhaps the Sentencing Commission was listening to Posner's call for a study to give judges the information they needed. Certainly the Supreme Court was watching the results of the Sentencing Commission's study done after the Seventh Circuit's decision and before Supreme Court review of it and relied on it for the conclusive negative answer to the question at hand of whether an offender under the failure to report or walkaway scenario is significantly more likely through his conduct to pose the "serious potential risk of physical injury" described in the statute. The Court noted in its opinion that Posner had urged the Commission to conduct the study.

The Court through Justice Alito in *Hein*, however, wanted none of Posner's suggestions for resolving the issue of whether *Flast v. Cohen*[82] limited standing to taxpayers claiming violations of the establishment clause. At issue were conferences set up and funded by the executive branch to promote religious groups over secular ones. Where the money came from mattered, since the taxpayers would have standing to challenge the conferences only if their funding came from Congress. That the funding was linked to the executive branch rather than to Congress did not trouble Posner. For him there was no functional difference between the sources. Justice Alito in response easily rejected the distinction-without-a-difference argument and held that *Flast*'s reference to congressional funding meant that executive branch expenditures did not fall within its ambit. For Alito and the Court it was all very simple, notwithstanding Posner's analysis looking to function and purpose. Posner for the Seventh Circuit had not applied *Flast*. He had extended *Flast*, an extension the Court would not countenance.

Cited by Name

In the decade, Posner is cited by name by circuit judges outside the Seventh Circuit 266 times and cited parenthetically by name 527 times. Of those occasions in which he is cited by name, he is used to describe core purpose of the "time at liberty" doctrine;[83] to explain why the FTC has concurrent jurisdiction to enforce the Clayton Act;[84] to explain the nature of the equitable tolling doctrine;[85] to express the underlying practical considerations for a rule that a judge may not forbid all discussion of a client's ongoing testimony during a substantial recess;[86] to state the restraining principle in assessing prosecutorial misconduct by judging its relevance in relation to the extent that it "may shed light on the materiality of the infringement of the defendants' rights";[87] to give an example of when a patentee's conduct transcends the confines of the patent and attempts to get around antitrust law;[88] to show a principle (consolidating criminal cases for sentencing) by way of a hypothetical;[89] to describe "state-created danger exception" to the rule that the Constitution as a charter of negative liberties protects people from the government, not from each other or themselves;[90] to explain the reasoning behind the rule that most jobs required regular and reliable attendance;[91] to explain the purpose of a rule imposing liability on subsidiaries by showing how things work in practice;[92] and to explain the nature of antitrust behavior ("almost any market can be cartelized if the law permits sellers to establish formal, overt mechanisms for colluding, such as exclusive sales agencies").[93]

He provides a test or measure for abuse of discretion when judges depart from the guidelines,[94] a test of the undisclosed relationship that must exist so as to cast serious doubt on an arbitrator's impartiality,[95] a test for the best of available interpretations of "prevailing party,"[96] and a test for what prisoners must prove when they bring deliberate indifference claims in federal court.[97]

Judges follow his test of actionable statements of fact, that "if it is plain that the speaker is expressing a subjective view, an interpretation, a theory, conjecture, or surmise, rather than claiming to be in possession of objectively verifiable facts, the statement is not actionable."[98] And they follow his proposed model "safe harbor" language for debt collectors.[99] They follow his analysis that lawyers cannot seek appellate review every time they are scolded by a judge but only when sanctions have been imposed,[100] agree with his reasoning in interpreting 42 U.S.C. sec. 1997e(e) and finding it fully applicable to 42 U.S.C. sec. 1997e(a),[101] and expressly follow Posner's reasoning and conclusion that appellate jurisdiction of tax court judgments that do not dispose of the entire case exists if the tax court has determined that certain claims are final and immediately appealable.[102] They agree with his analysis that courts are to apply an objective test for deciding in bankruptcy cases whether a payment arrangement was made "according to ordinary business terms."[103] They follow his Ponzi scheme analysis that, once the scheme is established, supposed profits received by investors qualify as fraudulent transfers as a matter of law,[104] his "cat's paw" analysis in employment discrimination cases that courts will not blindly accept the titular decisionmaker as the true one,[105] and his assessment that labor law's doctrine of an arbitrator's jurisdiction is not dead even though it may appear so. Courts adopt his definition of monopoly power,[106] and they follow his approach to religious holidays.[107]

His help gives voice to judges who share some of his frustrations with the way certain types of cases are handled. His view that administrative law judges in Social Security disability cases underperform is echoed by other judges, as is his complaint that lawyers should not think themselves qualified to play doctor in assessing disabilities.[108] On the immigration front, courts point to his unhappiness with the government's handling of such cases to support their own unhappiness, and courts quote his observation that it has been irresponsible, incoherent, and astonishing for the Board of Immigration Appeals for years to fail to define the standard it uses to review decisions from administrative law judges.[109] Courts have also invoked him for his complaint that immigration judges give too much weight to country reports from the State Department[110] and in their objections to how slowly the government processes claims under black-lung legislation.

Evaluations

The *Almanac of the Federal Judiciary*'s 2002 edition reported that most lawyers interviewed for the evaluation believed that Posner's demeanor at oral argument had "mellowed slightly with time." They remarked that Posner during argument could be courteous, even-handed, and polite—and in two comments even courtly and smiling throughout an argument. One described him as a mensch. Another thought that Posner was aware "that he is in the limelight and would like to enjoy a reputation of being civil toward attorneys." A dissenting minority, however, maintained that he was overly aggressive in questioning, probing, and punishing weaknesses and that he could be testy and nasty. One complained of the law professor / law student dynamic and said Posner "treats his courtroom as one long Socratic method discourse." Providing a version of balance, one lawyer noted that the morning he found out that Posner was on his panel he thought he was going to be sick. "But I was pleasantly surprised," he continued, "because he treated me in a genuinely civil manner." It was more of the same in the 2007 edition evaluations.

While Posner's and Easterbrook's evaluations had in prior editions sounded similar when it came to how each behaved during oral argument, things changed in the latest editions, with Easterbrook's evaluations worsening, highlighting the difference between the two judges. In the 2002 edition only a minority of the lawyers interviewed spoke well of him. Those who did not commented that "he is one of the meanest human beings you will ever encounter," that he treats lawyers "with utter contempt," that he "lies in wait [for lawyers] and treats them mercilessly," and that "he displays a brutal lack of civility." He was described as arrogant, even to other judges. "His intellectual ability is so superior he seems to feel everyone is beneath him, and he treats them accordingly." While some lawyers said that Easterbrook was not nasty and that he kept them on their toes, others noted that he was "absolutely intolerant" and that "he has a superiority complex and delights in humiliating lawyers." In the 2007 edition we hear again of Easterbrook playing to his clerks. "He likes to circle his kill and gives a nod and a wink to his clerk when he catches his prey." Another lawyer describes how he "berates lawyers and shows off to his clerks how powerful and smart he is. If he is on your side it can be fun, but if his position opposes yours, watch out. The rules of civility have not worked on him." We read about Easterbrook badgering lawyers. "It is almost a game to him."

Law Clerks

Law clerks from the decade provide an insider's view of Posner and of the contrast between Posner and Easterbrook at oral argument.[111] One clerk thought as a general matter that Posner was not driven by mean-spiritedness. "I think he is genuinely frustrated—I think he has higher standards. I think he is frustrated with the legal profession and ... some rules of evidence or some rules of convention that he thinks are useless or waste time."

On the oral argument issue, one clerk noted that Posner would get frustrated with attorneys on a semiregular basis if he thought that the lawyers were trying to bluff and stonewall him. "He didn't like that," one clerk said, noting that Posner thought he was there to get a real answer but the lawyers did not want to give him one. Other clerks pointed out that Posner did not like it if he asked a direct question and did not get a direct response to the question in return. He especially did not like asking questions that had yes or no answers and not get either one-word answer in response. One clerk noted that "in all the time I was clerking for him I never saw him lose his cool. I think he would definitely get frustrated and he would sound somewhat annoyed with the attorney like he'd be annoyed with a child who is misbehaving, something like that, but it never got to the point where I thought to myself, he is really becoming emotionally mad ... , and he certainly never set any sanctions against anyone while I was clerking for him." To the contrary, the clerk added, "No matter how frustrated he got with the attorney during the argument, when the argument was over, it was like a switch and he was back to being mild-mannered, friendly Dick Posner. He would always sort of say, 'Thank you very much for your argument,' even if he has hated the person's argument and it was useless to him."

In contrast, clerks reported that Easterbrook would get angry and dismissive with lawyers. Posner would push for answers to his questions from withholding lawyers, but Easterbrook would just give up. As one clerk put it, "He would think to himself, apparently, 'You're never going to give me an answer that's useful to me,' so he'd just sort of ignore the attorney after that. He'd just sit back and not ask any more questions in that argument. This person was not worth his time anymore."

Writing about Judging

Readers of Posner's judicial opinions who also read his 2008 *How Judges Think*[112] would recognize the complaints found there of judges. In *How Judges Think* Posner confronts the reader with a realistic assessment of how judges think, what judges do and the many techniques they use to distance themselves from what they do, and how they respond to both the demands of individual cases and the demands of judging itself, all as part of an argument that realism about judging is good for all, including judges themselves. He goes through, as background, nine theories of judging, such as, to mention just two, the attitudinal model featuring a judge's political preferences as the driving force in decision-making and the economic theory of judging, which treats the judge as a "rational, self-interested utility maximizer."[113] Posner discusses why we do not have a realistic understanding of judges and the judicial function and why it matters that we indulge in myths about judging rather than in the reality of it. Because judges are like everyone else in the way they approach their jobs, bringing personality and prior experience and prejudices to decision-making, no one is better off thinking otherwise, especially law students being taught by professors who continue to tell them the fairy tale that judges and Justices write their own opinions or that the Justices are all intellectual powerhouses and driven by disinterestedness and a scholarly approach to law. It is, he writes, "high time some realism about judging was injected into the teaching of law."[114] If nothing else, lawyers would be better off when they argue their cases if they had a realistic understanding of how judges work. Judges will also be better off if it is acknowledged that they are "limited human intellects navigating the seas of uncertainty."[115] Maybe if the judges recognized this, they would be more inclined to roll up their sleeves and write their own opinions and embrace the challenges of learning more to keep up with scientific and technological challenges that cases so often present today. The message was bracing enough as it appeared in the articles covering the 2004–8 period and seems even more so when put between hard covers.

District judges might well have been embarrassed to read some of the assessments handed out. In one case a judgment was declared "radically defective."[116] Another featured "an *appallingly* bad injunction."[117] One district judge was told not harshly but firmly when he refused to let the government dismiss a criminal case that he had assumed the role of the US Attorney, whose job it was to exercise prosecutorial discretion. "It is no doubt a position that he can fill with distinction, but it is occupied by another person."[118] Fingers are pointed sharply on the ever-delicate subject of dawdling judges. About a simple tort case that reached its tenth birthday Posner writes that "it is high time the district judge, who has presided over [the case] from the beginning, grabbed it by the neck, gave it a good shake, and placed it on the path to a speedy decision."[119] Rather than implying that a judge's ability to control his docket might be in question, Posner makes the point explicitly in a straightforward case, writing, "We note with regret that the almost two-year interval between the entry of the order of default and the entry of the final judgment, in a case involving simple facts and modest stakes, argues poor case management."[120]

Other judges are praised. One judge, though he was reversed for granting summary judgment in a complex case, is praised for "his patient shepherding of this formidable litigation."[121] One is praised for a meticulous thirty-five-page opinion that "thoroughly considered and correctly resolved" all the issues that the appellate court could as a result ignore, leaving Posner to in effect incorporate by reference the district judge's opinion into his.[122] And when a judge takes a page from criminal trial management in a complex civil case and severs two potentially confusing claims in a civil case and impanels two juries to hear the two different claims, he is praised for his innovation but reversed nonetheless. "Imaginative procedures for averting jury error, as long as they do not violate any legal norm, are to be encouraged rather than discouraged," Posner writes.[123] A judge who reviews complaints as they are filed to weed out the frivolous ones is commended but reminded that the review must be conscientious and be done by the district judge and not a law clerk.[124]

Posner's criticism of judges (and also lawyers) is part of his jurisprudence on how law works, and it complements if not overshadows his jurisprudence on specific subjects such as negligence or antitrust because it goes to the core of how law works. The criticism, in a more important way, though, reflects aspects of Posner's personality and his belief that he has a better way of doing things—all things. His constant push to get the law to bend to his will—a function of his personality and sense of self—plays out in the first half of the next decade with Posner on and off the bench displaying frustration, exasperation, and apparent irritation at the limits of his influence on the law. It is a bracing sight.

6

Push for Change and Measurement Taking (2010–2014)

IT WAS CLEAR FROM the beginning of the 2010s that Posner was changing tack from the previous decade. On the public intellectual front, Posner in 2010's *The Crisis of Capitalist Democracy*, his second book on the 2008 financial crisis, continued on much as he had in *A Failure of Capitalism* in charting and analyzing the economic crisis and using material from his *Atlantic Monthly* blog and his Becker-Posner Blog, but only for the book's first half. His public intellectual functions as narrator and explicator drop away in the book's second half, not to be seen again, here or in other books. His two other books in the first four years of the decade, *Reflections on Judging* and *The Behavior of Federal Judges* (written with William Landes and Lee Epstein), are more like his other traditionally academic books in which previously published articles are reworked. On the judicial front, early in the decade Posner reported that he was approaching his job differently. He wrote in his foreword to David Dorsen's biography of Friendly that what he had learned in reading about Friendly "induced [him] to make certain changes in [his] judicial practice," though he did not elaborate."[1] In a 2013 interview Posner expanded on the topic and said that he had not realized that Friendly was "quite as super" as he had thought and that he wanted to be as good as Friendly, though he recognized that Friendly had practical experience as a lawyer that he did not have. There was, though, nothing wrong with having being as good as Friendly as a goal. He then set out, he says, to reallocate his time so that he spent more of it on his judicial work. "I think it shows," he said, "[m]y performance has improved."[2] With regard to style and structure at least, though, the only difference before and after reading the Friendly biography is that many opinions during this period are shorter, but that's only because he abruptly ends them. Even the abrupt conclusions came to an end after a year or two, leaving Posner where he was before the beginning of the decade and his Friendly-provoked self-assessment. The question of what improved performance means looms over the 2010s.

As he had in prior years, Posner was concerned on the bench and in his academic writing with the performance of judges and lawyers. He continued with his criticisms of the judiciary in his 2013 *Reflections on Judging*, which, despite taking a lighter, more anecdotally driven approach at times, even more directly confronted judges with their underperformance than had *How Judges Think*. The federal docket was presenting judges with increasingly complex issues reflecting the modern world, but judges were not responding to the challenge with harder work and a greater interest in mastering the scientific and technological issues of their cases. A sectional heading in the chapter on technological and scientific challenges captures both the subject and tone: "Judicial Insouciance about the Real."[3] More to the point, the heading captures Posner's attitude toward his fellow federal judges. Posner also pulls no punches with a chapter titled "Coping Strategies" that describes ways judges seek to avoid confronting complexity and the need to know more, such as by making appeals to judicial self-restraint and originalism.

In his opinions, where he is able to point fingers, a trial judge's unwillingness to roll up his sleeves and learn some statistics draws sharp comment in a diversity breach-of-contract case featuring a jury damage award based on expert testimony presenting a regression analysis that was deeply flawed but went over the head of the judge.[4] The judge could have educated himself by appointing a neutral expert, as allowed under the rules, or he could have insisted that the lawyers explain the statistical evidence in plain English rather than in the technical language of statistics, though that approach would probably not have worked well since the transcript of the proceedings in the district court indicated that none of the lawyers understood regression analysis either. The other option, made painfully plain for the trial judge, was that he could have consulted a guide to statistics published by the Federal Judicial Center. If he had done this, he would have realized that the "regression analysis [at issue] was fatally flawed."[5] Posner then explains the nature of regression analysis to show what the judge would have learned if he had consulted the statistics primer and even produces and explains his own regression analysis drawn from the trial testimony to show what the correct analysis looks like. The judge's laziness on the statistics front is implied but not stated.

The theme of judges not holding up their end deepens with an interesting prisoner civil rights case involving a prison's failure to spot hypertension in an inmate in which the entire profession—judges and lawyers—is hit with collective punishment, if punishment can be understood as a scolding of lawyers and judges who think of science and technology as beyond their understanding in cases with scientific or technological issues.[6] Posner recounts that this aversion has long been familiar with lawyers, who joke about the "math block" that deterred many a lawyer from going into a technical field. But with "the extraordinary rate of scientific and other technological advances that figure in litigation,"[7] the failure of the profession to master the necessary statistical and scientific skills that their various cases require has become intolerable. The lawyers, the magistrate judge, and then the district judge were thrown by the reference to hypertension, a serious condition, as part of a claim that a nurse practitioner and a correctional counselor were deliberately indifferent to an inmate, in the cruel-and-unusual punishment sense, by failing to provide him with his prescribed medication for a three-week period. No one in the case recognized that at most the inmate's blood pressure was slightly elevated for part of the three-week period and that such an elevation was of no medical significance. The plaintiff's lawyer admitted at oral argument that he had not conducted any research into hypertension, and he cited no medical literature in his brief. Nor did either judicial officer cite any medical literature, and no one understood the insignificance of the temporary interruption in the inmate's medication. That's because "to determine the effect on the plaintiff's health of a temporary interruption in his medication, the lawyers in the first instance, and if they did their jobs the judges in the second instance, would have had to make some investment in learning about the condition." This they chose not to do, leading to the observation that "the legal profession must get over its fear and loathing of science."[8]

Supreme Court Review

The Supreme Court in reviewing Posner's opinions continued its resistance to the approaches he was taking. The Supreme Court in the 2010–14 period reviewed four Posner panel opinions, affirming one, reversing two, and vacating one. The affirmance case of *Sandifer v. U.S. Steel*,[9] written by Justice Scalia, was an adventure in definitions and statutory interpretation that began with the Fair Labor Standards Act of 1938 and its provision that labor and management in their contracts can decide for themselves that they do not want to treat as compensable the time workers spend getting dressed and undressed for work, known as donning and doffing in labor law jargon. Going against their own union, the plaintiffs argued nonetheless that they fit within an exception that made the time compensable if, as they argued, the clothes at issue qualified as protective gear. Posner's commonsensical approach when the case was at the Seventh Circuit looked to what the workers were doing rather than considering particular items they put on, such as hardhats and safety glasses. For Posner, getting ready for work is just that, not work itself. Scalia in the Supreme Court's review of Posner's panel opinion pointedly found his approach inadequate and looked instead to dictionaries from the historical period of the legislation's enactment and the relationship between the clothes donned and doffed and what the statute described as the principal activities for which the workers were employed. Both opinions found that the clothes exception did not apply and that the donning and doffing time was not compensable. But beyond the different ways Posner and Scalia tried to understand what people ordinarily mean when they talk about work clothes, Posner also both emphasized the economic negotiation dynamics that must have gone on in a union contract that exempted donning and doffing as work and highlighted how this union concession was financially compensated for in other ways in contract negotiations. That the employer and union knew what they were doing lent additional reason not to impose a strained definition. This approach received no consideration from Scalia in his majority opinion.

More so than in the donning and doffing case, Posner's approach to statutory construction did not sell well in a case involving sex offender registration. In *United States v. Carr* the issue was how much courts should look to the plain meaning of a statute and its use of a verb tense and how much courts should look to the purpose of a statute to understand particular parts of it.[10] The defendant had moved from the state of his conviction to Indiana before the Sex Offender Registration and Notification Act (SORNA) was enacted in 2006 and argued that the present-tense formulation of the verb "to travel" in the statute suggested that liability under the act for its reporting requirement did not attach prior to the act's passage. This is what the Tenth Circuit had held in 2008, that the act does not refer to travel that has already occurred.[11] Posner, however, thought that the verb choice in the statute was "not very revealing" and that the Tenth Circuit opinion did not come to terms with the purpose of the statute. It was for him to protect the public from sex offenders, which made it irrelevant whether the travel took place before or after the act's enactment. Rather than looking to verb tenses, he relied instead on the parallel between SORNA and the federal "felon in possession of a statute," 18 U.S.C. sec. 922(g), and its interstate commerce element. That statute, he explained, also used a present-tense verb formulation, but courts interpreting the statute ignored the verb's temporal implications and held that movement of the weapon or ammunition before or after the statute's enactment imposed criminal liability. The Supreme Court, through Justice Sotomayor, however, followed the argument of the Tenth Circuit and cited several cases on the importance of Congress's choice of verb tenses and statutory interpretation, omitting Posner's citation to authority going the other way. Jabbing Posner's approach, Justice Sotomayor looked to a 1993 Supreme Court case for the proposition that "vague notions of a statute's basic purpose are inadequate to overcome the words of its text regarding the *specific* issue under consideration." The registration section at issue is only one provision of SORNA, Justice Sotomayor emphasized, and was part of broader scheme aimed at fixing the problems with prior registration laws that had enabled sex offenders to exploit statutory loopholes. Recognizing this, the emphasis in statutory interpretation had to be on interpreting specific provisions such as the one at issue here with strict regard to statutory language. The penultimate paragraph positively pushed back the interpretive approach Posner had used, noting, "We have stated time and again that courts must presume that a legislature says in a statute what it means and means in a statute what it says there. When the statutory language is plain, the sole function of the courts— at least where the disposition required by the text is not absurd—is to enforce it according to its terms."[12]

Posner was also reversed in a disparate impact employment discrimination case involving Chicago firefighters and written qualifying tests.[13] Posner had looked to the statute's purpose as a guide to interpretation, while the Court wanted to follow only the words of the statute, putting the burden on Congress if a strict reading of the statute produced an odd result. The case was about whether the statute of limitations began to run when the city of Chicago adopted its discriminatory practice with its test results and a declaration that firefighters with scores below a certain level would not be hired, or whether it began to run when the city later began to use its practice in rounds of hiring. For Posner, but not for the Supreme Court, this timing issue turned on the difference between disparate impact claims on the one hand, which did not require proof of an intent to discriminate, and on the other hand disparate treatment cases, which did require proof of discriminatory intent.

It had been the acknowledged rule that in disparate treatment cases there was indeed a difference between executing and using a policy and that the claim of an executed policy had to be brought within the charging period. Posner had reasoned that since disparate impact and disparate treatment were fundamentally similar, the charging period for disparate impact cases of the Chicago firemen sort should be no different, which would require that the claim about the executed policy must fall within the charging period, which it hadn't. Posner in his panel opinion quoted one of his earlier opinions, though without naming himself as the author, for the predicate argument that the purpose of employment discrimination was the same for both disparate impact and disparate treatment situations. Why the charging period should change depending on the theory alleged, he wrote, escaped him.[14] The Court, though, said that drawing an equivalence between the two forms of discrimination should be ignored if seeing the two forms similarly gets in the way of Congress's intention as derived from the statute's language. That intention could be derived here because the statute stated that an

unlawful practice based on disparate impact is established by demonstrating that an employer "uses a particular employment practice that
causes a disparate impact." The verb "uses" ends the inquiry. That the
legislation would give life to one theory but not another is something
that is up to Congress, the Court said. The logic of the legislation defers
to the meaning of the statute as properly read. To go the other way, as
had the Seventh Circuit, would be to rewrite the statute "so that it covers only what we think is necessary to achieve what we think Congress
really intended."[15]

Even though the case counts as a remand rather than a reversal,
Posner got more rejection—sternly worded rejection—in *Black v.
United States*,[16] which involved whether the defendants had forfeited
their right to claim on appeal that the judge should have used a special verdict form rather than a general verdict form to have the jurors
indicate which of the alternate theories of criminal liability they convicted on, that is, whether they convicted on the theory of conventional
fraud involving money or property or on the theory of "honest services"
fraud. The problem as Posner saw it was that the defendants wanted it
both ways. The government had proposed a special jury verdict that
would have required the jury to indicate which theory it was convict-
ing on if it came to that, but the defendants objected, hoping to raise,
Posner speculated, the ambiguity of the general verdict upon a conviction, which in fact they did at trial and then at the Seventh Circuit.[17] To
keep this maneuver from succeeding, Posner concluded that, by spurn-
ing the opportunity to use the special verdict form that the government
had advocated, the defendants forfeited their right to complain later
about the general verdict form. This went too far, the Supreme Court
said, rather sternly, describing the forfeiture as "judicial invention." The
defendants had no obligation to request a special verdict and as a result
could not forfeit their objections to the pecuniary fraud instructions.
The Court understood Posner's forfeiture conclusion as an unwarranted
sanction on the defendants "unmoored to any federal statute or criminal."[18] The government moreover had the ability to trigger this sanction
just by proposing a special verdict. And worst of all ("to boot!"), Posner's
approach applied this forfeiture sanction without giving the defendants
any notice that they would in fact be forfeiting the right to object later
to the jury instruction just by not agreeing with the government to use

the special verdict. "There is a Rule designed to ward off judicial invention of the kind present here. Federal Rule of Criminal Procedure 57(b) admonishes: '[n]o sanction or other disadvantages may be imposed for noncompliance with any requirement not in federal law [or] federal rules . . . unless the alleged violator was furnished with actual notice of the requirement before the noncompliance.'"[19]

A Critic Takes Action

In addition to what we have seen occurring in prior decades, Posner in the first four years of the decade moved in an unprecedented way to criticize the system in which he worked and to reshape it to make it more like what he thought it should be. We see this on several fronts.

Supreme Court

Posner had his own kind of response to the Supreme Court in the 2010s. In unprecedented fashion Posner often and in a wide variety of publications—including his book *The Behavior of Federal Judges*, cowritten with William Landes and Lee Epstein—leveled stinging criticism at the Supreme Court, both generally and at specific Justices. He launches his attacks not just in academic writing, with its limited audience, but in the online magazine *Slate*,[20] with its large audience. He writes that the opinions, almost all clerk-written, are well-written but much too long, with this length a function of the Justices having too much time on their hands because they have too few cases and too many law clerks. The opinions lack a necessary element for successful opinions—candor—as the Justices even when they reach decisions on pragmatic or prudential grounds don't want to admit this. In Posner's view, almost all constitutional interpretation reflects the Justices' prior experiences and dispositions rather than some true reading of the document, so the Court should admit that this is how interpretation works.

That the Justices have too much free time, at least as when their workload and staff sizes are contrasted with the workload and staff sizes of fifty years ago, has led to some bad habits, he points out. It has probably led the Justices to ask far too many questions at oral argument, where there is too much clowning around, making for an undignified

spectacle. Some Justices have also gotten involved in public intellectual activities, such as the regrettable practice of having judges preside
over mock trials, taking the Justices and their judge counterparts in
the lower levels of the judiciary to places their intellectual credentials
should never take them. What, for example, does a judge or Justice
know about whether Shakespeare is the author of the plays attributed
to him? The good news is that as badly as the Justices have performed
on public intellectual fronts—oral arguments, mock trials, writing
books for large advances—it is all inconsequential because the Court's
reputation is a function of it as an institution, not as a function of what
the public thinks of its particular Justices. Yet it all matters to someone
like him, Posner tells us, a self-identified "fusspot."

Two Justices in particular are singled out for criticism. First he criticizes Chief Justice Roberts for either poor management skills or an
indifference to the managerial component of his position. He points
out that there is no reason for the Court to turn out opinions in a flurry
of activity at the end of the term just so that the Court can clear its
docket. He mentions that it takes up to five years for the Court's opinions to make their way into the official volumes of the *U.S. Reports* and
thinks something suspicious is going on with the Court's practice of
making changes to its opinions without public notice of the changes as
the opinions await publication. But beyond management issues, Posner
in an eyebrow-raising way challenges both Roberts's honesty and his
candor in stating the actual reasons for his decisions. Posner takes the
campaign finance case *McCutcheon v. Federal Election Commission*[21] and
asks if Roberts is really as naive about campaign contributions as he
sounds, suggesting through his skepticism that Roberts is not so naive
and that what he has written about politicians not rewarding donors
with particular votes is disingenuous, radically so, given that he is writing a Supreme Court opinion.

If Roberts is criticized, Scalia is evicerated. He needles Scalia for
not saying what an originalist-textualist would ordinarily say in cases,
such as in the DOMA[22] case in which Scalia in his dissent argued for
the virtue of consistency in federal law. Posner writes that it would
seem that Scalia would want to point out (but doesn't) that there is
nothing in the Constitution about discrimination generally or about
gay marriage and that the framers would have thought it, as Posner

puts it, preposterous to propose constitutional protection for gay sex acts, to say nothing of gay marriage or gay marriage benefits. All of this, Posner implies, means that Scalia is an originalist-contextualist of convenience. Posner looks at Scalia's dissent in the Arizona immigration case[23] and all but calls it reckless. For him, Scalia took a polarizing subject, immigration, in an election year in which immigration was an important and highly charged issue and used campaign-type language to the effect that it boggles his mind that the president refuses to enforce federal immigration policy—all this without presenting any evidence to support his claims about immigrants in Arizona invading private property, straining social services, and even putting the lives of citizens in jeopardy. An even more pointed criticism comes in response to Scalia's concurring opinion comment in *Decker v. Northwest Environmental Defense Center*[24] that he was unable to affirm the details of a section of the majority opinion on his own knowledge or even on his own belief, as the section of the opinion at issue went into what he describes as the fine details of molecular biology. For that reason he could not join that part of the majority opinion. There were two issues for Posner. How could it be, he asked, that Scalia did not understand the section of the opinion he could not join while saying at the same time that he had studied the opinions from the lower court and the expert briefs presented to the Supreme Court and was able to affirm that the two strains of DNA at issue were identical and that a third strain is a synthetic creation? How was he competent to opine on the legal and expert briefs and not be able to opine on the section of the brief he did not join? More important to Posner's criticism was Scalia's declaration of an ignorance about science that he was not willing to remedy. He uses, Posner argues, the so-called familiar tools of interpretation, which do not require any scientific understanding. What Scalia—and judges generally—should be doing is learning a little science.

Scalia Alone

Perhaps better known than Posner's attacks on the Court was his well-publicized tangle with Justice Scalia, in which Justice Scalia on one occasion said that Posner in his criticisms was writing above his station and on another occasion called Posner a liar for his suggestion in a book review that Scalia used legislative history in one of his opinions.

Posner's June 27, 2012, criticisms in *Slate* of Scalia's dissenting opinion in the Arizona immigration case play an important part in the dust-up over Posner's review of Scalia and Bryan Garner's *Reading Law*.[25] Scalia a month later gave an interview to Fox News and Chris Wallace in which Wallace asked Scalia about Posner's comment that Scalia's dissent, stating that the president was declining to enforce federal immigration law in Arizona, gives it "the air of a campaign speech." When asked for his response, Scalia in response said, "[h]e is a court of appeals judge, isn't he? . . . He doesn't sit in judgment of my opinions, as far as I'm concerned." When then asked if he sits in judgment Posner's opinions, he answered, "[t]hat's what happens."[26] Posner's review in the *New Republic* followed about a month later, and then three more weeks later Scalia and coauthor Garner gave an interview to Thomson Reuters and Stephen Adler. Adler described having read all the reviews he could find of *Reading Law* (citing Posner's review as one of the most critical) and confronts Scalia with Posner's comment that Scalia used legislative history in his majority opinion in the Second Amendment gun case of *District of Columbia v. Heller*.[27] Scalia rejected the notion that he had used legislative history in his opinion and distinguished what he described as a history of the times, which for him meant what people thought the Second Amendment meant "immediately after its enactment," from the history of the enactment of the bill, which he described as including floor speeches and prior drafts of committees. He said that only in writing for a nonlegal audience could Posner have accused him of using legislative history. Going further, he said that "to say that I use legislative history in how—is—simply, to put it bluntly, a lie." Posner's response when queried by Reuters to Scalia's charge of lying was to point to what Scalia had written in *Heller* with the argument that no matter how you cut it, Scalia used legislative history in the opinion.[28]

Posner used his review of *Reading Law* to report that Scalia's commitment to textualism in statutory interpretation has not always been what he wants us to think it has been and that, not surprisingly, his book with Garner on interpretation distorts the examples they use to make their points about their preference for textualism. His review is something of a précis of his view of judging contrasted with Scalia's view. Posner's approach, consistent with what he has written both on and off

the bench, is that "judges tend to deny the creative—the legislative—
dimension of judging, important as it is in our system, because they do
not want to give the impression that they are competing with legislators, or engaged in anything but the politically unthreatening activity
of objective, literal-minded interpretation, using arcane tools of legal
analysis."[29] Scalia in contrast will have none of this and insists instead
on casting himself as the defender of contextual originalism and the
opponent of legislative history.

We can only assume that Scalia, as Garner's coauthor, was familiar
with and supported the defenses Garner put forth. Garner's ostensible
complaint was that Posner got his facts wrong in his criticisms of various cases he and Scalia had used to applaud textualism properly done
and to ridicule the results of textualism ignored. His response in the
New Republic has both an oddly aggrieved quality and an inexplicable
haughtiness that comes through when he complains that Posner did
not respond—as though it were an obligation—to the criticisms he and
Scalia give of him in their book.

There matters stood until Tony Mauro of *National Law Journal*
reported in May 2014 that Garner had commissioned what he called
an objective arbiter to review *Reading Law* and Posner's *New Republic*
review of it to determine if Posner's complaints were valid. The arbiter
was Steven Hirsch, a San Francisco lawyer and longtime acquaintance of Garner's. He was paid $500 but was able to come to his own
conclusion. His conclusion, as reported by Mauro, was that eight of
Posner's twelve criticisms were unwarranted but that the remaining
four had varying degrees of merit, though none of the criticisms, he
oddly added, was "a valid ground for attacking the authors' integrity."[30] In addition, Hirsch wrote that he was struck "by the need-
lessly ad hominem nature of Posner's attack."[31] When asked by Mauro
about Garner's turn toward an arbiter, Posner wrote, "[p]lease convey my congratulations to Bryan Garner on inventing a new form
of arbitration. Two parties have a dispute; one appoints an arbitrator
to resolve the dispute; the other disputant is not consulted." "How
beautifully," he continued, "that simplifies arbitration! No need for
the parties to agree on an arbitrator, or the American Arbitration
Association to list possible arbitrators and the disputants cross out the
ones they don't like."[32] Garner, when presented with Posner's response

by Mauro, returned to the criticisms of Posner found in *Reading Law* and said, "[i]sn't it interesting that Judge Posner has never tried to defend the few passages of his that *Reading Law* criticizes—and shows to be preposterous." According to Garner, "[t]he report speaks for itself."[33]

Garner's haughtiness is of a piece with Scalia's, though likely for different reasons. Scalia's position, as made plain in his comment about Posner's criticism of his *Heller* decision—that Posner as a lower-court judge does not sit in judgment of his opinions—goes to Scalia's apparent belief in a hierarchy that jumps from the three levels of the federal judiciary—trial judges, appellate judges, and Supreme Court Justices—to the intellectual world at large. His angry if not furious response at being caught out for using legislative history when he has so often inveighed against it seems to inform Garner's response to Posner in the pages of the *New Republic*. Moreover, even if legislative history could be defined as narrowly as Scalia wants it defined, and even if we ignore what Scalia actually wrote about the tenor of the times when the Second Amendment was passed, accusing Posner of lying could never hold water. At the very most Posner simply interpreted the meaning of legislative history in a way Scalia objects to, all of which suggests that Scalia's complaint about Posner and legislative history is about something else.

In an interview with the *ABA Journal* Posner disagreed with the suggestion that he had attacked Scalia. "I don't think *attacking* is the word. He writes a book about judicial interpretation. His book has errors. . . . I'm not saying the authors are bad people—that they're greedy or that they're lying. I'm saying that it's an inaccurate book. I also happen to disagree with Justice Scalia's philosophy of originalism. I think that's legitimate criticism."[34] Posner in an interview with me thought Scalia's reaction to the review had two explanations. The first is that, for Scalia, "junior judges shouldn't be criticizing their senior judges." The second is that "he's utterly convinced of not only the correctness of his position, but that nobody could possibly disagree with it in good faith. Anybody who studied the issue would agree with him, so if someone doesn't agree with him it's for a bad reason. It might be envy, a sense of rivalry, or an attempt to destroy the Court, but it couldn't be in good faith."[35]

Championing Patent Law Reform

As a complement of sorts to Posner's criticism of the federal judiciary, the Supreme Court, and Justice Scalia, Posner seemingly acted on his complaint that patent law needed reforming, first by implementing drastic changes in existing patent law in a case he was presiding over as a district court judge and then by undertaking something of a media blitz raising awareness of the problems he saw with patent law and making a number of proposals for change along the way.

Posner drew attention to himself and his views on patent litigation when as a trial judge in 2012 sitting by designation he presided over a patent case involving Apple and Google-owned Motorola and smartphone patents they respectively owned. The case ended suddenly when just prior to trial Posner dismissed it with prejudice based on the inability of each side to prove damages.[36] The absence of damages also precluded Motorola from seeking injunctive relief against Apple. One of Posner's innovations related to damages as a general matter in a high-technology patent case and more specifically the need for evidence of marketplace damages relating to the specific patent at issue. Another innovation was a stricter test on admissible expert testimony by seemingly setting out a per se rule at odds with what had become a near standard operating procedure directing that experts could not be qualified as such if they worked for their respective companies.

Posner then took to the media following the trial to make a pitch to reshape patent law to make it more responsive to the world of high technology in which patents were too often used offensively and in which it could be questioned whether patents were even needed for software and high-technology industries, as illustrated by Apple and Motorola and their respective smartphone technologies. He contributed articles to online and traditional magazines after the Apple case in which he decried the state of the nation's patent law and offered possible reforms. He wrote for *Slate* on October 15, 2012, about mischief caused by companies—known as patent trolls—who buy up blocks of patents and then threaten to bring infringement suits against companies using technology implicated by the patents. Posner argued that the law should be changed so that only companies actively using their patents can sue for infringement. He wrote in the July 2012 *Atlantic*

Monthly about why there are too many patents in America and how too many patents ironically hurt innovation. He offered a number of proposals for reform, the most important of which was changing the law to distinguish between industries so that only the industries that need patent protection—such as the pharmaceutical industry—get it, while high-technology industries with rapid change and low invention costs do not. He wrote about patent trolls in a July 21, 2013, entry for the Becker-Posner Blog restating for a more economically savvy audience what he had written for *Slate*. He wrote another entry on September 30, 2012, on patents and copyrights in which he worked through the economic analysis to show that too many of either was bad for business. He gave interviews to Reuters and to *SRR Journal* within a month of the Apple case's conclusion in which he described the ills of the current patent system, which extended to the Federal Circuit, and explained that patent appeals should be returned to the regional circuit courts, that jury trials in patent cases should be abolished, and that more district judges should volunteer to try patent cases after being trained to handle patent litigation.[37] In the Reuters interview he went through the problems and possible solutions again, also making the point that the companies themselves should not be faulted for taking advantage of a broken system. "It is a constant struggle for survival," he said. "As in any jungle, the animals will use all the means at their disposal, all their teeth and claws that are permitted by the ecosystem."[38] Business journalist and op-ed columnist Joe Nocera in a *New York Times* piece based on a Posner interview specifically linked Posner's interest in shaking up patent law with the Apple trial. He begins with Posner's observation that he thought it would be fun to do patent trials before explaining that Posner has been volunteering to serve as a district judge in patent cases. Then, in the paragraph making the point without it having to come from Posner himself, which might have been too provocative, we read, "[b]ut 'fun' is hardly Posner's only motive. To put it more bluntly than he ever would, he is adjudicating patent cases in an effort to change a legal system that now gives companies rich incentives to bring costly, time-consuming and often prideful patent lawsuits. It desperately needs to be done."[39] On the change in damages that he wants to bring to patent litigation requiring precise calculation relating to the infringing technology and market demand for the product in which it is used, Posner said that "if they can meet that challenge, then fine. But it's difficult."[40]

The Federal Circuit took a different view of the case and patent law when the case reached it for review not quite two years later and held that Posner had gone too far with each of his innovations. The opinion, with rather pointed language pushing Posner back, noted that "a judge must be cautious not to overstep its [*sic*] gatekeeping role and weigh facts, evaluate the correctness of conclusions, impose its own preferred methodology, or judge credibility, including the credibility of one expert over another. These tasks are solely for the fact finder."[41]

Campaign against the Brazen

Descriptions of Posner's opinions in a group of cases from the decade, mostly from 2014, help bring together for review the full complement of his stylistic and jurisprudential traits and show Posner taking particular aim at parties making brazen arguments. In *United States v. Slaight*,[42] the defendant had pleaded guilty to the charge of receipt and possession of child pornography shipped in interstate or foreign commerce while reserving his right to challenge the trial court's denial of his motion to suppress incriminating statements he had made when questioned by the police. The facts described an instance of the collision between the right of the *Miranda* rule—that a suspect in custody must be advised of his rights before police questioning and that if not so advised his statements are inadmissible—and the reality of certain police practices designed to avoid the rule. At issue are police who "are sometimes restive under the restraints imposed by the [*Miranda*] rule" and the particular facts of the case showing what Posner describes as "ingenious, pertinacious, but ultimately (as it seems to us) transparent efforts to disguise a custodial interrogation as noncustodial."[43] Law enforcement knew from searching Internet peer-to-peer sites that Slaight had downloaded child pornography and, with a force of nine officers, drove to Slaight's house and "broke in with a battering ram, strode in with pistols and assault rifles at the ready, and when they found him naked in his bed ordered him, in an 'authoritative tone' and guns pointed at him, to put his hands up."[44] They searched his home and seized his computer and then effectively insisted that he accompany them to the police station to be interviewed. They had for this purpose already booked "a tiny windowless interview room."[45] This interrogation setting plus the police show of force indicated that the defendant was not free to leave—the test of whether someone is in custody—even though the police said that he could. The defendant knew the police had all the evidence they needed to convict him and that as a result they were not about to let him leave. Despite this, the government insisted that Slaight had not been in custody.

The opinion, with its theme of exposing chutzpah-like pretext, shows Posner using the full range of his favorite techniques and raising some of his familiar issues. Lawyers for both sides are chided for not putting the dimensions of the interview room into the record with the observation that "we've previously noted with displeasure lawyers' indifference to exact measurements,"[46] though here the surveillance video of the interrogation provided enough information to confirm the room's small size. He gives the government lawyer high marks for candor, though, for acknowledging at oral argument that the police officers in fact had wanted to question Slaight without the *Miranda* warnings because they wanted to get from him the particular admission, which they did, that no one else had access to his computer as a way of blocking that avenue of defense. He uses casual language when he writes that when Slaight was finally given his *Miranda* warnings at the direction of the prosecutor, he "promptly clammed up—too late."[47] He adds dramatic flair when he parenthetically imagines the difficulty Slaight would have had in actually leaving the cramped room and the need to say something to the effect of "Officer, may I please squeeze by you?"[48] He wittily mocks the police for arguing that one reason they wanted to interview the defendant at the police station rather than at his home was that the windows at his home were covered with trash bags and that there was very little natural light in the house, writing after noting that the house had electricity that "the officers gave no reason why an interview, unlike painting a landscape, requires natural light."[49] A police argument that another reason for not wanting to interview the defendant at his home was that the house had a strong smell of cats brought Posner to the defense of the cats. He described the argument as laughable and pointed out that "police smell much worse things in the line of duty."[50] He also uses a literary allusion in a powerful closing paragraph that goes to the core issue and decides the case, writing that "the key facts are the show of force at Slaight's home, the protracted questioning of him in the claustrophobic setting of the police station's Lilliputian interview room, and the more than likelihood that he would be formally placed under arrest if he tried to leave because the government already had so much evidence against him. These facts are incontrovertible and show that the average person in Slaight's position would have thought himself in custody. Any other conclusion would leave *Miranda* in tatters."[51]

In *Baskin v. Bogan*,[52] he calls out the states of Indiana and Wisconsin on the brazenness of their empty arguments attempting to defend the constitutionality of their respective statutes not recognizing gay marriage. The states did not make the usual arguments against gay marriage, declining to argue that homosexuality is not an immutable trait or that a moral objection of gay marriage was sufficient to carry the constitutional day. Nor did they argue that gay marriage must be prohibited because it undermines or threatens heterosexual marriage. Indiana argued instead that the only point of state-authorized marriage was to channel procreative sex and its resulting unwanted children into marriage by making marriage more attractive through various benefits than it otherwise would be and that gays had no need of marriage because the problem of unwanted children did not attach to them. Posner in his opinion mocks the states at nearly every turn for their arguments and for their responses to hypotheticals, writing of the unwanted children argument that it is so full of holes that it cannot be taken seriously,[53] that the "the grounds advanced by Indiana and Wisconsin for their discriminatory policies are not only conjectural; they are totally implausible,"[54] and that he doubts "that [Indiana] is serious" in "arguing that the only governmental interest derives from the problem of accidental births."[55] Moreover, "The state's [Indiana's] argument that a marriage of first cousins who are just past child-bearing age provides a 'model [of] family life for younger, potentially procreative men and women' is impossible to take seriously."[56] "Go figure," he mocks.

The proof of the disingenuousness (or chutzpah) of the states was that in making the child welfare arguments the states simply ignored that each state allowed gays to adopt children—that gays disproportionally adopted children in fact, clearly a social good—but that children adopted by gays were less well off because unlike the children of straight parents they could not say that their parents were married and that as a result they were like everyone else. Posner wrote that the laws of the two states on gay marriage were simply irrational and that while gays, because of immutable traits defining sexual orientation, would otherwise qualify and pass the analytical tests using suspect classifications, such an approach was not necessary because the statutes at issue were simply irrational. He deployed extensive statistics relating to unwanted children and to straight and gay adoption to make his points; he related social science scholarship to show that homosexuality is an immutable characteristic and went even further with a perhaps unnecessary discussion of what is going on in the body that determines sexual orientation; and he invokes Holmes's observation that it is revolting to have no better reason for a rule of law than tradition. He clinches the argument against a moral opposition to gay marriage, even though the states do not make it, by discussing John Stuart Mill's idea in *On Liberty* that distinguishes between someone's distress caused by an act, such as a crime upon a person, and someone's distress caused by behavior that disgusts but does not harm him because it is too far temporally removed, as with the English not being affected by polygamy in Utah, even though the English opposed the practice. For a harm to be the basis of moral or legal concern, Posner explained, it must be tangible, secular, and material rather than moral or spiritual. His point for gay marriage purposes was that heterosexuals may disapprove of gay marriage but it will not harm them in a way that states would be justified in acting on through legislation.

The abortion restriction case *Planned Parenthood of Wisconsin, Inc. v. Van Hollen*,[57] which involved a Wisconsin statute modeled on statutes from several other states requiring physicians performing abortions to have admitting privileges within thirty miles of their clinic, came to the Seventh Circuit on the issue of a preliminary injunction rather than full review on the merits and prompted Posner to make plain that the statute was interested in restricting abortion availability rather than the health of the patient, as the state claimed. The statute was passed on a Friday and was to take effect on the following Monday, giving physicians just the weekend to accomplish what usually took months, even assuming that obstacles were not put in their way to gain otherwise expected admitting privileges. The harm factor that was one-half of the sliding-scale approach to the question of whether the preliminary injunction that the district judge had put in place should continue prior to trial was so one-sidedly in favor of women seeking abortions, who would have seen two and one-half of the four Wisconsin clinics close without the injunction, that little attention needed to be paid to the remaining factor of the eventual likelihood of the suit's success. Nonetheless, Posner extensively analyzed the case on the merits, though always with the caveat that the available evidence could change, to argue that the statute was irrational and there was, in fact, a looming equal protection argument based on the different manner in which different admitting privilege rules applied to physicians performing abortions (with the thirty-mile admitting privilege rule) and to physicians performing similar or more invasive surgical procedures (with no such rules applying to them). The state's attempt at constitutionality was twice noted as feeble, perhaps to the state's irritation. In petitioning unsuccessfully for review with the US Supreme Court the state twice referred to the "feeble" characterization as part of the error.

Panel member Judge Manion concurred in the judgment but that was it. Seeing what he thought was Posner's argument on the merits as unfair assistance to the abortion doctors via his unnecessary constitutional analysis, he fought back in his concurring opinion with his own constitutional analysis and assistance to the state when the case eventually got to trial. Manion's analysis differed completely from Posner's. He provided a different gloss to "rationally related" concept and argued that the needed evidence did not have to be of the "as practiced" or field studies sort as required by Posner (by which standard the state would lose) but could be evidence of a speculative sort. He then went further and provided that evidence in the form of an American Medical Association position paper. He also challenged the opinion's undue burden argument and culled cases from other jurisdictions to show that the number of extra miles that would need to be driven and the number of extra trips that woman would need to make, due to the new admitting privileges restrictions, had been held in other cases not to be an undue burden. What he did not attempt to counter was Posner's market analysis explanation that the hospital industry is changing and that hospitals are making admitting-privileges decisions based on the amount of business a physician can bring to hospitals and thus presenting physicians with obstacles unrelated to the legislature's continuity-of-care assumptions about the effect of requiring admitting privileges for abortion doctors. That the legislature knew so little about the hospital industry generally and admitting privileges specifically was further proof for Posner that, even though the issue was not before his court, Wisconsin's intention in its legislation was not concern for the health of the patient but a legislative end run to restrict abortion availability with no resulting healthcare benefit to the patient. Manion, on the other hand, was content with the idea that Wisconsin could say one thing and mean another.

A Push to Go outside the Record and Meeting Resistance

Consistent with Judge Manion's implicit criticism of Posner's majority opinion in the Wisconsin abortion case, that it went beyond what was needed to resolve the case, a dissenting opinion in a 2014 Fair Labor Standards Act case raised an issue accusing Posner of going outside the appellate record and then using the information found there to affect the result in *Mitchell v. JCG Industries,*[58] a case like *Sandifer* involving clothing and the time it took for workers to put on and take off (donning and doffing) certain items of clothing to help determine whether that time was compensable. The parties gave two very different estimates of how much time it took to don and doff. The plaintiff by way of affidavit said fifteen minutes, while the defendant said the time was de minimis. Out of curiosity, as Posner put it, and to better understand the case, Posner and two of his law clerks acquired the clothing (or gear) in question and videotaped (and of course timed) themselves in trial runs of donning and doffing. Taking the gear off took fifteen seconds and putting it on took a minute. This convinced Posner that there was no genuine issue of material fact and that the trial judge had been correct in granting summary judgment for the defendant employer. Chief Judge Wood in her dissent went after the propriety of the donning-and-doffing experiment and wrote, "I am startled, to say the least, that an appellate court would resolve such a dispute based on a post-argument experiment conducted in chambers."[59] She seemed to accept Posner's acknowledgment in his majority opinion that the results of the experiment did not qualify as evidence on which he could rely but then implicitly doubted the explanation (why else would she bring it up?) before writing that "to the extent (even slight) that the court is relying on this experiment to resolve a disputed issue, I believe that it has strayed beyond the boundaries established by Federal Rule of Civil Procedure 56."[60]

Other judges then joined in when the plaintiff petitioned for an en banc rehearing, which was denied. Four judges—three Democratic appointees and one Republican appointee—dissented from the denial, and Judge Williams wrote a dissent that Judge Wood and Judges Rovner and Hamilton joined, again bringing up the donning-and-doffing experiment and making the same claim that explicitly rejecting the plaintiff's affidavit evidence and confirming the defendant's version "ignored the evidence in the light most favorable to the employees and therefore did not conduct a proper Rule 56 analysis."[61]

Apparently seeing these as fighting words, Posner took the unusual route of concurring in the denial of rehearing en banc, beginning his opinion with the procedural oddity of his concurrence, seemingly indicating that there was a strongly felt need to respond to those who had dissented from the en banc rehearing denial. He next explained, as noted by Judge Wood in her dissent, that the donning-and-doffing experiment did not result in evidence upon which he relied. And then Posner responded to Judge Rovner's dissent by explaining at length that the experiment shed light on an evidentiary puzzle—how much time donning and doffing took—not susceptible to a jury determination given the gap between the estimates from the two parties. If, as the experiment suggests, no reasonable jury could credit the appellants' contentions on donning and doffing, the appellate court was required to affirm the district judge's grant of summary judgment.[62]

Posner and his law clerks had been conducting independent research for years. Posner's law clerk manual in fact tells clerks that one of the first things they should do when a new case comes in is to Google all the parties to learn as much as they can. Lawyers complained about his use of independent research, and in 2013, in response to Posner's own article justifying independent research,[63] distinguished law professor Frederick Schauer described Posner's approach as problematic because the two usual justifications for independent research—a judge looking into facts about which a court can take judicial notice or looking into legislative facts, that is, facts that are not case specific—did not seem to fit what Posner was up to.[64] Then as part of a 2014 interview Posner gave a startling answer to a question about the independent research he conducts. "I understand the criticism [of going outside the record, but not for adjudicative fact]," he began, "because the lawyers want to control the case. They invoke the glories of the adversary system. I think the adversary system is overrated. Not that I want to convert to the inquisitorial system that prevails in Europe (except the U.K.) and most of the rest of the world, but I want to see the adversary system taken down a peg."[65]

Oral Arguments

While it had certainly happened before, Posner more recently seems to have intensified, at least in a few high-profile cases, his demand that lawyers respond in oral argument to questions that can range well beyond the record to what the lawyer personally thinks or feels rather than to what the client's position is with regard to policy-based questions. Sparks can fly when the lawyers confronted with such a question attempt to beg off on the grounds of not having an opinion or not knowing or, in legislative interpretation cases, claiming no knowledge of the legislature's intention. The sparks fly in the form of Posner's frustration or irritation at the refusal of the lawyer to engage, to drop the lawyer's pretense, so to speak, to answer questions designed to get at the solution for a particular problem. Lawyers aggressively trying to beg off answering or trying to challenge the nature of the question can get the harshest responses, with Posner demanding, sometimes with a raised and irritated voice, that the lawyers answer his questions.

He takes this approach in the recent gay marriage case and the Wisconsin abortion clinic case, though the dynamic at work could be seen in a 2006 unpleasant prison disciplinary case turning on what punishment could be meted out to a prisoner who refused to eat and took all sorts of disruptive steps such as smearing feces on the walls of his cell as a protest against eating specifically and prison regulations generally.[66] A few minutes into the argument Posner asked the lawyer for the state what she thought the prison should do with someone like the inmate. Before the lawyer has a chance to respond, he extended the question to "[i]f you were running the prison, what would you do?" A more unfair question could not be asked.

The lawyer for the state of Indiana faced the same kind of pressure in the 2014 gay marriage case.[67] Posner was pressing the argument, resisted by Indiana's lawyer, that the adopted children of gay parents would be better off if their adopted parents were married. To the question of whether the children would be better off, the state's lawyer said that he did not know. "Let's think about the answer," Posner began before asking the lawyer to think back to when he was six to query whether children at that age are affected, given peer pressure, by whether their parents are married. The state's lawyer stiffened his spine and said that it was not his job to answer that kind of question, to which Posner responded by asking if he had an opinion on the matter. Following the answer of no, he mocked the lawyer by snippily saying that it must be a matter of indifference to him. The lawyer for Wisconsin had his own troubles to deal with.[68] Posner on occasion raised his voice with him and with irritation said that the lawyer was not answering his question about what the legislature was intending with its legislation. "Look, answer my question," he commanded. The lawyer's repeated answer that he could not speak to legislative choices was never sufficient. The lawyer representing the state of Wisconsin in the abortion clinic case ran into the same problem when he in response to Posner's questions about legislative intent said that he couldn't speak to what was not in the record when it came to legislative choices.[69] As a last example of recent cases, in a case involving whether in a civil rights case brought by an inmate the trial judge should have appointed a lawyer for the inmate,[70] Posner made the query directly personal when the issue turned on the skills needed to try the case, asking the state's lawyer whether he would have been competent to try the moderately complex case, which turned on cross-examination of conflicting accounts and case preparation. The lawyer candidly answered that he wasn't, a concession that could have shown up in the opinion as proof that the inmate plaintiff was not up to representing himself at trial. The state's lawyer dodged a bullet, though, when rather than point to the lawyer's concession Posner in his opinion looked primarily to the obstacles the inmate faced in trying to prepare his case from his prison cell to conclude that the inmate needed to have a lawyer to make it a fair trial.

Posner's asking lawyers what they think about a particular issue and his irritation at their unwillingness to join him on the policy plane on which he wants to discuss the case needs to be distinguished from a general irritation at the unwillingness of lawyers to answer other types of questions and his irritation with the personality type that seeks to best him in argument by what Posner calls fencing. The recent case involving Notre Dame University, turning on its compliance with certain provisions of the Affordable Care Act, illustrates this point.[71] The University's lawyer, seeming to enjoy his parries and thrusts a bit too much, was refusing to answer in a straightforward fashion questions Posner was posing him. They went back and forth several times, with Posner increasingly annoyed with the lawyer's performance. He then rather startlingly told the lawyer that if he did not answer his questions, he would not let him continue with his argument. This stern and perhaps overly aggressive move was reported in the national press. Bad manners or losing composure during oral argument, though, is not the same as asking lawyers questions that require them to step outside their roles as lawyers. The idea that oral argument is the occasion for lawyers to help judges reason through problems not as advocates but as people engaged, knowledgeable, and interested in the case at hand runs counter to the adversary system, in which the case is contained within the four corners of the record and the lawyers are there to advance their client's position with respect to the law and facts of the case.

Taking Measurements

That Posner was thinking about being as good as Henry Friendly of course recalls what Posner had written to Aaron Director upon learning of his nomination to the Seventh Circuit, that he would get the chance to measure himself on the appellate bench against Learned Hand and Friendly. What of that measurement? Posner had written in his book measuring Cardozo's greatness that statistics were important in the same way that statistics were an important measure of greatness in baseball. There are difficulties, though, in using statistics to measure baseball players or judges of different generations. In baseball, the liveliness of the ball itself has varied over time, for example, as has the height of the pitching mound, affecting both pitching and hitting statistics. And of course there have been rule changes, such as the designated hitter rule, which affect statistics. In judging, a measure that looks to the number of times a judge has been cited by name either as a stand-alone invocation in the text or in a case citation, as in "(Posner, J.)," has been affected by changing citation and opinion-writing styles. Judges until approximately fifty years ago did not tend to use the parenthetical inclusion of a judge's name as a tip-of-the-hat reference from which we can infer influence or respect. Friendly seems to have started or at least accelerated the practice in the 1960s. Certainly there is a difference in how often we see such parenthetical citation references in the *Federal Reporter* once we get into the 1960s and 1970s. The same is true of an opinion-writing style that makes reference to a judge by name in the text.

There were 102 times between 2010 and 2014 when Posner was cited by name by judges outside the Seventh Circuit. Judge Easterbrook, his closest rival, was cited by name outside the Seventh Circuit 55 times. More important, when we look to total citations by name through 2014, Posner was cited by name in the text of an opinion by judges outside the Seventh Circuit 724 times. Judge Easterbrook, coming in second, was cited 322 times. But there's more.

Until now we have not been able to measure Posner's engagement with the law and the extent to which that engagement has influenced other judges. But with the help of the Westlaw editorial team (in particular Robert Smits and David Carlson) and its remarkable willingness to spend hundreds of hours coding and running searches of its dazzling databases and its digest and key number system, upon which it can be argued that law as practiced by lawyers and judges itself pivots, we can get at where Posner has traveled in the law and the extent that others have followed him. We can also contrast Posner's numbers with the numbers for Hand, Friendly, and Easterbrook.

The breadth of Posner's engagement with the law can be measured by looking to the number of distinct principles of law as translated into key numbers he has used in his opinions. The digest system as a whole, with its 414 topics, contains some 115,000 distinct principles of law or key numbers. Posner has used 9,573 distinct principles of law as translated into key numbers in his 2,885 majority opinions. Many he has used only once, some fifty times. Altogether he has used these principles of law 24,574 times; that is, Posner's opinions contain 24,574 headnotes. These headnotes have in turn been cited by judges using the digest system for research some 213,474 times. Put differently, in the digest marketplace, Posner headnotes (though of course his name is not attached to the headnotes) have been cited 213,474 times. Coming in second, Judge Easterbrook's headnotes, based on 6,182 distinct key number principles of law, have been cited some 138,662 times. Judge Friendly's headnotes, based on 4,151 distinct key number principles of law, have been cited 63,915 times.

Conclusion

IN MEASURING HIS INFLUENCE we need to consider Posner's recent initiatives—in oral argument, criticisms of the judiciary, criticisms of patent law, and going outside the record—some of which are clearly transgressive. What is he up to? Getting older—he is now seventy-seven—could have something to do with it, though there's little direct evidence of his age having an effect. He seems not to be much different now than in earlier decades, though he travels less now. He said in a 2002 interview that he works seven days a week and repeated as much in a 2014 interview. "As long as my physical health holds up and senility holds off," he said recently, "I will continue to work as I have. I am one of those people who dread retirement. I hope I won't overstay my welcome."[1]

Unlike Learned Hand, who moved increasingly to the right as he got into his seventies and eighties, Posner has moved to the left on several issues. He noted in a recent interview that these days he is more concerned than he had been about long prison sentences, consumer protection, the environment, and income inequality. He is now "less trustful of purely economic analysis," in part because of the "2008 crash and the ensuing economic downturn. That shook some of my faith in economic analysis. And developments in psychology have required qualification of the 'rational choice' model of economic behavior."[2] He also changed his mind about gay marriage from when he first wrote about it in 1992 in *Sex and Reason*. He had argued then that not enough was known to favor it, while of course his recent opinions in the Wisconsin and Indiana cases argue for marriage equality for gays.

While explanations for what seems to be a concerted campaign for change might be difficult to come by, it is true that if nothing else Posner's recent initiatives are consistent with the balance of Posner's career in which he has always moved against the grain. Clues to this phenomenon—and by extension to his recent behavior—can be found in his archive correspondence.[3] There he describes not just his less than tight fit with law in general but more particularly his many traits and characteristics, one of which is as a provocateur and metaphorical bomb thrower.

He disparages pretty much everything about the teaching and practice of law. He writes to Larry Kramer, "Modern scholarship! Ugh! The vast bulk of modern scholarship, in law as in certain other embattled fields of the humanities such as English literature, is *bullshit*." Critical theory can be blamed. He writes, "If it lasts, there really is no God. The entire cerebral cortex of bright people like Frank Michelman has been *destroyed* by fumes emanating from Paris." The larger issue, which pops up several times in the correspondence, is that for him the whole field of academic law is weak. Pulling no punches, he tells Kramer, who was then trying to sort out his career path, that "academic law is a very defective field, full of bullshit and capable of turning capable people into bullshitters. It's also very much an every-man-a-king field; no one is content to do 'ordinary science.' Economists seem very *sober* in contrast." He fails to see the point of what some legal academics do. To support his dismissal he contrasts inquiry that considers the positive theory of judicial behavior with what he calls "the unedifying (when not played in a lawsuit or a law school classroom) lawyer's game of rationalizing a predetermined result," that is, looking back at judicial opinions and discerning their reasoning, an approach often skewed by the biases of the law professor sorting through the opinion. He sees this as a sort of game, writing that "when I read [the work of two well-known academics], I sense that the latter is the game they're playing because they leave out so much that I would think important to the positive-theory game (and what exactly are they *explaining* when they're *criticizing* judicial decisions)."

Going beyond the walls of the academy, he writes that the practice of law is also beset with problems for the intellectually inclined. "A very intelligent *lawyer* understands that the greatest lawyer is on a plane of creativity far below that of a great scientist, philosopher, or artist," he writes to Larry Kramer. Perhaps more to the point, he writes that the way the profession is organized today limits more than it offers. "I am afraid that the modern practice of law does not offer a great deal of scope for the poetic imagination," he writes to a correspondent inquiring about law practice as a career. "The reason is intense specialization, which fosters tunnel vision. But we must do what we can." When a friend on the English department faculty describes the difficulties his son was facing in trying to sort out whether law was the career path he should choose, Posner writes, "I have often shared your son's doubts, but have learned to live with them. Oliver Wendell Holmes by the way was also much assailed by doubts that law was a worthwhile calling for people of sensibility." And when a new college graduate writes to inquire about law, in the context of a literary sensibility in particular, he writes, in a sort of summing up of his view on the important issue, "I would caution you however that in most of its purlieus and declivities the law really is a very limited field for a person of literary bent. Holmes was right that 'a man may live greatly in the law as elsewhere,' but I would underline 'may' to introduce the proper note of dubiety." He goes on to say that "there is no dependable career track for teaching or judging, the fields of law with the most literary potential. Most law graduates end up willy-nilly in some form of practice, and it can be dreary even when it's lucrative. Do you know Melville's story 'Bartleby the Scrivener'? And Tolstoy's 'The Death of Ivan Ilych'? These are cautionary tales about the lawyer's life. I don't recommend law to people unless they have a bent for it or can think of nothing better to do with their lives. But you make your own decisions of course." "Even legal academics," he adds elsewhere, "are livelier than practicing lawyers. It is a profession that dulls most of its practitioners."

Turning to judging, he rates himself with regard to what legal professionals like to see in a judge's work, writing that he is "incurably idiosyncratic" and that he has "never been fully socialized in law." By this latter comment he means that he does not share the profession's rather low-bar demand for superficial justification that can be had with the established formulations. As he puts it, it is "the soundness that interests me, not the plumage." This belief is complemented by an observation that goes to his sense of identity. It comes up as part of a discussion with Larry Kramer about whether judging rather than practice or teaching is perhaps a career path he should choose. Kramer points to the idea as part of his argument that judging for Posner is the most important part of his professional life. But Posner disagrees with this. He writes, "I think of judging as my 'day job,' as they say in Hollywood. Don't get me wrong. I love it, and I give it the first call on my time. But I think it is exceedingly difficult for a federal judge (below the Supreme Court) to have a significant impact on the law, legal thought, social thought, or whatever." This then leads to a general summing up of his career to date. "Hand and Friendly could do it in part," he writes, "because they (Hand especially) lived in a period of less academic specialization (today it is very hard for a judge to know anywhere near as much about a field as some law professors do), in part because of the concentration of certain types of federal law, such as copyright and securities, in New York (that's changing), in part because the workload was much lighter, allowing for much greater depth. Friendly wrote—what?—30 opinions a year; I write three times as many. I would like to make a mark with my opinions but I'm not optimistic. It's different with my academic writing. My work on economic analysis of law has had a big impact. I think my work on law and literature and especially on jurisprudence will also have some impact."

He describes himself variously. He frequently describes himself as having led a sheltered life. It takes the lead, for example, in his description of himself as "a sheltered, cossetted, timid, diaspora Jewish American intellectual," and for proof he offers up in various letters that he has never heard of yeast infections ("do you believe me now when I say I have led a sheltered life") and that he had to look up "cystitis" in the dictionary ("such is the sheltered character of my life"). The real proof that he has led a sheltered life, though, comes in his surprise and even shock in finding out about the ways people he knows of act in their tawdry affairs, cruel treatment of others, and masks of deceit to fool the world as to who they really are. After learning of the serial philandering of a sometime colleague, he writes that "nothing that happened in my circle of acquaintances *should* have come as a shock to me, but my capacity to be shocked appears unimpaired. I must have had a sheltered childhood, which makes it difficult for me to understand, except in the most arid purely cognitive sense, what is going on in the world." He is stunned to learn that another sometime colleague sends venomous anonymous letters and writes, "It had never occurred to me that I would ever meet a person who writes anonymous letters—which we judges encounter as hate mail and threats—any more than I would ever meet a murderer. My knowledge of human nature is incomplete." After giving analysis and advice on the messy breakup of a marriage with lesbian and adultery angles, he writes, "But I say this as someone who has no direct experience with such situations and doesn't consider Henry James a realist novelist, so maybe I don't know what I'm talking about." To a correspondent who writes especially compelling letters about his professional and personal entanglements, he writes, "Your vignettes about your own relationships and those of people you know are fascinating—eye-opening to me, because I've lived such a sheltered life." A few days later, after receiving another letter from this same correspondent containing even more entanglement descriptions, he writes that "these letters are deeply fascinating. They open a glimpse into a world of strong emotion that I barely know except from books that I don't take quite as seriously as you do. I know people have secret lives but the awareness is rarely brought home to me."

The significance of the Jewish element in the phrase Jewish American intellectual is not settled, though, by the factual accuracy that Posner was born to Jewish parents. The several references to Posner's Jewishness suggest that it was something of a complicated issue for him. He gives every indication that he wants to distance himself from his Jewish roots. After saying that for him the Jewish holidays are what he calls "a real yawn" and after writing that the only religious holiday he likes is Christmas, because of the carols, trees, lights, and the like, he writes that he is "the prime example of the assimilated Jew (though not the anti-Semitic variety, which is common too), and unlike others of my ilk do not find as I grow older any tugging at my ethnic roots—but maybe I'm just not old enough yet." He then adds, "I dislike ethnicity as much as religion and of course in Judaism the two are intertwined." He does not self-identify as a Jewish judge and was taken aback when Stephen Breyer described himself when new to the

Court as an American Jew. "Now that Jews and Catholics are so thoroughly mainstreamed in American society," he writes, "they don't have to draw attention to themselves qua Jews and Catholics." Driving home the point, he writes, "I believe in the robe as a symbol of neutrality, and that judges should so far as possible shed gender, race, and religion not only in their judging but in all their public utterances." But against all of this, especially his statement that he dislikes ethnicity as much as religion, he nonetheless got irritated when as part of an exchange over the interpretation of literature he was called authoritarian, "which sounds close to 'fascist,' which I've also been called and which makes the Jew in me bridle." Disliking ethnicity, the letters suggest, is not the same as denying its application on some level. He believes that he understands Kafka as part of his claim that "Kafka is another who cannot be fully appreciated by non-Jews, that one must be ethnically Jewish to appreciate the *humor* in Kafka."

He enjoys challenging and even upsetting the status quo, providing a shock of sorts. Examples abound. When Martha Nussbaum in an exchange over his book *Sex and Reason* suggested that it was bizarrely irrational to discuss, as Posner had, sex in economic terms, he had a ready answer that has application far beyond this particular book. "That's my method of *épater les bourgeois*," he explains, likely delighting in Nussbaum's response to his approach. He describes to Larry Lessig giving a "fouling the nest" talk to the American Enterprise Institute on pragmatism where he "was roundly denounced by a string of really dumb rightwingers before the television cameras of C-Span. I had fun." He concludes the letter wittily: "I am now anathema to the left and the right. I have achieved centrality."

As another example, he offends or shocks people in social settings and seems to enjoy writing about it in his letters. In one letter to Nussbaum he describes a dinner party at which as part of dinner he attributed the high IQ of Jews "to the Darwinian winnowing performed by pogroms, etc., culminating in the Holocaust." This shocked some of the guests, as did his suggestion that if the Jews do eventually disappear through intermarriage, it wouldn't matter that much because they "would have had a good run—longer than the Romans, for example." The paragraph then ends with "I am a monster." This reference to himself as a monster appears several times in the correspondence and gets a definition of sorts when he engages with Nussbaum on the idea of the fully human. He argues that Nussbaum will not recognize as fully human a life without laughter, without play, without empathy, without family relationships, without a feeling for nature. There is for her no trade-off among the elements—it is all or nothing. "But this seems to rule out," he writes, "precisely the most interesting, creative—I would say, the most worthwhile—human beings: monsters like Wagner, Tolstoy, Nietzsche, Wittgenstein, Proust, Kafka, Newton, and Michelangelo, etc.—as specimens of warped humanity, each radically deficient in one or more of the items on your checklist, who nevertheless, it seems to me, outrank in human terms those bland and cheerful sheep whom your list conjures up." We do not get, however, a connection between Posner's self-identification as a monster and any particular element. We have instead the instances in which he describes himself as a monster, such as when Nussbaum introduces him to a philosophy professor friend of hers of a liberal sensibility. He jokes and notes, "I daresay he was treading warily in the presence of such a monster as I must appear to him to be." In another letter to Nussbaum he explains that he is going to Georgetown University to receive an honorary degree and then jokes, "I daresay they, good Catholics that they are, will cancel it when they discover what sort of monster they propose to honor." In a letter to Richard Rorty he describes a trip to Harvard in which he gave a lecture followed by an exchange with Michael Sandel in a class with seven hundred students enrolled. "The consensus, I think, is that I am a monster." He tells Nussbaum in a letter about a radical feminist he had met at a conference who had thought of him, he speculated, as "the usual type of Republican monster ('conservative dinosaur')" until she looked at his book *Sex and Reason* and recognized that he was receptive to other points of view and was not "a fetal-life" buff.

He's willing to report on what he finds when he assesses himself. He provides support for the famous identification he gave in the *New Yorker* profile of himself with a cat when he writes, "I don't like to stay in other people's houses ordinarily. I much prefer hotels (my cold, feline nature)." He thinks of himself as a Milton Friedman type of libertarian. He considers himself a pragmatist, "meaning that I don't believe in metaphysical certainties, but do believe in truth (with a small t)." In reassuring a colleague that he is not going to blab some gossip just confided to him, he writes, "I like to think of myself as one of those close-mouthed lawyer types, like Tulkinghorn in *Bleak House.*" He might not be a total skeptic, he says, but he feels affinities with the skeptics and what he describes as moderate skepticism. Moderate skepticism he believes makes a person less prone to anger and provides what he describes as "detachment, distancing, and perspective." The moderate skeptic thinks more clearly "by virtue of avoiding emotional entanglements with ideas." As a reduced strength skeptic, he feels none of what his correspondent describes as a lessened willingness to endure hardship for loved ones. He wittily writes, "I would not risk my life to defend the Coase Theorem, but I hope I would be prepared to endure hardship for my family."

He does not think of himself as hard, metallic, or irritable in the way that a correspondent sees himself and goes on to say, "But neither do I consider myself undisclosed (lawyers use the term 'undisclosed principal' to describe the case where an agent does not indicate to the person he's contracting with that he's acting on behalf of another). The truth is that I am *au fond* perfectly conventional—a one-cat household." He repeats and expands the sentiment when the issue is why he did not know, earlier than he did, about an affair one much younger colleague was having with a much older colleague. He explains that one reason is that "I am *au fond* extremely conventional, although somewhat open-minded." Someone studying the allocation of his time among his various activities would conclude that he was "doing a pretty consistent job maximizing my expected utility." He does not see himself as rich, since "[r]ich begins somewhere above one's own income, whatever it is." He is reluctant to get worked up about a friend who is acting badly. "But that is because my outlook is basically aesthetic rather than ethical. I am inclined to blame, but not to care." This attitude is consistent with the way he reads literature, caring only about the aesthetic element as opposed to, for example, any ethical element. "Almost my entire interest in literature is aesthetic (I agree with Oscar Wilde that there are not moral or immoral books, just good and bad books), so that I am very forgiving of literature that supports positions I don't like, whether revolution or anti-Semitism."

He reveals what might be called regret when, after writing that he is in awe of scientists in general and the scientist under discussion, Robert

Trivers, in particular, he writes, "I wish I were as smart as Trivers or [Gary] Becker, and that I had made an earlier and fuller commitment to an academic career and honed my quantitative skills (such as they are) better." He explains why he roams so widely intellectually, writing that "people like me who ooze across fields do so out of restlessness." He is not a good teacher by University of Chicago standards, "which are very high indeed." Honor societies, he writes, "are perfect nonsense, and if I had character I would refuse them *and* honorary degrees." He also writes assertively, in the context of a famous philosopher who does not know anything about the realities upon which social policy is based, that "no doubt I live largely in my own dream world too, but the judging and the economics, and the consulting and government work I used to do, give me some insight into policy questions; or so I flatter myself."

He uses a joke about cats at the same time he gets at the core issue of an academic writing style not intended to engage. "To be completely honest," he writes to Nussbaum, "I think the basic reason I write in a callous tone is that I am rather callous toward the nonfeline population." Continuing with the feline theme, he does not go in for public displays of emotion, and, like cats, he is not comfortable around babies. He talks to his cat Dinah when no one is around but explains jokingly that he tries to restrict his conversation to topics of interest to the cat. When he is discussing the vagueness of "anger" in modern American usage, he offers, "I have, for what little it may be worth, a simple view of anger. It's a useless, albeit inevitable, emotion. It's bad for the stomach and interferes with clear thinking. It's not even valuable for revenge: the *implacable* avenger—the most feared and effective sort—is not angry." He acknowledges his submission to middle-class manners and usages and recognizes that it "sounds extraordinarily stuffy, but I bristle a bit (inwardly—you know I don't make scenes) when I see a middle-aged man of the educated middle class dressed in his working milieu, the classroom, for example, like a student or worker." He does not describe himself as an economist when invited to write a paper on "How Economists Work," writing that he has never taught in an economics department, though when he is cited in the journal *The Margin* as one of the top twenty-five most cited economists, he writes to the journal's editor, "I do like to think of myself as an economist as well as a lawyer, though I have no formal training in economics; and the 'real' economists have been on the whole generous enough to consider me one of their own."

How he sees himself on stage gives perhaps a more concrete sense of self. When he is presented with the opportunity to participate in a short stage performance, he writes with enthusiasm, "I like the idea of play reading" before explaining that he had done some acting in high school and college. "I would like to act men with government jobs, like me: Claudius, Julius Caesar—and of course Coriolanus." He comes back to Shakespeare twice more. When in the aftermath of the Clinton win in 1992 there was some talk that he might make it onto Clinton's shortlist for the Supreme Court, he rejected the idea out of hand when a correspondent brought it up, explaining why Clinton would not want him and why he would not want Clinton and the other politicians who would be involved in a nomination. He writes with what seems to be pride that "no one has ever written so much pleasing to so few and offensive to so many. Also the idea of kowtowing to senators and other politicos is very offensive to me; I may have mentioned that another Shakespearean character with whom I identify, besides Hamlet, is Coriolanus." He had in fact pointed to Hamlet and Coriolanus when Nussbaum had asked him if he felt affinities with any of Shakespeare's characters. The bombshell response has him writing, "I don't think of myself as a single Shakespearean character, but of having the traits of many of them—but I suppose Hamlet most of all, with a little Macbeth and a fair amount of Coriolanus."

In a comment that can go by too quickly because it is connected to the issue of men dressing their age, he describes a tension in his life. When the issue of clothes comes up, he reveals that he feels himself as torn when it comes to the way he dresses and the way he really is. On the one hand he feels that people "should dress their age and that he likes to dress like a successful businessman or professional, not all the time, such as at home, but in public." A part of him "wants to be a conservative establishment figure." "Part of me," he continues, "wants to be a Promethean intellectual hero." His conservative side has won on the sartorial front, he writes, "to the greater profit of Brooks Brothers." He closes the paragraph noting, "That is as close as I get to confession."

That Posner has thought of himself as a Promethean intellectual hero explains much if not all of the contrariness of his career, the belief in being right, and the urge to give instruction and guidance to improve the performance of others. Setting out a belief that he would like to see the adversary system taken down a peg as a way of diminishing the role of lawyers and increasing the role of judges, while not the equivalent of giving fire to man as Prometheus did, does represent—as do all of Posner's smaller transgressive acts—a remarkable attempt to shake things up in the hope of realigning the pieces into a better fit. The same is true for bringing economic analysis to law. For Posner it has been a career's work. That he has been so respected by his fellow judges not for his economic analysis but for his take on the world as he has encountered it—as ever the critic at large—is perhaps a grand irony.

ACKNOWLEDGMENTS

I am indebted to a number of people for their help with this book, beginning with all the people (more than two hundred) I either spoke with or heard from for the book.

John Langbein, Jeffrey Cole, and Richard Posner read an early draft of the book and improved it with their suggestions. Posner did double duty and read the final draft and caught several errors.

Posner was wonderfully cooperative from the beginning. He gave me access to his archive at the University of Chicago Regenstein Library, sat for interviews, shared family memorabilia with me, answered my dozens of email queries, and provided me with a copy of his Yale thesis.

The Special Collections staff at the University of Chicago Regenstein Library was courteous and helpful and helped move my project along with its policy of allowing cell phone photographs of documents. The University of Chicago Law School Library staff was also helpful and courteous and helped track down some of Posner's hard to find articles.

The Westlaw editorial team, led by Robert Smits and David Carlson, responded to my request for help on the issue of quantifying of a judge's influence on other judges with a generous expenditure of its resources to produce unprecedented research into the issue.

I am most indebted to Kathleen Peach, my wife. She read every draft of the book and spent scores of hours transcribing interviews I had conducted. I could not have written this book without her. I couldn't have written, in fact, any of my now five books without her help.

NOTES

———

Introduction
1. Richard Posner, draft letter to Aaron Director, July 27, 1981. Letters used in this introduction and elsewhere come from the Richard Posner archive at the University of Chicago Library and are used with its permission.
2. Richard Posner and Philip B. Heymann, "Tap Dancing: A TNR Online Debate with Philip B. Heymann," *New Republic Online*, January 31, February 2, February 5, 2006, http://www.tnr.com/user/nregi.mhtml?i=wo 60130&s=heymannposner013106.
3. Posner to Larry Kramer, July 12, 1991.
4. Posner to Martha Nussbaum, December 9, 1992.
5. Posner to Martha Nussbaum, June 5, 1992.

Chapter 1
1. Except as otherwise noted, information for this section about Posner's first nine years comes from 2012 interviews with Posner and childhood memorabilia shared with me as part of our interviews.
2. *New York Times*, March 4, 1941, p. 25.
3. Amy Swerdlow's *Women Strike for Peace* (Chicago: University of Chicago Press, 1993), p. 111.
4. 2003 interview with Nathan Lewin.
5. Posner to Frank Clancy, December 7, 1992. This and other correspondence comes from the Posner archive and is used with the permission of the University of Chicago Library.
6. Posner to Frank Clancy, December 22, 1992.
7. Posner to Ronald Schwartz, August 15, 1997.
8. Posner to Martha Nussbaum, October 2, 1996.

9. Posner to Beryl Levy, July 7, 1993.

10. Except as otherwise noted, information for this high school section comes from interviews with and emails from a dozen of Posner's classmates, 2012 interviews with Posner, and documents found in his University of Chicago archive and used with the University's permission.

11. Posner to Robert Ferguson, June 27, 1994.

12. Except as otherwise noted, information for this college section comes from 2012 interviews with Posner, Yale memorabilia he shared with me during the interviews, interviews with and emails from fifteen of Posner's Yale classmates between 2013 and 2014 and Justin Zaremby, *Directed Studies and the Evolution of American General Education* (New Haven: Whitney Humanities Center Yale University, 2006).

13. Posner to Martha Nussbaum, April 17, 1997.

14. *Yale Daily News*, November 5, 1958, p. 2.

15. *Yale Daily News*, March 3, 1958, p. 2.

16. Id.

17. Id.

18. Richard Posner, "Yale, a Confusion of Values," 3 *Criterion* 14, 16 (1958).

19. The program is described in Walter Goldfrank, "The Scholars of the House Program at Yale: Praise from the Faculty, Student Criticism," *Harvard Crimson*, November 22, 1958.

20. Posner to Steven Umin, March 6, 1989.

21. Posner to Martha Nussbaum, June 17, 1994.

22. Except as otherwise noted, information for this section about Harvard Law School comes from my interviews with Posner, from interviews with and emails from more than two dozen of Posner's law school classmates, from interviews with Harvard faculty members, and from memorabilia Posner shared with me during our interviews.

23. Richard Posner, *Reflections on Judging* (Cambridge: Harvard University Press, 2013), p. 20.

24. Id.

25. Id.

26. Posner to Martha Nussbaum, January 21, 1993.

27. Id.

28. Pierre N. Leval, Tribute to Judge Richard A. Posner, 61 *New York University Annual Survey of American Law* 9 (2005).

29. Richard Posner, "The Bluebook Blues," 120 Yale Law Journal 850, 858 fn. 9 (2011).

30. This information comes from 2013 interviews with three Stanford faculty members involved in the hiring process.

31. Richard Posner, "Bork and Beethoven," 42 *Stanford Law Review* 1365 (1990).

32. Erwin Griswold to Posner, October 17, 1990.

33. Richard Posner, review of Myres McDougal et al., *Law and Public Order in Space*, 77 *Harvard Law Review* 1370 (1964).

34. *United States v. Philadelphia National Bank*, 374 U.S. 321, 83 S.Ct. 1715 (1963).

35.   Richard Posner, "The Future of the Student-Edited Law Review," 47
      Stanford Law Review 1131 (1995); Richard Posner, "Against the Law
      Reviews," *Legal Affairs*, November–December 2004, p. 57; Richard Posner,
      "Law Reviews," 46 *Washburn Law Journal* 155 (2006); "The Peer Review
      Experiment," 60 *South Carolina Law Review* 821 (2009).
36.   Richard Posner, "Oligopoly and the Antitrust Laws: A Suggested
      Approach," 21 *Stanford Law Review* 1562 (1969).
37.   Except as otherwise noted, information for this Supreme Court clerkship
      section comes from interviews with Posner, an interview with fellow clerk
      Robert O'Neil, and interviews with law clerks to other Justices for the 1962
      term.
38.   Posner to William Brennan, July 24, 1990.
39.   William Brennan to Posner, August 6, 1990.
40.   373 U.S. 1, 83 S.Ct. 1068 (1963).
41.   372 U.S. 391, 83 S.Ct. 822 (1963).
42.   371 U.S. 415, 83 S.Ct. 328 (1963).
43.   374 U.S. 321, 83 S.Ct. 1715 (1963).
44.   372 U.S. 293, 83 S.Ct. 745 (1963).
45.   Richard Posner, "Tribute to Mr. Justice Brennan," 1981 *New York University
      Annual Survey of American Law*, no. 4, at xi.
46.   Richard Posner, "A Tribute to Justice William J. Brennan, Jr.," 104 *Harvard
      Law Review* 13 (1990).
47.   Posner to Kenneth Bamburger, September 3, 1997.
48.   Posner to Cass Sunstein, August 11, 1997.
49.   Richard Posner, "In Memoriam: William J. Brennan," 111 *Harvard Law
      Review* 9, 13 (1990).
50.   Id. at 13.
51.   Richard Posner, *Reflections on Judging* (Cambridge: Harvard University
      Press, 2013), p. 21.
52.   Except as otherwise noted, information in this FTC section comes from
      interviews with Posner and interviews with other lawyers who worked at
      the FTC at or about the time Posner did.
53.   74 *Yale Law Journal* 652 (1965).
54.   Norman I. Silber, ed., *With All Deliberate Speed: The Life of Philip Elman*
      (Ann Arbor: University of Michigan Press, 2004), p. 344.
55.   Id. at 342.
56.   *Federal Trade Commission v. Procter & Gamble*, 63 FTC 1465 (1963).
57.   Norman I. Silber, ed., *With All Deliberate Speed: The Life of Philip Elman*
      (Ann Arbor: University of Michigan Press, 2004), p. 4.
58.   Except as otherwise noted, information for this Office of the Solicitor
      General section comes from interviews with Posner and from interviews
      with a dozen lawyers working in the office during Posner's time there or
      slightly before or after.
59.   Archibald Cox Oral History, Columbia University Libraries Oral History
      Research Office, part 1, p. 90.

60. Roger Newman, ed., *The Yale Biographical Dictionary of American Law* (New Haven: Yale University Press, 2009), p. 106.
61. Richard Posner, *Reflections on Judging* (Cambridge: Harvard University Press, 2013), p. 23.
62. Id.
63. Author interview with Erwin Griswold, December 30, 1993.
64. Except as otherwise noted, the information for this section comes from 2012 interviews with Posner and interviews with or emails from five former members of the task force.
65. Message from President Lyndon B. Johnson to Congress, *Communications Policy*, 3 Weekly Compilation of Presidential Documents, No. 33, 1135, 1146 (August 14, 1967), also available at http://www.presidency.ucsb.edu/ws/ ?pid=28390.
66. Richard Posner, "The Decline and Fall of AT&T: A Personal Recollection," 61 *Federal Communications Bar Journal* 11, 12 (2008).
67. Edmund Kitch, "The Fire of Truth: A Remembrance of Law and Economics at Chicago, 1932–1970," 26 *Journal of Law and Economics* 163, 226 (1981).
68. Letter from Richard M. Nixon to James Broyhill of the Subcommittee on Communications and Power of the House Committee on Interstate and Foreign Commerce, May 20, 1969.
69. Except as otherwise noted, information for this Stanford Law School section came from interviews with Posner, interviews with about a dozen former Stanford Law School students who had taken various of his classes, and interviews with half a dozen Stanford professors who overlapped with Posner at Stanford.
70. Posner to Ronald Coase, April 11, 1997.
71. "Natural Monopoly and Its Regulation," 21 *Stanford Law Review* 548 (1969).
72. Id. at 549.
73. "Oligopoly and the Antitrust Laws: A Suggested Approach," 21 *Stanford Law Review* 1562 (1969).

Chapter 2

1. This model is described in Edmund Kitch, "The Fire of Truth: A Remembrance of Law and Economics at Chicago, 1932–1970," 26 *Journal of Law and Economics* 163 (1981).
2. Posner to Gareth Jones, April 13, 1976. All correspondence and other documents referred to in this chapter unless otherwise noted come from the Posner archive at the University of Chicago Library and are used with its permission.
3. Posner to Arthur Leff, February 6, 1976.
4. "Some Thoughts on Legal Education," *University of Chicago Law School Record*, winter 1972, p. 19.
5. Id. at 20.

6. Information in the balance of this paragraph comes from an interview with Douglas Laycock on July 2, 2014.

7. Posner memorandum to Arnold Harberger, May 17, 1977.

8. Posner to Richard Epstein, November 5, 1979.

9. Posner to Charles Meyer, February 24, 1975.

10. Posner to Stanley Katz, November 4, 1974.

11. Posner to Frank Easterbrook, March 7, 1975.

12. Posner to Phillip Areeda, February 25, 1974.

13. Posner to James Atwood, November 26, 1979.

14. Posner memorandum to faculty, May 25, 1976.

15. Posner memorandum to Harris Weinstein, February 6, 1978.

16. Posner memorandum to Frank Ellsworth, January 6, 1976.

17. Posner memorandum to Ed Kitch, June 9, 1980.

18. Posner, "Diary," *Slate*, January 17, 2002.

19. Email from Robert Frank to author, July 31, 2014.

20. Author interview, Franklin Zimring, February 27, 2014.

21. Author interview with Gerhard Casper, July 24, 2012.

22. Id.

23. Id.

24. Author interview with Geoffrey Stone, April 9, 2014.

25. Posner to Thomas H. Elliot, August 30, 1976.

26. Posner to Dean Casper, February 27, 1980; Posner to William Cannon, April 15, 1980.

27. Posner memorandum to faculty, April 30, 1980.

28. Posner to Duncan Kennedy, March 28, 1978.

29. Posner to James White, May 23, 1978.

30. Id.

31. Richard Posner to Bruce Ackerman, October 18, 1978.

32. Id.

33. 64 *American Economic Review* 384 (1974).

34. Posner memorandum to Ronald Coase, November 28, 1973.

35. Richard Posner, "Oligopolistic Pricing Suits, the Sherman Act, and Economic Welfare (Symposium): A Reply to Professor Markovits," 28 *Stanford Law Review* 903, 907 (1976).

36. Id. at fn. 15.

37. Richard Posner emails to author, May 13 and 14, 2014.

38. Id.

39. Author interview with William Landes, April 11, 2014.

40. Email to author, May 11, 2014, from source preferring not to be named.

41. Richard A. Posner, "The New Institutional Economics Meets Law and Economics," 149 *Journal of Institutional and Theoretical Economics* 73 (1993). See also Richard A. Posner, "Nobel Laureate: Ronald Coase and Methodology," 7 *Journal of Economic Perspectives* 195 (1993).

42. Ronald H. Coase, "Coase on Posner on Coase: Comment," 149 *Journal of Institutional and Theoretical Economics* 96 (1993).

43. Posner to Aaron Director, January 5, 1994.
44. Richard A. Posner, Keynes and Coase, 54 *Journal of Law and Economics* 31 (2011).
45. Id. at 39.
46. Interview with Richard A. Posner, *Reason*, April 2001, at p. 39.
47. Ronald Coase, Law and Economics at Chicago, 36 *Journal of Law and Economics*, 239 (1993).
48. Draft of undated and unaddressed letter in archive.
49. Richard Posner, "Volume One of the Journal of Legal Studies—An Afterword," 1 *Journal of Legal Studies* 437 (1972).
50. Id.
51. Draft of undated and unaddressed letter in archive.
52. Emails of William Landes and Isaac Ehrlich to author, April 27, 2014.
53. Richard Posner, "Killing or Wounding to Protect a Property Interest," 14 *Journal of Law and Economics* 201 (1971).
54. Richard Posner, "A Theory of Negligence," 1 *Journal of Legal Studies* 29 (1972).
55. Richard Posner, "Killing or Wounding to Protect a Property Interest," 14 *Journal of Law and Economics* 201, 208 (1971).
56. Id.
57. Id.
58. Id.
59. Id., quoting O. W. Holmes, "Common Carriers and the Common Law," 13 *American Law Review* 608, 630 (1879).
60. Id. at 209.
61. Id.
62. Id.
63. Richard Posner, "A Theory of Negligence," 1 *Journal of Legal Studies* 29 (1972).
64. Id. at 34.
65. Posner email to author, December 8, 2012.
66. Richard Posner, *Economic Analysis of Law* (Boston: Little, Brown, 1973).
67. Id. at ix–x.
68. Posner to James Krier, January 20, 1975.
69. Id.
70. Richard Posner, *Economic Analysis of Law* (Boston: Little, Brown, 1973), p. x.
71. Id.
72. Posner to Charles J. Meyers, November 6, 1972.
73. In addition to the reviews discussed herein, other reviews include James M. Buchanan, "Good Economics. Bad Law," 60 *Virginia Law Review* 483 (1974); James E. Krier, 122 *University of Pennsylvania Law Review* 1664 (1974); John Palmer, Book Review, 1 *Canadian Public Policy* 268 (1975); Book Review, 26 *Stanford Law Review* 711 (1974); D. N. Dewees, Book Review, *University of Toronto Law Journal* 320 (1974); and Donald H. J. Hermann, Book Review, 1974 *Washington University Law Quarterly* 354 (1974).

74. Peter A. Diamond, "Posner's Economic Analysis of Law," 5 *Bell Journal of Economics and Management Science* 294 (1974); 15 *Jurimetrics Journal* 60 (1974).

75. Gordon Tullock, Book Review, 17 *Public Choice* 122 (1974).

76. Malcolm Feeley, 71 *Political Science Review* 422 (1977).

77. 87 *Harvard Law Review* 1655 (1974).

78. Arthur Miller, "Economic Analysis of Law by Richard A. Posner," 10 *Journal of Economic Issues* 179, 180 (1976).

79. Id. at 179.

80. Arthur A. Leff, "Economic Analysis of Law: Some Realism about Nominalism," 60 *Virginia Law Review* 451, 452 (1974).

81. Id. at 481.

82. Id.

83. Posner to Victor Ferrall, August 5, 1974.

84. Posner to Victor Ferrall, November 11, 1974.

85. Posner to Dean Gordon Christenson, April 4, 1980.

86. Dennis Carlton, William Landes, and Richard Posner, "Benefits and Costs of Airline Mergers: A Case Study," 11 *Bell Journal of Economics and Management Science* 65 (1980).

87. William Landes and Richard Posner, "Market Power in Antitrust Cases," 94 *Harvard Law Review* 937 (1981).

88. Richard Posner, "The Federal Trade Commission: A Retrospective," 72 *Antitrust Law Journal* 761 (2005).

89. Richard Posner, "The Federal Trade Commission," 37 *University of Chicago Law Review* 47 (1969).

90. Id. at 88.

91. Id.

92. Id. at 89.

93. Richard Posner, "The Federal Trade Commission: A Retrospective," 72 *Antitrust Law Journal* 761, 764 (2005).

94. Richard Posner, *Cable Television: The Problem of Local Monopoly* (Rand Memorandum RM-6309-FF, at iii, May 1970).

95. Richard Posner, "Regulatory Aspects of National Health Insurance Plans," 39 *University of Chicago Law Review* 1 (1971).

96. Charles J. Meyers and Richard Posner, *Market Transfers of Water Rights: Toward an Improved Market in Water Resources*, National Water Commission, Legal Study No. 4, Final Report, July 1, 1972, published by National Technical Information Service.

97. Richard Posner, "Taxation by Regulation," 2 *Bell Journal of Economics and Management Science* (1971); Richard Posner, "Theories of Economic Regulation," 5 *Bell Journal of Economics and Management Science* 335 (1974).

98. Richard Posner, "Theories of Economic Regulation," 5 *Bell Journal of Economics and Management Science* 344 (1974).

99. Posner to Paul MacAvoy, March 17, 1975.

100.   Panel Discussion, in Martin Greenberger, ed., *Computers, Communications, and the Public Interest* (Baltimore: Johns Hopkins University Press, 1971), pp. 242–56.

101.   Richard Posner, "Certificates of Need for Health Care Facilities: A Dissenting View," in Clark C. Havighurst, ed., *Regulating Health Facilities Construction* (Washington, D.C.: American Enterprise Institute for Public Policy Research 1974), p. 113.

102.   Id. at 123.

103.   *Regulation of Advertising by the FTC* (American Enterprise Institute, 1973).

104.   Richard Posner, *The Robinson-Patman Act: Federal Regulation of Price Differences* (American Enterprise Institute, 1976).

105.   Id. at 52.

106.   Richard Posner, "A Statistical Study of Antitrust Enforcement," 13 *Journal of Law and Economics* 365 (1970).

107.   Richard Posner, "A Program for the Antitrust Division," 38 *University of Chicago Law Review* 500 (1971).

108.   Id. at 501.

109.   Id. at 530, n. 97.

110.   Richard Posner, "Antitrust Policy and the Supreme Court: An Analysis of the Restricted Distribution, Horizontal Merger and Potential Competition Decisions," 75 *Columbia Law Review* 282 (1975); Richard Posner, "The Supreme Court and Antitrust Policy: A New Direction?," 44 *Antitrust Law Journal* 141 (1975).

111.   *United States v. Philadelphia National Bank*, 374 U.S. 321, 83 S.Ct. 1715 (1963).

112.   Richard Posner, "The Supreme Court and Antitrust Policy: A New Direction?," 44 *Antitrust Law Journal* 141, 145 (1975).

113.   384 U.S. 270, 88 S.Ct. 1478 (1966).

114.   Richard Posner, "The Supreme Court and Antitrust Policy: A New Direction?," 44 *Antitrust Law Journal* 141, 146 (1975).

115.   Richard Posner, "The Antitrust Decisions of the Burger Court," 47 *Antitrust Law Journal* 819 (1979).

116.   Id. at 825.

117.   Richard Posner, "The Supreme Court and Antitrust Policy: A New Direction?," 44 *Antitrust Law Journal* 141, 143 (1975).

118.   Richard Posner, "The Rule of Reason and the Economic Approach: Reflections on the *Sylvania* Decision," 45 *University of Chicago Law Review* 1 (1977); *Continental T.V., Inc. v. G.T.E. Sylvania Inc.*, 433 U.S. 36, 97 S.Ct. 2549 (1977); *United States v. Arnold, Schwinn & Co.*, 388 U.S. 365, 87 S.Ct. 1856 (1967).

119.   Richard Posner, "The Rule of Reason and the Economic Approach: Reflections on the *Sylvania* Decision," 45 *University of Chicago Law Review* 1, 2 (1977).

120.   Richard Posner, "The Economic Approach to Law," 53 *Texas Law Review* 758 (1975).

121.   Id. at 764.

122. "Utilitarianism, Economics, and Legal Theory," 8 *Journal of Legal Studies* 103 (1979).

123. Id. at 119.

124. Ronald Dworkin, "Is Wealth a Value?," 9 *Journal of Legal Studies* 191, 194 (1980).

125. Richard Epstein, "Ronald Dworkin: A Tribute from the Other Side of the Political Spectrum," *Ricochet*, found at http://richot.com/profile/1480, posted February 19, 2013.

126. Email from Stephen Williams to author, July 4, 2014.

127. Richard Posner, "The Ethical and Political Basis of the Efficiency Norm in Common Law Adjudication," 8 *Hofstra Law Review* 487 (1980).

128. Id.

129. Richard Posner, *The Problems of Jurisprudence* (Cambridge: Harvard University Press, 1990), p. 375.

130. James Hackney, *Legal Intellectuals in Conversation* (New York: New York University Press, 2012), p. 52.

131. Richard Posner, *Economic Analysis of Law* (Boston: Little, Brown, 1973), p. 357.

132. Anthony T. Kronman and Richard A. Posner, eds., *The Economics of Contract Law* (Boston: Little, Brown, 1979).

133. Richard Posner, *Antitrust Law: An Economic Perspective* (Chicago: University of Chicago Press, 1976).

134. Richard Posner, *The Economics of Justice* (Cambridge: Harvard University Press, 1981).

135. Richard Posner, *Antitrust Law: An Economic Perspective* (Chicago: University of Chicago Press, 1976), p. vii.

136. Id. at ix.

137. Thomas Kauper, Review of *Antitrust Law: An Economic Perspective* by Richard Posner, 75 *Michigan Law Review* 768 (1977).

138. William Baxter, Review of *Antitrust Law: An Economic Perspective* by Richard Posner, 8 *Bell Journal of Economics and Management Science* 609 (1977).

139. Terry Calvani, "Mr. Posner's Blueprint for Reforming the Antitrust Laws," 29 *Stanford Law Review* 1311, 1312–13 (1977).

140. Thomas Kauper, Book Review, 75 *Michigan Law Review* 768, 804 (1977).

141. Peter O. Steiner, Book Review, 44 *University of Chicago Law Review* 873, 875 (1977).

142. Id. at 877.

143. Aside from the reviews mentioned here, other reviews include Jules Coleman, "The Normative Basis of Economic Analysis," 34 *Stanford Law Review* 1105 (1982); Michael McPherson, Book Review, 2 *Law and Philosophy* 129 (1983); Alexander J. Field, Book Review, 20 *Journal of Economic Literature* 73 (1982); Derek Morgan, Book Review, 41 *Cambridge Law Journal* 206 (1982); Thomas Sharpe, Book Review, 93 *Economic Journal* 248 (1983); Eli M. Noam, Book Review, 7 *American Bar Foundation Research Journal* 269 (1982); Peter J. Hammond, Book Review, 91 *Yale Law Journal* 1493 (1982); Donald H. J. Hermann, Book Review,

33 *Hastings Law Journal* 1285 (1982); M. Neil Browne, John H. Hoag, and S. M. Ashiquzzaman, Book Review, 16 *Georgia Law Review* 767 (1982); and Thomas D. Barton, Book Review, 80 *Northwestern University Law Review* 476 (1985).

144.   Richard Posner, *The Economics of Justice* (Cambridge: Harvard University Press, 1981), p. 1.

145.   Id.

146.   Bradley Honoroff, "Reflections of Richard Posner," 18 *Harvard Civil Rights–Civil Liberties Law Review* 287, 295 (1983).

147.   Peter Reuter, "A Just Use or Just Use Economics," 70 *California Law Review* 850, 869 (1982).

148.   Bradley Honoroff, "Reflections of Richard Posner," 18 *Harvard Civil Rights–Civil Liberties Law Review* 287, 292 (1983).

149.   Izhak Englard, "The Failure of Economic Justice," 95 *Harvard Law Review* 1162, 1176 (1982).

150.   Richard Schmalbeck, "The Justice of Economics," 83 *Columbia Law Review* 488, 489 (1983).

151.   Id.

152.   Id., quoting Richard Posner, "A Reply to Some Recent Criticisms of Efficiency Theory of the Common Law," 9 *Hofstra Law Review* 775, 791 (1981).

153.   Bradley Honoroff, "Reflections of Richard Posner," 18 *Harvard Civil Rights–Civil Liberties Law Review* 287, 288 (1983).

154.   Id. at 295 n. 26, quoting Richard Posner, *The Economics of Justice* (Cambridge: Harvard University Press, 1981), p. 76.

155.   Richard Posner, "Reflections on Consumerism," *University of Chicago Law School Record*, spring 1973, p. 19.

156.   Richard Posner, "Problems of a Policy of Deconcentration," in Harvey J. Goldschmid et al., eds., *Industrial Concentration: The New Learning* (Boston: Little, Brown, 1974), p. 393.

157.   Richard Posner, *Affirmative Action: The Answer to Discrimination?* (American Enterprise Institute Round Table, 1975) (with Ralph K. Winter Jr., Owen Fiss, Vera Glaser, William Raspberry, and Paul Seabury).

158.   Richard Posner, "The Economic Approach to Law," 53 *Texas Law Review* 758 (1975).

159.   Richard Posner, "The Supreme Court and Antitrust Policy: A New Direction?," 44 *Antitrust Law Journal* 141 (1975).

160.   Richard Posner, "The Federal Trade Commission's Mandated-Disclosure Program: A Critical Analysis," in Harvey J. Goldschmid, ed., *Business Disclosure: Government's Need to Know* (New York: McGraw-Hill, 1979), p. 331.

161.   Richard Posner and Andrew Rosenfield, "Impossibility and Related Doctrines in Contract Law: An Economic Analysis," 6 *Journal of Legal Studies* 83 (1977).

162. Richard Posner, "The Rule of Reason and the Economic Approach: Reflections on the *Sylvania* Decision," 45 *University of Chicago Law Review* 1 (1977).

163. Richard Posner, "The Right of Privacy," 12 *Georgia Law Review* 393 (1978).

164. Richard Posner, "Privacy, Secrecy, and Reputation," 28 *Buffalo Law Review* 1 (1979).

165. Richard Posner, "The Chicago School of Antitrust Analysis," 127 *University of Pennsylvania Law Review* 925 (1979).

166. Richard Posner, "Some Uses and Abuses of Economics in Law," 46 *University of Chicago Law Review* 281 (1979).

167. Richard Posner, "Information and Antitrust: Reflections on the *Gypsum* and *Engineers* Decisions," 67 *Georgia Law Journal* 1187 (1979).

168. The various activities and work products described in this paragraph are part of a folder marked as "Practice" in the Posner archive.

169. *National Broiler Marketing Association v. United States*, 436 U.S. 816 (1978).

170. The information on hours and billing is also found in the Practice folder.

171. The information in this paragraph comes from interviews with Andrew Rosenfield, William Landes, George Saunders, Christopher DeMuth, Mark Klamer, and Greg Sidak on March 18, 2014.

172. William Landes, "The Art of Law and Economics: An Autobiographical Essay," 41 American Economist 31, 39 (1997).

173. Three former faculty members in interviews described this to me.

174. Author interview with Stanley Katz, March 4, 2014; Elisabeth Landes and Richard Posner, "The Economics of the Baby Shortage," *The Journal of Legal Studies* 323 (1978).

175. Author interview with Stanley Katz, March 4, 2014.

176. Author interview with William Landes, April 11, 2014.

177. Posner to author, December 11, 1997.

178. July 27, 1981, draft of a letter from Posner to Aaron Director.

179. Author interview with Posner, June 12, 2012.

Chapter 3

1. Except as otherwise indicated, information in this section comes from 2013 and 2014 interviews with and emails from eight Posner law clerks from the 1980s.

2. C-SPAN interview, October 18, 2011.

3. Id.

4. There are approximately 106 pages of letters making up approximately fifteen thousand words in the Harvard Law School archives. Henry Jacob Friendly Papers, Harvard Law School Library, Harvard University, Series VI Correspondence Files, 1965–1986, Subseries B, 221-7, Friendly-Posner Correspondence 1982–1986. The correspondence file contains sixty-two letters.

5. Richard A. Posner, "In Memoriam: Henry J. Friendly," 99 *Harvard Law Review* 1724 (1986).

6. Friendly to Posner, May 12, 1982, as quoted in Henry Jacob Friendly Papers, Harvard Law School Library, Harvard University, Series VI Correspondence Files, 1965–1986, Subseries B, 221-7, Friendly-Posner Correspondence 1982–1986.

7. Friendly to Posner, June 14, 1982, as quoted in William Domnarski, "The Correspondence of Henry Friendly and Richard A. Posner, 1982–86," 51 *American Journal of Legal History* 395, 399 (2012). Hereinafter known as "Correspondence."

8. Friendly to Posner, August 28, 1983, as quoted in "Correspondence," at 400.

9. Friendly to Posner, September 19, 1984, as quoted in "Correspondence," at 400.

10. Friendly to Posner, September 9, 1985, as quoted in "Correspondence," at 400.

11. Friendly to Posner, May 13, 1985, as quoted in "Correspondence," at 412.

12. Posner to Friendly, December 9, 1985, as quoted in "Correspondence," at 413.

13. Friendly worried that Posner would rebuke him for his opinion in *Business Services by Manpower, Inc. v. NLRB*, 785 F.2d 442 (2d. Cir. 1986) in light of Posner's opinion in *NLRB v. Browning-Ferris Industries*, 700 F.2d 385 (7th Cir. 1983).

14. Tom Dagger to Posner, February 27, 1986, as quoted in "Correspondence," at 413.

15. Posner email to author, April 25, 2010.

16. David Dorsen, *Henry Friendly: Greatest Judge of His Era* (Cambridge: Harvard University Press, 2012), pp. 339–345.

17. *Edgewater Nursing Center, Inc. v. Miller*, 678 F.2d 716, 718 (7th Cir. 1982).

18. *N.L.R.B. v. Loy Food Stores, Inc.*, 697 F.2d 798, 800 (7th Cir. 1983).

19. *N.L.R.B. v. Res-Care, Inc.*, 705 F.2d 1461, 1469 (7th Cir. 1983).

20. *Johnson v. C.I.R.*, 720 F.2d 963, 964 (7th Cir. 1983).

21. *A/S Apothekernes Laboratorium for Specialpraeparater v. I.M.C. Chemical Group, Inc.*, 725 F.2d 1140, 1143 (7th Cir. 1984).

22. *McDonald v. Schweiker*, 726 F.2d 311, 316 (7th Cir. 1983).

23. *General Leaseways, Inc. v. National Truck Leasing Ass'n*, 744 F.2d 588, 592 (7th Cir. 1984).

24. *Matterhorn, Inc. v. NCR Corp.*, 763 F.2d 866, 871 (7th Cir. 1985).

25. *American Nurses' Ass'n v. State of Ill.*, 783 F.2d 716, 730 (7th Cir. 1986).

26. *Olympia Equipment Leasing Co. v. Western Union Telegraph Co.*, 797 F.2d 370, 373 (7th Cir. 1986).

27. *International Union, United Auto., Aerospace and Agricultural Implement Workers of America v. N.L.R.B.*, 802 F.2d 969, 974 (7th Cir. 1986).

28. *Matter of Lindsey*, 823 F.2d 189, 192 (7th Cir. 1987).

29. *Mars Steel Corp. v. Continental Illinois Nat. Bank and Trust Co. of Chicago*, 834 F.2d 677, 684 (7th Cir. 1987).

30. *Crowley Cutlery Co. v. United States*, 849 F.2d 273, 275 (7th Cir. 1988).

31. *State of Illinois ex rel. Hartigan v. Panhandle Eastern Pipe Line Co.*, 852 F.2d 891, 894 (7th Cir. 1988).

32. *McLaughlin v. Union Oil Co. of California*, 869 F.2d 1039, 1043 (7th Cir. 1989).

33. *By-Prod Corp. v. Armen-Berry Co.*, 668 F.2d 956, 961 (7th Cir. 1982).

34. *Sur v. Glidden-Durkee, a Div. of S.C.M. Corp.*, 681 F.2d 490, 501 (7th Cir. 1982).

35. *Lloyd v. Loeffler*, 694 F.2d 489, 496 (7th Cir. 1982).

36. *Matter of Chicago, Milwaukee, St. Paul and Pacific R. Co.*, 713 F.2d 274, 278 (7th Cir. 1983).

37. *Medtronic, Inc. v. Intermedics*, 725 F.2d 440, 443 (7th Cir. 1984).

38. *Matter of Special March 1981 Grand Jury*, 753 F.2d 575, 577 (7th Cir. 1985).

39. *Tarkowski v. Lake County*, 775 F.2d 173, 175 (7th Cir. 1985).

40. *Swietlik v. United States*, 779 F.2d 1306, 1310 (7th Cir. 1985).

41. *Tagatz v. Marquette University*, 861 F.2d 1040, 1043 (7th Cir. 1988).

42. *Cote v. Wadel*, 796 F.2d 981, 983 (7th Cir. 1986).

43. *United States v. Pallais*, 921 F.2d 684, 692 (7th Cir. 1990).

44. *Indianapolis Colts, Inc. v. Metropolitan Baltimore Football Club Limited Partnership*, 34 F.3d 410, 413 (7th Cir. 1994).

45. *University Life Ins. Co. of America v. Unimarc*, 699 F.2d 846, 853 (7th Cir. 1983).

46. *Barkauskas v. Lane*, 878 F.2d 1031, 1032 (7th Cir. 1989).

47. *Albright v. Oliver*, 975 F.2d 343, 346 (7th Cir. 1992).

48. For more examples, see Robert F. Blomquist, ed., *The Quotable Judge Posner: Selections from Twenty-Five Years of Judicial Opinions* (Albany: State University of New York Press, 2010).

49. *Attorney Registration and Disciplinary Com'n of the Supreme Court of Illinois v. Schweiker*, 715 F.2d 282, 286 (7th Cir. 1983).

50. *Minority Police Officers Ass'n of South Bend v. City of South Bend, Indiana*, 721 F.2d 197, 202 (7th Cir. 1983).

51. *United States v. Torres*, 751 F.2d 875, 880 (7th Cir. 1984); *Bash v. Firstmark Standard Life Ins. Co.*, 861 F.2d 159, 162 (7th Cir. 1988).

52. *Tagatz v. Marquette University*, 861 F.2d 1040, 1044 (7th Cir. 1988).

53. *Greenwalt v. Indiana Dept. of Corrections*, 397 F.3d 587, 591 (7th Cir. 2005).

54. *United States v. Silverstein*, 732 F.2d 1338, 1341 (7th Cir. 1984).

55. *Afram Export Corp. v. Metallurgiki, S.A.*, 772 F.2d 1358, 1366 (7th Cir. 1985).

56. *United States v. LeFevour*, 798 F.2d 977, 985 (7th Cir. 1986).

57. *Matter of Wagner*, 808 F.2d 542, 544 (7th Cir. 1986).

58. *Pomer v. Schoolman*, 875 F.2d 1262, 1263 (7th Cir. 1989).

59. *United States v. Masters*, 924 F.2d 1362, 1365 (7th Cir. 1991).

60. *Blue Canary Corp. v. City of Milwaukee*, 251 F.3d 1121, 1124 (7th Cir. 2001).

61. *School Dist. of Wisconsin Dells v. Z.S. ex rel. Littlegeorge*, 295 F.3d 671, 676 (7th Cir. 2002).

62. *Freeman v. Berge*, 441 F.3d 543, 544 (7th Cir. 2006).

63. *United States v. Bullion*, 466 F.3d 574, 575 (7th Cir. 2006).

64. *Jay E. Hayden Foundation v. First Neighbor Bank, N.A.*, 610 F.3d 382, 384 (7th Cir. 2010).
65. *Waldron v. McAtee*, 723 F.2d 1348, 1351 (7th Cir. 1983).
66. *Grip-Pak, Inc. v. Illinois Tool Works, Inc.*, 694 F.2d 466, 469–70 (7th Cir. 1982).
67. *Azeez v. Fairman*, 795 F.2d 1296, 1299 (7th Cir. 1986).
68. *Joseph v. Brierton*, 739 F.2d 1244, 1249 (7th Cir. 1984).
69. *Taylor v. Meirick*, 712 F.2d 1112, 1118 (7th Cir. 1983).
70. *United States v. Tucker*, 773 F.2d 136, 140 (7th Cir. 1985).
71. *DF Activities Corp. v. Brown*, 851 F.2d 920, 923 (7th Cir. 1988).
72. *Edmond v. Goldsmith*, 183 F.3d 659, 665 (7th Cir. 1999); *Malhotra v. Cotter & Co.*, 885 F.2d 1305, 1312 (7th Cir. 1989).
73. *Malhotra v. Cotter & Co.*, 885 F.2d 1305, 1312 (7th Cir. 1989).
74. *Reimnitz v. State's Attorney of Cook County*, 761 F.2d 405, 407 (7th Cir. 1985).
75. *Rodi Yachts, Inc. v. National Marine, Inc.*, 984 F.2d 880, 886 (7th Cir. 1993).
76. *Wolin v. Smith Barney Inc.*, 83 F.3d 847, 853 (7th Cir. 1996).
77. *United States v. Cranley*, 350 F.3d 617, 621 (7th Cir. 2003).
78. *Sodal v. County of Cook*, 942 F.2d 1073, 1078 (7th Cir. 1991).
79. *Fagan v. Washington*, 942 F.2d 1155, 1157 (7th Cir. 1991).
80. *Eaglin v. Welborn*, 57 F.3d 496, 501 (7th Cir. 1995).
81. *Boyve v. Fernandes*, 77 F.3d 946, 950 (7th Cir. 1996).
82. *Miller v. Taylor Insulation Co.*, 39 F.3d 755, 761 (7th Cir. 1994).
83. *Wolin v. Smith Barney Inc.*, 83 F.3d 847, 852 (7th Cir. 1996).
84. *Howard v. Wal-Mart Stores, Inc.*, 160 F.3d 358, 360–61 (7th Cir. 1998).
85. *Jack Walters & Sons Corp. v. Morton Building, Inc.*, 737 F.2d 698, 704 (7th Cir. 1984).
86. *United States v. Herrera-Medina*, 853 F.2d 564, 567 (7th Cir. 1988).
87. *Colby v. J.C. Penney Co., Inc.*, 811 F.2d 1119, 1122 (7th Cir. 1987).
88. *Autotrol Corp. v. Continental Water Systems Corp.*, 918 F.2d 689, 695 (7th Cir. 1990).
89. *Avitia v. Metropolitan Club of Chicago, Inc.*, 49 F.3d 1219, 1225 (7th Cir. 1995).
90. *Warner/Elektra/Atlantic Corp. v. County of DuPage*, 991 F.2d 1280, 1287 (7th Cir. 1993).
91. *Boer v. Crown Stock Distribution, Inc.*, 587 F.3d 787, 797 (7th Cir. 2009).
92. *Ustrak v. Fairman*, 781 F.2d 573, 577 (7th Cir. 1986).
93. *Del Raine v. Carlson*, 826 F.2d 698, 702 (7th Cir. 1987).
94. Id.
95. *McCollum v. Miller*, 695 F.2d 1044, 1046 (7th Cir. 1982).
96. *McKeever v. Israel*, 689 F.2d 1315, 1323 (7th Cir. 1982) (Posner, J., dissenting).
97. *People of State of Ill. v. General Electric Co.*, 683 F.2d 206, 214 (7th Cir. 1982).
98. *United States v. Rockford Memorial Corp.*, 898 F.2d 1278, 1286 (7th Cir. 1990).

99. *Johnson v. C.I.R.*, 720 F.2d 963, 964–65 (7th Cir. 1983).

100. *United States v. Patel*, 835 F.2d 708, 709 (7th Cir. 1987).

101. *Tinker-Bey v. Meyers*, 800 F.2d 710 (7th Cir. 1986).

102. *Savage v. C.I.A.*, 826 F.2d 561, 563–64 (7th Cir. 1987).

103. *Omega Satellite Products Co. v. City of Indianapolis*, 694 F.2d 119, 124 (7th Cir. 1982).

104. *McCollum v. Miller*, 695 F.2d 1044, 1049 (7th Cir. 1982).

105. *Stoleson v. United States*, 708 F.2d 1217, 1222 (7th Cir. 1983).

106. *Matter of Continental Illinois Securities Litigation*, 962 F.2d 566, 572 (7th Cir. 1992).

107. *Matter of Continental Illinois Securities Litigation*, 962 F.2d 566, 572 (7th Cir. 1992).

108. *W. T. Rogers Co., Inc. v. Keene*, 778 F.2d 334, 346; *Omega Satellite Products Co. v. City of Indianapolis*, 694 F.2d 119, 124 (7th Cir. 1982).

109. *Village of Bellwood v. Dwivedi*, 895 F.2d 1521, 1534 (7th Cir. 1990).

110. *Bartlett v. Heibl*, 128 F.3d 497, 501 (7th Cir. 1997).

111. *N.L.R.B. v. Kemmerer Village, Inc.*, 907 F.2d 661, 663 (7th Cir. 1990).

112. *Nicolet Instrument Corp. v. Lindquist & Vennum*, 34 F.3d 453, 456 (7th Cir. 1994).

113. *United States v. Costello*, 666 F.3d 1040, 1050 (7th Cir. 2012).

114. *F.T.C. v. Think Achievement Corp.*, 312 F.3d 259, 261 (7th Cir. 2002).

115. *Reich v. Continental Gas Co.*, 33 F.3d 754 (7th Cir. 1994).

116. 2 H. & C. 906, 159 Eng. Rep. 375 (Ex. 1864).

117. 9 L.R. Exch. 215 (1874).

118. 9 L.Q. Rev. 197 (1893).

119. 2 H. & C. 722, 159 Eng. Rep. 299 (Ex. 1863).

120. *Aguirre v. Turner Const. Co.*, 582 F.3d 808, 811 (7th Cir. 2009).

121. Francis Biddle, *Justice Holmes, Natural Law and the Supreme Court* (New York: Macmillan, 1961), p. 422.

122. *McMunn v. Hertz Equipment Rental Corp.*, 791 F.2d 88, 93 (7th Cir. 1993).

123. Id.

124. *Friedrich v. City of Chicago*, 888 F.2d 511, 514 (7th Cir. 1989).

125. *United States v. Crawley*, 837 F.2d 291, 292 (7th Cir. 1988).

126. *Marozsan v. United States*, 852 F.2d 1469, 1482 (7th Cir. 1988).

127. *Crawford v. Indiana Dept. of Corrections*, 115 F.3d 481, 485–86 (7th Cir. 1997).

128. *Twisdale v. Snow*, 325 F.3d 950, 953 (7th Cir. 2003).

129. *Miller v. McCalla, Raymer, Padrick, Cobb, Nichols, and Clark, L.L.C.*, 214 F.3d 872, 875 (7th Cir. 2000).

130. *United States v. Mannava*, 565 F.3d 412, 417 (7th Cir. 2009).

131. 697 F.2d 796 (7th Cir. 1983).

132. Id. at 797.

133. Id. at 798.

134. *Roberts v. Sears, Roebuck and Company*, 723 F.2d 1324, 1347 (7th Cir. 1983).

135. Id. at 1348.

136. 683 F.2d 1022 (7th Cir. 1982).

137. 780 F.2d 589 (7th Cir. 1986).

138. *American Hospital Supply Cor. v. Hospital Products, Ltd.*, 780 F.2d 589, 594 (7th Cir. 1986).

139. 812 F.2d 298 (7th Cir. 1987).

140. 506 U.S. 56, 113 S.Ct. 538 (1992).

141. 686 F.2d 616 (7th Cir. 1982).

142. Id. at 618.

143. 812 F.2d 298 (7th Cir. 1987).

144. 489 U.S. 189, 109 S.Ct. 998 (1989).

145. 706 F.2d 1435, 1441 (7th Cir. 1983).

146. 692 F.2d 1083 (7th Cir. 1982).

147. Id. at 1096.

148. Id. at 1100.

149. 752 F.2d 261 (7th Cir. 1984).

150. Id. at 266.

151. Id. at 272.

152. 737 F.2d 698, 713–714 (7th Cir. 1984).

153. 844 F.3d 1310 (7th Cir. 1988).

154. *Davenport v. DeRoberts*, 844 F.3d 1310, 1317 (7th Cir. 1988) (Cudahy, J., dissenting in part and concurring in part).

155. 697 F.2d 761 (7th Cir. 1983).

156. 17 *Journal of Contemporary Health Law and Policy* xxxi (2000).

157. 780 F.2d 589 (7th Cir. 1986).

158. *American Hosp. Supply Corp. v. Hospital Products Ltd.*, 780 F.2d 589, 609–10 (1986) (Swygert, J., dissenting).

159. 782 F.2d 1429 (7th Cir. 1986).

160. 972 F.2d 792 (7th Cir. 1992).

161. 475 U.S. 292, 106 S.Ct. 1066 (1986).

162. *Hudson v. Teachers Union Local No.* 1, 743 F.2d 1187 (7th Cir. 1984).

163. 431 U.S. 209, 97 S.Ct. 1782 (1977).

164. 469 U.S. 241, 105 S.Ct. 687 (1985).

165. 484 U.S. 219, 108 S.Ct. 538 (1988).

166. *Forrester v. White*, 484 U.S. 219, 230, 108 S.Ct. 538, 545 (1988), quoting from *Forrester v. White*, 792 F.2d 647, 660 (7th Cir. 1986) (Posner, J., dissenting).

167. 490 U.S. 826, 109 S.Ct. 2218 (1989).

168. *Newman-Green, Inc. v. Alfonzo-Larrain*, 854 F.2d 916, 919 (7th Cir. 1988).

169. *Newman-Green, Inc. v. Alfonzo-Larrain*, 490 U.S. 826, 837, 109 S.Ct. 2218, 2225 (1989), quoting *Newman-Green, Inc. v. Alfonzo-Larrain*, 854 F.2d 916, 925 (7th Cir. 1988).

170. 473 U.S. 1, 105 S.Ct. 3012 (1985).

171. "Statutory Construction—In the Classroom and in the Courtroom," 50 *University of Chicago Law Review* 800, 822 (1983).

172. Id.

173. *The Federal Courts: Crisis and Reform* (Cambridge: Harvard University Press, 1985). The book draws on the following articles: "The Present Situation in Legal Scholarship," 90 *Yale Law Journal* 1113 (1981); "Economics, Politics, and the Reading of Statutes and Constitutions," 49 *University of Chicago Law Review* 263 (1982); "Toward an Economic Theory of Federal Jurisdiction," 6 *Harvard Journal of Law and Public Policy* 41 (1982); "Will the Federal Courts Survive until 1984? An Essay on Delegation and Specialization of the Judicial Function," 56 *Southern California Law Review* 761 (1983); "Statutory Construction—in the Classroom and in the Courtroom," 50 *University of Chicago Law Review* 800 (1983); and "The Meaning of Judicial Self-Restraint," 59 *Indiana Law Journal* 1 (1983).

174. *The Federal Courts: Crisis and Reform* (Cambridge: Harvard University Press, 1985), p. 293.

175. Samuel Estreicher, "Conserving the Federal Judiciary for a Conservative Agenda?," 84 *Michigan Law Review* 569 (1986).

176. Jack Beermann, "Crisis? What Crisis," 80 *Northwestern University Law Review* 1383, 1405 (1986).

177. Paul Bator, "The Judicial Universe of Richard Posner," 52 *University of Chicago Law Review* 1146, 1146–47 (1985).

178. *F. & H.R. Farman-Farmaian Consulting Engineers Firm v. Harza Engineering Co.*, 882 F.2d 281, 283 (7th Cir. 1989).

179. *Newman-Green, Inc. v. Alfonzo-Larrain R., Inc.*, 854 F.2d 916, 923 (7th Cir. 1988).

180. *Louis Vuitton S.A. v. Lee*, 875 F.2d 584, 587 (7th Cir. 1989).

181. *Jack Walters & Sons Corp. v. Morton Building, Inc.*, 737 F.2d 698, 713 (7th Cir. 1984).

182. *Tagatz v. Marquette University*, 861 F.2d 1040, 1045 (7th Cir. 1988).

183. *Central Soya Co., Inc. v. Epstein Fisheries, Inc.*, 676 F.2d 939, 941 (7th Cir. 1982).

184. *Dimmitt & Owens Financial, Inc. v. United States*, 787 F.2d 1186, 1189 (7th Cir. 1986).

185. *Duckworth v. Franzen*, 780 F.2d 645, 650 (7th Cir. 1985).

186. *Hospital Corp. of America v. F.T.C.*, 807 F.2d 1381, 1384 (7th Cir. 1986).

187. *Cote v. Wadel*, 796 F.2d 981, 984 (7th Cir. 1986).

188. *Hill v. Norfolk and Western Ry. Co.*, 814 F.2d 1192, 1194–95 (7th Cir. 1987).

189. *United States v. Mazzone*, 782 F.2d 757, 765 (7th Cir. 1986).

190. *Stotler and Co. v. Able*, 837 F.2d 1425, 1427 (7th Cir. 1988).

191. *Sparks v. N.L.R.B.*, 835 F.2d 705, 707 (7th Cir. 1987).

192. *Foy v. First National Bank of Elkhart*, 868 F.2d 251, 258 (7th Cir. 1989).

193. *Pearce v. Sullivan*, 871 F.2d 61, 63 (7th Cir. 1989).

194. *S.E.C. v. Suter*, 832 F.2d 988, 991 (7th Cir. 1987).

195. *Fox Valley AMC/Jeep, Inc. v. AM Credit Corp.*, 836 F.2d 366, 368 (7th Cir. 1988).

196.   Peter Carstensen, "Explaining Tort Law: The Economic Theory of Landes
        and Posner," 86 *Michigan Law Review* 1161 (1988).
197.   J. M. Balkin, "Too Good to Be True: The Positive Economic Theory of
        Law," 87 *Columbia Law Review* 1447 (1987).
198.   John J. Donohue and Ian Ayers, "Posner's Symphony No. 3: Thinking the
        Unthinkable," 39 *Stanford Law Review* 791 (1987).
199.   Id. at 798.
200.   Id. at 800–801.
201.   *Economic Analysis of Law* (Boston: Little, Brown, 1986), p. xx.
202.   Richard Posner, *Law and Literature: A Misunderstood Relation*
        (Cambridge: Harvard University Press, 1988).
203.   Richard Posner, "Law and Literature: A Relation Reargued," 72 *Virginia
        Law Review* 1351 (1986).
204.   Richard Posner, *Law and Literature* (3rd ed., Cambridge: Harvard
        University Press, 2009), p. 6.
205.   69 *Boston University Law Review* 1067 (1989).
206.   Stanley Fish, "Don't Know Much about the Middle Ages," 97 *Yale Law
        Journal* 777, 788–89 (1988).
207.   J. M. Balkin, "The Domestication of Law and Literature," 14 *Law and
        Social Inquiry* 787 (1989).
208.   Richard Posner, "The Present Situation in Legal Scholarship," 90 *Yale Law
        Journal* 1113 (1981).
209.   Richard Posner, "Legal Scholarship Today," 45 Stanford Law Review
        1647 (1993); Richard Posner, "Legal Scholarship Today," 115 Harvard
        Law Review 1314 (2002); and "The State of Legal Scholarship Today," 97
        Georgetown Law Journal 845 (2009).
210.   William Domnarski, "The Friendly-Posner Correspondence 1982–86," 51
        Journal of American Legal History 395, 411 (2012).
211.   Ronald K. L. Collins, "The Man behind the Robes—A Q&A with
        Richard Posner," Concurring Opinions, December 1, 2014, found at
        www.concurringopinions.com/ archives/ 2014/ 12/ the- man- behind- the-
        robes- a- qa- with- richard- posner.html.
212.   Information in this paragraph is based on six interviews with Reagan
        administration officials familiar with the Supreme Court selection process
        and the extent to which Posner was considered.

Chapter 4

1.   Richard Posner, *The Problems of Jurisprudence* (Cambridge: Harvard University
      Press, 1990). The book brought together and reworked the following
      articles: "The Concept of Corrective Justice in Recent Theories of Tort Law,"
      10 *Journal of Legal Studies* 187 (1981); "Lawyers as Philosophers: Ackerman
      and Others," 1981 *American Bar Foundation Research Journal* 231 (1981);
      "Wealth Maximization Revisited," 2 *Notre Dame Journal of Law, Ethics,
      and Public Policy* 85 (1985); "The Decline of Law as an Autonomous

Discipline: 1962–1987," 100 *Harvard Law Review* 761 (1987); "Legal Formalism, Legal Realism, and the Interpretation of Statutes and the Constitution," 37 *Case Western Reserve Law Review* 179 (1987); "The Regulation of the Market in Adoptions," 67 *Boston University Law Review* 59 (1987); "The Law and Economics Movement," 77 *American Economic Review Papers and Proceedings* 1 (May 1987); "Conventionalism: The Key to Law as an Autonomous Discipline?," 38 *University of Toronto Law Journal* 333 (1988); "The Jurisprudence of Skepticism," 86 *Michigan Law Review* 827 (1988); and "Conservative Feminism," 1989 *University of Chicago Legal Forum* 191.

2. 100 *Harvard Law Review* 761 (1987).

3. Richard Posner, "The Jurisprudence of Skepticism," 86 *Michigan Law Review* 827, 829 (1988).

4. Richard Posner, *The Problems of Jurisprudence* (Cambridge: Harvard University Press, 1990), p. 468.

5. Unless otherwise noted, all correspondence described in this chapter comes from the Posner University of Chicago archive and is used with the University's permission.

6. Luckily, Henry Friendly kept Posner's letters from 1982–1986 and deposited them in his Harvard archive.

7. Richard Posner, *Cardozo: A Study in Reputation* (Chicago: University of Chicago Press, 1990).

8. Richard Posner, "The Learned Hand Biography and the Question of Greatness," 104 *Yale Law Journal* 511 (1994).

9. Richard Posner, ed., *The Essential Holmes: Selections from the Letters, Speeches, Judicial Opinions, and Other Writings of Oliver Wendell Holmes, Jr.* (Chicago: University of Chicago Press, 1992).

10. Richard Posner, "Objectivity and Hagiography in Judicial Biography," 70 *New York University Law Review* 502 (1995).

11. 248 N.Y. 339, 162 N.E. 99 (1928).

12. 217 N.Y. 382, 111 N.E. 1050 (1916).

13. Mark Arkin, "Judging by Reputation," 60 *Fordham Law Review* 739, 740 (1992).

14. Donald Logan, "The Man in the Mirror," 90 *Michigan Law Review* 1739 (1992).

15. Id. at 1769.

16. Id. at 1770.

17. Jeffrey O'Connell and Thomas O'Connell, review of *The Essential Holmes*, 44 *DePaul Law Review* 513 (1995) and "Review," 106 *Harvard Law Review* 1703 (1993).

18. David E. Van Zandt, review of *The Essential Holmes*, 104 *Ethics* 643, 644 (1994).

19. Id.

20. Richard Posner, "The Learned Hand Biography and the Question of Greatness," 104 *Yale Law Journal* 511, 514 (1994).

21. *United States v. Adeniji*, 179 F.3d 1028, 1030 (7th Cir. 1999).

22. *Matter of New Era, Inc.*, 135 F.3d 1206, 1209 (7th Cir. 1998).

23. *United States v. Stafford*, 136 F.2d 1109, 1113 (7th Cir. 1998).

24. *United States v. Oberhellmann*, 946 F.2d 50, 54 (7th Cir. 1991).

25. *Anderson v. Romero*, 42 F.3d 1121, 1123 (7th Cir. 1994).

26. *United States v. Giovannetti*, 919 F.2d 1223, 1230 (7th Cir. 1990).

27. *Matter of Hendrix*, 986 F.2d 195, 200 (7th Cir. 1993).

28. *United States v. Zafiro*, 945 F.2d 881, 886 (7th Cir. 1991).

29. *United States v. Feliciano*, 45 F.3d 1070, 1073 (7th Cir. 1995).

30. *United States v. Daniels*, 902 F.2d 1238, 1245 (7th Cir. 1990).

31. *United States v. Grimes*, 173 F.3d 634, 636 (7th Cir. 1999).

32. *United States v. Gerber*, 999 F.2d 1112, 1117 (7th Cir. 1993).

33. *Matter of Continental Illinois Securities Litigation*, 962 F.2d 566 (7th Cir. 1992).

34. *Matter of Taxman Clothing Co.*, 49 F.3d 310, 316 (7th Cir. 1995).

35. *Publications Intern. v. Landoll, Inc.*, 164 F.3d 337, 343 (7th Cir. 1998).

36. *Spurlin v. Director, Office of Workers' Compensation Programs*, 956 F.2d 163 (7th Cir. 1992).

37. *United States v. Barnes*, 188 F.3d 893, 895 (7th Cir. 1999).

38. *Chicago & North Western Transportation Co. v. Railway Labor Executives' Ass'n*, 908 F.2d 144, 151 (7th Cir. 1990).

39. *Duff v. Marathon Petroleum Co.*, 985 F.2d 339, 341 (7th Cir. 1993).

40. *IDS Life Ins. Co. v. SunAmerica, Inc.*, 103 F.3d 524, 530 (7th Cir. 1996).

41. *Matter of Continental Illinois Securities Litigation*, 985 F.2d 867, 869 (7th Cir. 1993).

42. *United States v. Thomas*, 956 F.2d 165, 167 (7th Cir. 1992).

43. *United States v. Schneider*, 910 F.2d 1569, 1571 (7th Cir. 1990).

44. *United States v. McKinney*, 919 F.2d 495, 419, 429 (7th Cir. 1990) (Posner, J. concurring).

45. 972 F.2d 792, 796 (7th Cir. 1992).

46. 985 F.2d 327, 327 (7th Cir. 1993).

47. 683 F.2d 1022 (7th Cir. 1982).

48. 44 F.3d 538, 542 (7th Cir. 1995).

49. Id. at 542–43.

50. *Ayres v. City of Chicago*, 125 F.3d 1010, 1013–14 (7th Cir. 1997).

51. *Matter of Handy Andy Home Improvement Centers, Inc.*, 144 F.3d 1125, 1127 (7th Cir. 1998).

52. *Konradi v. United States*, 919 F.2d 1207, 1210 (7th Cir. 1990).

53. *Matter of Continental Illinois Securities Litigation*, 962 F.2d 566 (7th Cir. 1992).

54. *K.H. through Murphy v. Morgan*, 914 F.2d 846, 850 (7th Cir. 1990).

55. Author interview with Bruce Selya, 2014.

56. 120 F.3d 1045, 1060 (9th Cir. 1997) (Reinhardt, J., concurring).

57. 919 F.2d 405 (7th Cir. 1990).

58. *United States v. McKinney*, 919 F.2d 405, 409 (7th Cir. 1990) (Flaum, J.).

59. Id. at 411.

60.   *Villanova v. Abrams*, 972 F.2d 792, 796 (7th Cir. 1992).

61.   148 F.3d 812 (7th Cir. 1998).

62.   *Milner v. Apfel*, 148 F.3d 812, 818 (7th Cir. 1998) (Ripple, J., concurring in the judgment).

63.   506 U.S. 534, 113 S.Ct. 933 (1993).

64.   *United States v. Zafiro*, 945 F.2d 881, 885 (7th Cir. 1991).

65.   Id.

66.   *Zafiro v. United States*, 506 U.S. 534, 539, 113 S.Ct. 933, 938 (1993).

67.   *United States v. Zafiro*, 945 F.2d 881, 886 (7th Cir. 1991).

68.   499 U.S. 606, 111 S.Ct. 1539 (1991).

69.   *American Hospital Association v. N.L.R.B.*, 899 F.2d 651 (7th Cir. 1990).

70.   510 U.S. 266, 127 S.Ct. 114 (1994).

71.   *Albright v. Oliver*, 975 F.2d 343, 347 (7th Cir. 1992).

72.   512 U.S. 477, 114 S.Ct. 2364 (1984).

73.   *Heck v. Humphrey*, 997 F.2d 355 (7th Cir. 1993).

74.   520 U.S. 899, 117 S.Ct. 1793 (1997).

75.   *Bracy v. Gramley*, 81 F.3d 684 (7th Cir. 1997).

76.   506 U.S. 56, 113 S.Ct. 538 (1992).

77.   *Sodal v. County of Cook*, 942 F.2d 1073 (7th Cir. 1991).

78.   *Sodal v. County of Cook*, 942 F.2d 1073 (7th Cir. 1991).

79.   *Sodal v. Cook County, Ill.*, 506 U.S. 56, 113 S.Ct. 538 (1992).

80.   Id. at 506 U.S. 61, 113 S.Ct. 543 (1992).

81.   Id. at 506 U.S. 69, 113 S.Ct. 547 (1992).

82.   Id.

83.   499 U.S. 187, 111 S.Ct. 1196 (1991).

84.   *International Union, United Auto., Aerospace and Agriculture Implement Workers of America v. Johnson Controls, Inc.*, 886 F.2d 871 (7th Cir. 1989).

85.   500 U.S. 453, 111 S.Ct. 1919 (1991).

86.   *United States v. Marshall*, 908 F.2d 1312 (7th Cir. 1990).

87.   500 U.S. 291, 111 S.Ct. 1825 (1991).

88.   *In re Sanderfoot*, 899 F.2d 598 (7th Cir. 1990).

89.   "Evaluation of the United States Court of Appeals for the Seventh Circuit," 43 *DePaul Law Review* 673 (1994).

90.   Information from more than a dozen law clerks who worked for Posner in the 1990s are used in this section. Their preference was for anonymity.

91.   William M. Landes, Lawrence Lessig, and Michael E. Solimine, "Judicial Influence: A Citation Analysis of Federal Courts of Appeals Judges," 27 *Journal of Legal Studies* 271 (1998).

92.   Mitu Gulati and Veronica Sanchez, "Giants in a World of Pygmies? Testing the Superstar Hypothesis with Judicial Opinions in Casebooks," 87 *Iowa Law Review* 1141 (2002).

93.   29 *Journal of Legal Studies* 409, 424 tbl. 6 (2000).

94.   Richard Posner, *Sex and Reason* (Cambridge: Harvard University Press, 1992); Tomas J. Philipson and Richard Posner, *Private Choices and Public Health:*

The AIDS Epidemic in an Economic Perspective (Cambridge: Harvard University Press, 1993), and Richard Posner, *Aging and Old Age* (Chicago: University of Chicago Press, 1995).

95.   Richard Posner and Katharine Silbaugh, *A Guide to America's Sex Laws* (Chicago: University of Chicago Press, 1996).

96.   Richard Posner, *Sex and Reason* (Cambridge: Harvard University Press, 1992), p. 437.

97.   Id. at 30.

98.   Richard Posner, *Aging and Old Age* (Chicago: University of Chicago Press, 1995), p. 1.

99.   Richard Posner, *Overcoming Law* (Cambridge: Harvard University Press, 1995).

100.   Id. at 21.

101.   Id. at 8.

102.   Id. at viii.

103.   The book draws on the following essays: "Hegel and Employment at Will: A Comment," 10 *Cardozo Law Review* 1625 (1989); "The Depiction of Law in *The Bonfire of the Vanities*," 98 *Yale Law Journal* 1653 (1989); "What Has Pragmatism to Offer Law?," 63 *Southern California Law Review* 1653 (1990); "Bork and Beethoven," 42 *Stanford Law Review* 1365 (1990); "Duncan Kennedy on Affirmative Action," 1990 *Duke Law Journal* 1155; "Democracy and Distrust Revisited," 77 *Virginia Law Review* 641 (1991); "Foreword," James Fitzjames Stephen, *Liberty, Equality, Fraternity* 7 (Indianapolis: Liberty Fund, 1992); "Legal Reasoning from the Top Down and from the Bottom Up: The Question of Unenumerated Constitutional Rights," 59 *University of Chicago Law Review* 433 (1992); "Medieval Iceland and Modern Scholarship" (review of William Ian Miller, *Bloodtaking and Peacemaking: Feud, Law, and Society in Saga Iceland*), 90 *Michigan Law Review* 1495 (1992); "Ms. Aristotle," 70 *Texas Law Review* 1013 (1992); "Democracy and Dualism" (review of Bruce Ackerman, *We the People*, vol. 1: *Foundations*), *Transition* no. 56, at p. 68 (Summer 1992); "The Strangest Attack Yet on Law and Economics," 20 *Hofstra Law Review* 933 (1992); "Law as Politics: Horwitz on American Law, 1870–1960" (review of Morton J. Horwitz, *The Transformation of American Law: 1870–1960, The Crisis of Legal Orthodoxy*), 6 *Critical Review* 559 (1992); "Ronald Coase and Methodology," 7 *Journal of Economic Perspectives* 197 (1993); "The New Institutional Economics Meets Law and Economics," 149 *Journal of Institutional and Theoretical Economics* 73 (1993); "Richard Rorty's Politics," 7 *Critical Review* 33 (1993); "The Material Basis of Jurisprudence," 69 *Indiana Law Journal* 1 (1993); "Legal Scholarship Today," 45 *Stanford Law Review* 1627 (1993); "The Radical Feminist Critique of *Sex and Reason*," 25 *Connecticut Law Review* 515 (1993); "The Deprofessionalization of Legal Teaching and Scholarship," 91 *Michigan Law Review* 1921 (1993); and "What Do Judges and Justices Maximize? (The Same Thing Everybody Else Does)," 3 *Supreme Court Economic Review* 1 (1994).

104. Matthew H. Kramer, "The Philosopher-Judge: Some Friendly Criticisms of Richard Posner's Jurisprudence," 59 *Modern Law Review* 465 (1996).

105. Joshua Getzler, "Pragmatism and the End of Ideology," 17 *Oxford Journal of Legal Studies* 525 (1997).

106. Richard Posner, "The Path away from the Law," 110 *Harvard Law Review* 1039 (1997); Richard Posner, "The Problematics of Moral and Legal Theory," 111 *Harvard Law Review* 1637 (1998); Richard Posner, "Against Constitutional Theory," *New York University Law Review* 1 (1998); and Richard Posner, "Professionalisms," 40 *Arizona Law Review* 1 (1998).

107. Richard Posner, *The Problematics of Moral and Legal Theory* (Cambridge: Harvard University Press, 1999), p. vii.

108. Id. at vii.

109. Ronald Dworkin, *Law's Empire* (Cambridge: Harvard University Press, 1986), p. 161.

110. Richard Posner, *The Problematics of Moral and Legal Theory* (Cambridge: Harvard University Press, 1999), p. 241.

111. Id. at viii.

112. Id. at 81.

113. Id. at 80.

114. Id. at xi.

115. Id. at 262.

116. Daniel A. Farber, "Shocking the Conscience: Pragmatism, Moral Reasoning, and the Judiciary," 16 *Constitutional Commentary* 675, 676 (1999).

117. Id.

118. Richard Posner, *Law and Legal Theory in the UK and the USA* (Oxford: Oxford University Press, 1996), p. 3.

119. Richard Posner, *An Affair of State: The Investigation, Impeachment, and Trial of President Clinton* (Cambridge: Harvard University Press, 1999).

120. Id. at 127.

121. 487 U.S. 654 (1988).

122. 117 S.Ct. 1636 (1997).

123. Richard Posner, *An Affair of State* (Cambridge: Harvard University Press, 1999), p. 228.

124. Id. at 240.

125. Id. at 87.

Chapter 5

1. Unless otherwise indicated, all documents and correspondence referred to in this chapter, including not footnoted correspondence, comes from the Posner University of Chicago archive and is used with the University's permission.

2. Ken Auletta, *World War 3.0* (New York: Random House, 2001), pp. 309–62.

3. Ronald Dworkin, "Philosophy & Monica Lewinsky," *New York Review of Books*, March 9, 2000.

4. Id.

5. Id.

6. "*An Affair of State*: An Exchange," *New York Review of Books*, April 27, 2000.

7. Posner to Martha Nussbaum, September 13, 1993.

8. Richard A. Posner, "Tribute to Ronald Dworkin," 63 *New York University Annual Survey of American Law* 9, 11 (2007).

9. Id. at 9.

10. "Florida 2000: A Legal and Statistical Analysis of the Election Deadlock and the Ensuing Litigation," 2000 *Supreme Court Review* 1 (2001).

11. Richard Posner, *Breaking the Deadlock: The 2000 Election, the Constitution, and the Courts* (Princeton: Princeton University Press, 2003).

12. Id. at 199.

13. Id. at 186.

14. H. Jefferson Powell, "Overcoming Democracy: Richard Posner and *Bush v. Gore*," 17 *Journal of Law and Politics* 333, 335 (2001).

15. Larissa MacFarquhar, "Bench Burner," *New Yorker*, December 10, 2001, 78, 80.

16. Id. at 78.

17. Ronald K. L. Collins, "The Man behind the Robes—A Q&A with Richard Posner," Concurring Opinions, December 3, 2014, found at www.concurringopinions.com/archives/2014/12/the-judge-company-questions-for-judge-posner-from-judges-law-professors-a-journalist.html.

18. Richard Posner, *Public Intellectuals: A Study of Decline* (Cambridge: Harvard University Press, 2002).

19. Id. at 397.

20. Id. at 77.

21. Id. at 51.

22. Id.

23. Id.

24. David Brooks, "Notes from a Hanging Judge," review, *New York Times*, January 13, 2002, p. 9.

25. David J. Garrow, "A Tale of Two Posners," 5 *Green Bag 2d* 341, 342 (2002).

26. Thomas Nagel, "Sheltered Lives and Public Postures," *Times Literary Supplement*, January 25, 2002.

27. Gary S. Becker and Richard A. Posner, *Uncommon Sense: Economic Insights from Marriage to Terrorism* (Chicago: University of Chicago Press, 2009).

28. Ronald K. L. Collins, "The Man behind the Robes—A Q&A with Richard Posner," Concurring Opinions, December 3, 2014, found at www.concurringopinions.com/archives/2014/12/the-judge-company-questions-for-judge-posner-from-judges-law-professors-a-journalist.html.

29. "What Am I? A Potted Plant," *New Republic*, September 28, 1987, p. 23.

30. Richard Posner, "The Best Offense," *New Republic*, September 2, 2002, p. 30.

31. Richard Posner, "The End Is Near," *New Republic*, September 22, 2003, p. 31.

32. Richard Posner, *Catastrophe: Risk and Response* (New York: Oxford University Press, 2004).

33. Stanford, Calif.: Hoover Institution; Lanham, Md.: Rowman & Littlefield, 2005.

34. Stanford, Calif.: Hoover Institution; Lanham, Md.: Rowman & Littlefield, 2006.

35. Stanford, Calif.: Hoover Institution; Lanham, Md.: Rowman & Littlefield, 2007.

36. Stanford, Calif.: Hoover Institution, 2005.

37. New York: Oxford University Press, 2006.

38. Richard Posner, *Preventing Surprise Attacks: Intelligence Reform in the Wake of 9/11* (Stanford, Calif.: Hoover Institution; Lanham, Md.: Rowman & Littlefield, 2005), p. 87.

39. Richard Posner, *Remaking Domestic Intelligence* (Stanford, Calif.: Hoover Institution, 2005).

40. Richard Posner, *A Failure of Capitalism: The Crisis of '08 and the Descent into Depression* (Cambridge: Harvard University Press, 2008).

41. Id. at xiv.

42. 61 *New York University Annual Survey of American Law* (2005).

43. Robert A. Ferguson, "Tribute to Judge Richard A. Posner," 61 *New York University Annual Survey of American Law* 1, 2 (2005).

44. *The Economic Structure of Intellectual Property Law* (Cambridge: Harvard University Press, 2003) (coauthored with William M. Landes).

45. George L. Priest, "What Economists Can Tell Lawyers about Intellectual Property," 8 Research in Law and Economics 19 (1986).

46. 537 U.S. 186, 123 S.Ct. 769 (2003).

47. Mark Weinstein, "Review," 41 *Journal of Economic Literature* 239 (2003).

48. Richard Posner, *Law, Pragmatism, and Democracy* (Cambridge: Harvard University Press, 2003), p. 14 .

49. Id. at 13.

50. Id. at 50.

51. Richard Rorty, "More Than Compromise," *Dissent*, Fall 2003, p. 101.

52. *The Federal Courts: Challenge and Reform* (2d ed., Cambridge: Harvard University Press, 2009).

53. Richard Posner, *Law and Literature* (3d ed., Cambridge: Harvard University Press, 2009), p. xv.

54. *Antitrust Law* (2d ed., Chicago: University of Chicago Press, 2001).

55. *Law and Economics* (3 vols.) (Cheltenham: Edward Elgar, 1997), coedited with Francesco Parisi; *The Collected Economic Essays of Richard A. Posner*, vol. 1: *The Economic Structure of the Law* (Cheltenham: Edward Elgar, 2001) (edited by Francesco Parisi); *The Collected Economic Essays of Richard A. Posner*, vol. 2: *The Economics of Private Law* (Cheltenham: Edward Elgar, 2001) (edited by Francesco Parisi); *The Collected Economic Essays of Richard A. Posner*, vol.

3: *The Economics of Public Law* (Cheltenham: Edward Elgar, 2001) (edited by Francesco Parisi); *The Economics of Private Law: The Collected Economic Essays of Richard A. Posner* (Francesco Parisi ed. 2001); *The Economics Structure of the Law: The Collected Economic Essays of Richard A. Posner,* vol. 1 (Francesco Parisi ed. 2001); *Economic Foundations of Private Law* (Cheltenham: Edward Elgar, 2002) (coedited with Francesco Parisi); *The Coase Theorem* vol. 1: *Origins, Restatements and Extensions* (Cheltenham: Edward Elgar, 2013) (coedited with Francesco Parisi); and *The Coase Theorem* vol. 2: *Criticisms and Applications* (Cheltenham: Edward Elgar, 2013) (coedited with Francesco Parisi).

56. *Van De Sande v. Van De Sande,* 431 F.3d 567 (7th Cir. 2005).

57. Id. at 570.

58. *Mesman v. Crane Pro Services,* 409 F.3d 846, 849–50 (7th Cir. 2005).

59. *Sheridan v. Marathon Petroleum Co. LLC,* 530 F.3d 590, 593 (7th Cir. 2008).

60. *Blue Cross Blue Shield of Illinois v. Cruz,* 495 F.3d 510, 511 (7th Cir. 2007).

61. *Metheny v. United States,* 469 F.3d 1093, 1096 (7th Cir. 2006).

62. *Ty, Inc. v. Publications International, Ltd.,* 292 F.3d 512 (7th Cir. 2002).

63. *Peaceable Planet, Inc. v. Ty, Inc.,* 362 F.3d 986 (7th Cir. 2004).

64. *Ty, Inc. v. Perryman,* 306 F.3d 509 (7th Cir. 2002).

65. 366 F.3d 554, 560 (7th Cir. 2004) (Evans, J., dissenting).

66. 375 F.3d 508 (7th Cir. 2004), 543 U.S. 22, 125 S.Ct. 738 (2005).

67. 542 U.S. 296, 124 S.Ct. 2531 (2004).

68. 553 U.S. 181, 128 S.Ct. 1610 (2008).

69. *Crawford v. Marion County Election Board,* 472 F.3d 949 (7th Cir. 2007).

70. 531 U.S. 32, 121 S.Ct. 447 (2000).

71. *Edmond v. Goldsmith,* 183 F.3d 659 (7th Cir. 1999).

72. 528 U.S. 562, 120 S.Ct. 1073 (2000).

73. *Olech v. Village of Willowbrook,* 160 F.3d 386, 387–88 (7th Cir. 1998).

74. 530 U.S. 15, 120 S.Ct. 1951 (2000).

75. *In re Stoecker,* 179 F.3d 546, 552 (7th Cir. 1999), quoting *Bull v. United States,* 295 U.S. 247, 260, 55 S.Ct. 695 (1935).

76. 534 U.S. 316, 122 S.Ct. 775 (2002).

77. *Thomas v. Chicago Park Dist.,* 227 F.3d 921, 924 (7th Cir. 2000).

78. 555 U.S. 122, 129 S.Ct. 687 (2009).

79. 551 U.S. 587, 127 S.Ct. 2553 (2007).

80. *Freedom from Religion Foundation, Inc. v. Chao,* 433 F.3d 989 (7th Cir. 2006).

81. *United States v. Chambers,* 473 F.3d 724, 726 (7th Cir. 2007).

82. 392 U.S. 83, 88 S.Ct. 1942 (1968).

83. *Dunne v. Keohane,* 14 F.3d 335, 337 (7th Cir. 2009); *Espinoza v. Sabol,* 558 F.3d 83, 88 (1st Cir. 2009).

84. *Hosp. Corp. Of Am. v. FTC,* 807 F.2d 1381, 1386 (7th Cir. 1986); *Federal Trade Commission v. Whole Foods, Inc.,* 548 F.3d 1028, 1043 (D.C. Cir. 2008).

85. *Cada v. Baxter Healthcare Corp.,* 920 F.2d 446, 449 (7th Cir. 1990), cited by *Garcia v. Brockway,* 503 F.3d 1092, 1107 (9th Cir. 2007).

86. *United States v. Santos,* 201 F.3d 953, 965 (7th Cir. 2000); *United States v. Triumph Capital Group, Inc.,* 487 F.3d 124, 132 (2d Cir. 2007).

87. *United States v. Boyd*, 55 F.3d 239, 241 (7th Cir. 1995); *Conley v. United States*, 415 F.3d 183, 190 (1st Cir. 2005).

88. *Asahi Glass Co., Ltd. v. Pentech Pharmaceuticals, Inc.*, 289 F.Supp.2d 986, 991 (N.D.Ill. 2003); *Schering-Plough Corp. v. F.T.C.*, 402 F.3d 1056, 1074 (11th Cir. 2005).

89. *United States v, Joseph*, 50 F.3d 401, 403 (7th Cir. 1993); *United States v. Feathers*, 369 F.3d 1035, 1037–38 (8th Cir. 2004) (Heaney, J., concurring).

90. *Bowers v. DeVito*, 686 F.2d 616, 618 (7th Cir. 1982); *Ye v. United States*, 484 F.3d, 634, 637 (3d Cir. 2007).

91. *Vande Zande v. Wisconsin Dep't of Admin.*, 44 F.3d 538, 544 (7th Cir. 1995); *Mason v. Avaya Communications, Inc.*, 357 F.3d 1114, 1120 (10th Cir. 2004).

92. *Papa v. Katy Industries*, 166 F.3d 937, 942 (7th Cir. 1999); *Engelhardt v. S.P. Richards, Oc., Inc.*, 472 F.3d 1, 8 (1st Cir. 2006).

93. *In re High Fructose Corn Syrup Litigation*, 295 F.3d 651, 655 (7th Cir. 2002); *Williamson Oil Co., Inc. v. Philip Morris USA*, 346 F.3d 1287, 1317 (11th Cir. 2003).

94. *United States v. Dean*, 414 F.3d 725, 729 (7th Cir. 2005); *United States v. Taylor*, 499 F.3d 94, 100 (9th Cir. 2007).

95. *Merit Insurance Co. v. Leatherby Insurance Co.*, 714 F.2d 673, 680 (7th Cir. 1983); *Positive Software Solutions, Inc. v. New Century Mortgage Corp.*, 476 F.3d 278, 287 (5th Cir. 2007).

96. *Richardson v. Penfold*, 900 F.2d 116, 119 (7th Cir. 1990), cited by *Radvansky v. City of Olmsted Falls*, 496 F.3d 609, 620 (6th Cir. 2007).

97. *Bowers v. DeVito*, 686 F.2d 616, 618 (7th Cir. 1982), cited by *Jensen v. Clarke*, 94 F.3d 1191, 1197 (8th Cir. 1996).

98. *Haynes v. Alfred A. Knopf, Inc.*, 8 F.3d 1222, 1227 (7th Cir. 1993), cited by *Gray v. St. Martin's Press, Inc.*, 221 F.3d 243, 248 (1st Cir. 2000).

99. *Herzberger v. Standard Ins. Co.*, 205 F.3d 327, 331 (7th Cir. 2000); *Brigham v. Sun Life of Canada*, 317 F.3d 72, 81 (1st Cir. 2003).

100. *Bolte v. Home Ins. Co.*, 744 F.2d, 573 (7th Cir. 1984), cited by *Baker v. Group, L.C. v. Burlington Northern and Santa Fe Ry. Co.*, 451 F.3d 484, 491 (8th Cir. 2006).

101. *Robinson v. Page*, 170 F.3d 747, 748–49 (7th Cir. 1999); *Lira v. Herrera*, 427 F.3d 1164, 1173 (9th Cir. 2005).

102. *Shepherd v. Comm'r*, 147 F.3d 633, 635 (7th Cir. 1998); *New York Football Giants, Inc. v. C.I.R.*, 349 F.3d 102, 106 (3d Cir. 2003).

103. *In re Rolona Pizza Products Corp.*, 3 F.3d 1029, 1032–33 (7th Cir. 1993); *In re Gulf City Seafoods, Inc.*, 296 F.3d 363, 368 (5th Cir. 2002).

104. *Scholes v. Lehmann*, 56 F.3d 750, 752 (7th Cir. 1995); *In re Slatkin*, 525 F.3d 805, 814 (9th Cir. 2008).

105. *Shager v. Upjohn Co.*, 913 F.2d 398, 405 (7th Cir. 1990); *Russell v. McKinney Hosp. Venture*, 235 F.3d 219, 228 (5th Cir. 2000).

106. *In re Brand Name Prescription Drugs Antitrust Litigation*, 123 F.3d 599, 603 (7th Cir. 1997); *United States v. LSL Biotechnologies*, 379 F.3d 672, 697 n.9 (9th Cir. 2004).

107.   *Metzl v. Leininger*, 57 F.2d 618, 623–24 (7th Cir. 1995); *American Civil Liberties Union of Kentucky v. McCreary County, Kentucky*, 354 F.3d 438, (6th Cir. 2003).

108.   *Schmidt v. Sullivan*, 914 F.2d 117, 118 (7th Cir. 1990); *Frank v. Barnhart*, 326 F.3d 618, 622 (5th Cir. 2003).

109.   *Ortiz-Salas v. INS*, 992 F.2d 105, 107 (7th Cir. 1993); *Ramirez-Alejandre v. Ashcroft*, 320 F.3d 858, 865 (9th Cir. 2003) (en banc).

110.   *Galina v. INS*, 213 F.3d 955, 959 (7th Cir. 2000); *Li Wu Lin v. I.N.S.*, 238 F.3d 239, 248 (3d Cir. 2001).

111.   The information in this section comes from interviews with and emails from seven Posner law clerks in the decade. The preference was for anonymity.

112.   Richard Posner, *How Judges Think* (Cambridge: Harvard University Press, 2008).

113.   Id. at 35.

114.   Id. at 212.

115.   Id. at 377.

116.   *Chase Manhattan Mortgage Corp. v. Moore*, 446 F.3d 725, 727 (7th Cir. 2006).

117.   *Chicago Board of Education v. Substance, Inc.*, 354 F.3d 624, 632 (7th Cir. 2003).

118.   *In re United States*, 345 F.3d 450, 453 (7th Cir. 2003).

119.   *Richman v. Sheahan*, 512 F.3d 876, 886 (7th Cir. 2008).

120.   *Lowe v. McGraw-Hill Companies, Inc.*, 361 F.3d 335, 338 (7th Cir. 2004).

121.   *In re High Fructose Corn Syrup Antitrust Litigation*, 295 F.3d 651, 666 (7th Cir. 2002).

122.   *Johnson Bank v. George Korbakes & Co.*, 472 F.3d 439, 444 (7th Cir. 2006).

123.   *In re High Fructose Corn Syrup Antitrust Litigation*, 361 F.3d 439, 441 (7th Cir. 2004).

124.   *Shah v. Inter-Continental Hotel Chicago Operating Corp.*, 314 F.3d 278, 282 (7th Cir. 2006).

Chapter 6

1.   Richard Posner, foreword, in David Dorsen, *Henry Friendly: Greatest Judge of His Era* (Cambridge: Belknap Press of Harvard University Press, 2012), p. xi.

2.   Author interview with Posner, May 8, 2013.

3.   Richard Posner, *Reflections on Judging* (Cambridge: Harvard University Press, 2013), p. 78.

4.   *ATA Airlines, Inc. v. Federal Express* Corp., 655 F.3d 882 (7th Cir. 2011).

5.   Id. at 889.

6.   *Jackson v. Pollion*, 733 F.3d 786 (7th Cir. 2013).

7.   Id. at 788.

8.   Id. at 790.

9.   _571_ U.S. __, 187 S.Ct. 729 (2014).

10. *United States v. Dixon*, 551 F.3d 578 (7th Cir. 2008), renamed *Carr v. United States*, 560 U.S. 438, 130 S.Ct. 2229 (2010) for Supreme Court review.

11. 545 F.3d 1240 (10th Cir. 2008).

12. *Carr v. United States*, 560 U.S. 438, 457, 130 S.Ct. 2229, 2242 (2010).

13. *Lewis v. City of Chicago*, 560 U.S. 205, 130 S.Ct. 2191 (2010).

14. *Lewis v. City of Chicago*, 528 F.3d 488, 492 (7th Cir. 2008).

15. *Lewis v. City of Chicago*, 560 U.S. 205, 213, 130 S.Ct. 2191, 2198 (2010).

16. 561 U.S. 465, 130 S.Ct. 2963 (2010).

17. *United States v. Black*, 530 F.3d 596, 603 (7th Cir. 2008).

18. *Black v. United States*, 561 U.S. 465, 474, 130 S.Ct. 2963, 2970 (2010).

19. Id.

20. Posner participated in *Slate*'s Supreme Court in Review roundtables for both 2012 and 2013.

21. 134 S.Ct. 1434 (2014).

22. *United States v. Windsor*, 133 S.Ct. 2675 (2013).

23. *Arizona v. United States*, 567 U.S. ___, 132 S.Ct. 2492 (2012).

24. 133 S.Ct. 1326 (2013).

25. *Antonin Scalia and Bryan A. Garner, Reading Law: The Interpretation of Texts (St. Paul: Thomson/West, 2012).*

26. "Justice Antonin Scalia on the Issues Facing SCOTUS and the Country," *Fox News Sunday*, July 29, 2012, found at http://foxnews.com/on-air/fox-news-sunday-chris-wallace/2012/07/29/justice-antonin-scalia-issues-facing-scotus-and country#p//v1760654457001.

27. 554 U.S. 570, 128 S.Ct. 2783 (2008).

28. "Richard Posner Responds to Antonin Scalia Accusation of Lying," found at http://www.newrepublic.com/article/107549/richard-posner-responds-antonin-scalia-accusation-lying.

29. Richard Posner, 'The Incoherence of Antonin Scalia," *New Republic*, August 24, 2012, found at http://www.newrepublic.com/article/magazine/books-and-arts/106441/scalia-garner-reading-the-law-textual-originalism; "The Spirit Killeth, but the Letter Giveth Life," *New Republic*, September 13, 2012, p. 18.

30. Tony Mauro, "New Study Revisits Scalia-Posner Feud," *Legal Times*, May 8, 2014, found at http://www.nationallawjournal.com/legaltimes/id=1202654511559 2/New-Study-Revisits-ScaliaPosner-Feud.

31. Id.

32. Id.

33. Id.

34. "An Interview with Judge Richard A. Posner," *ABA Journal*, July 2014, available at http://www.abajournal.com/magazine/article/an_interview_with_judge_richard_a_posner.

35. Posner interview with author, May 8, 2013.

36. *Apple v. Motorola, Inc.*, 869 F.Supp.2d 901 (N.D.Ill. 2012).

37. "An Interview of Judge Richard A. Posner on Patent Litigation,"
     SSR Journal, Fall 2013, found at http://www.srr.com.com/article/
     interview-judge-richard-posner-patent-litigation.

38. Dan Levine, "Judge Who Shelved Apple Trial Says Patent System out of
     Sync," July 5, 2012, found at http://www.reuters.com/article/2012/07/05/
     us-apple-google-judge-idUSBRE864OIQ20120705.

39. Joe Nocera, "Innovation Nation at War," *New York Times*, February 9,
     2013, p. A19.

40. Id.

41. *Apple v. Motorola, Inc.*, 757 F.3d 1286, 1314 (Fed.Cir. 2014).

42. *United States v. Slaight*, 620 F.3d 816 (7th Cir. 2010).

43. Id. at 817.

44. Id. at 820.

45. Id. at 818.

46. Id. at 819.

47. Id. at 820.

48. Id. at 819.

49. Id. at 818.

50. Id.

51. Id at 822.

52. *Baskin v. Bogan*, 766 F.3d 648 (7th Cir. 2014).

53. Id. at 656.

54. Id. at 671.

55. Id. at 664.

56. Id. at 662.

57. 738 F.3d 786 (7th Cir. 2013).

58. 745 F.3d 837 (7th Cir. 2014).

59. *Mitchell v. JCG Industries*, 745 F.3d 837, 849 (7th Cir. 2014) (Wood, J.,
     dissenting).

60. Id.

61. *Mitchell v. JCG Industries*, 753 F.3d 695, 698 (Rovner, J., dissenting from
     denial of en banc hearing).

62. *Mitchell v. JCG Industries*, 753 F.3d 695, 703 (7th Cir. 2014) (Posner, J.,
     concurring in denial of en banc rehearing).

63. Richard Posner, "Judicial Opinions and Appellate Advocacy—One Judge's
     View," 51 *Duquesne Law Review* 3 (2013).

64. Frederick Schauer, "The Decline of 'the Record': A Comment on Posner,"
     51 *Duquesne Law Review* 51 (2013).

65. Ronald K. L. Collins, "The Man behind the Robes—A Q&A with
     Richard Posner," Concurring Opinions, December 3, 2014, found at
     www.concurringopinions.com/archives/2014/12/the-judge-company-
     questions-for-judge-posner-from-judges-law-professors-a-journalist.html.

66. *Freeman v. Berge*, 441 F.3d 543 (7th Cir. 2006) (05-2820). This and
     the other oral arguments discussed in this section can be found at

http://media.ca7.uscourts.gov/oral/Arguments/oar.jsp using the docket number following the case citation.

67. *Baskin v. Bogan*, 766 F.3d 648 (7th Cir. 2014) (14-2386).
68. *Wolf v. Walker*, 766 F.3d 648 (7th Cir. 2014) (14-2388).
69. *Planned Parenthood of Wisconsin, Inc. v. J.B. Van Hollen*, 738 F.3d 786 (7th Cir. 2013) (13-2726).
70. *Junior v. Anderson*, 724 F.3d 812 (7th Cir. 2013) (11-2999).
71. *University of Notre Dame v. Sebelius*, 743 F.3d 547 (7th Cir. 2014) (13-3853).

Conclusion

1. Ronald K. L. Collins, "The Man behind the Robes—A Q&A with Richard Posner," Concurring Opinions, December 3, 2014, found at www.concurringopinions.com/archives/2014/12/the-judge-company-questions-for-judge-posner-from-judges-law-professors-a-journalist.html.
2. "An Interview with Judge Richard A. Posner," *ABA Journal*, July 2014, available at http://www.abajournal.com/magazine/article/an_interview_with_judge_richard_a_posner.
3. All quotations in this concluding section come from Posner's correspondence between 1990 and 1997 and are used with the permission of the University of Chicago Library.

INDEX

Atwood, James, 55, 56

Bator, Paul, 129–130
Baxter, William, 54, 55, 57, 86, 94, 95
Becker, Gary, 59, 60, 61, 66, 73, 112,
    144, 171, 196, 254
Bluebook, 37, 39, 111
Bok, Derek, 30, 38
Brennan, William. 40, 41
Brooks, Cleanth, 20, 26, 27, 134

Casper, Gerhard, 60, 63
Coase, Ronald, 2, 52, 54, 58, 59, 60, 65,
    66, 67, 68, 69, 73, 112
Cox, Archibald, 48
Cudahy, Richard, 96, 121, 122

Davidow, Joel, 45, 46
Demsetz, Harold, 60, 66, 68, 73, 88
Director, Aaron, 2, 54, 55, 57, 59, 60,
    66, 68, 69, 73, 80, 95
Douglas, William O, 41, 43
Dworkin, Ronald, 83, 84, 86, 87,
    171, 177, 179, 183, 186, 187,
    188, 201

Easterbrook, Frank, 62, 63, 96, 100,
    111, 169, 170, 171, 208, 214, 215,
    216, 244
Elman, Philip, 45–48
Epstein, Richard, 60, 83, 144, 145

Flaum, Joel, 96, 123, 125, 158, 159
Frankfurter, Felix, 36, 45
Friendly, Henry, 1, 2, 3, 95, 99–101,
    110, 111, 138, 139, 219, 220, 243,
    244, 249
Freund, Paul, 36, 38

Griswold, Erwin, 30, 31, 36, 37, 38,
    48, 51, 53

Hand, Learned, 1, 2 3, 95, 99–101, 110,
    111, 138, 139, 219, 220, 243,
    244, 249
Harvard Law School, 29, 30
Harvard Law Review, 33, 36
Hofrichter, Blanche (see Posner,
    Blanche)
Holmes, Oliver Wendell, 71, 95, 111,
    112, 160, 248

Johnson, Leland, 52, 53, 57

Keynes, Maynard, 6, 68, 197, 201

Landes, William, 60, 66, 67, 90, 91,
        133, 145
Laycock, Douglas, 61
Leval, Pierre, 31, 202

Manning, Bayless, 53, 56, 58
Marshall, Thurgood, 48
Meyers, Chalres, 61, 74
Mueller, William "Fritz," 47, 53

Neal, Phil, 57, 58, 60
New Criticism, 26, 28
Noll, Roger, 52
Novak, Alan, 51, 52
Nussbaum, Bernard, 33d

O'Neil, Robert, 40, 42

Posner, Blanche (Posner's mother),
        9–12, 14, 16, 22, 24, 171, 173, 174
Posner, Charlene, 39
Posner, Max (Posner's father), 9–10, 12,
        14, 19, 173
Posner, Richard
    A Failure of Capitalism, 199–201
    Aging and Old Age, 172–173
    An Affair of State, 179–182
    Cardozo, 148–149
    Catastrophe, 198
    early youth and education, 12–14
    Frontiers of Legal Theory, 203–204
    Garner, Bryan, 229–232
    Harvard Law School
        academic performance, 32, 39
        assessment by classmates, 34
        classroom performance, 31–32
        law review president, 33
        struggles with Erwin Griswold,
            30–31, 37–38
    How Judges Think, 216–217

Junior high and high school
        years, 15–19
Law, Pragmatism, and Democracy, 204
Not a Suicide Pact, 199
Preventing Surprise Attacks, 198–199
Private Choices and Public Health,
        171–172
Reflections on Judging, 220
Remaking Domestic Intelligence, 199
Self–assessment, 252–255
Self–description, 249–252
Sex and Reason, 172
The Behavior of Federal Judges, 226
The Crisis of Capitalist
        Democracy, 219
The Economics of Contract Law, 85
The Essential Holmes, 149–150
The Problems of Jurisprudence,
        140–141
Uncertain Shield, 198
Uncommon Sense, 196
Views of
    academics, 193–195, 247
    Chief Justice Roberts, 7, 227
    judging, 141–142
    Justice Scalia, 7, 197, 227, 228,
        229–232
    legal profession, 248
    moral and legal philosophers,
        192–193
    old age and death, 173–175
    patent law, 232–234
    Socratic method, 29–30,
    Supreme Court Justices, 226–227
Yale University
    academic performance, 20–22
    as iconoclast and radical, 24–26
    club and organizations, 23
    directed Studies Program, 19–20
    roommates and fellow
        students, 22–23
    scholar of the House thesis, 26–28

Rifkind, Robert, 32, 49, 50

Semple, Robert, 25
Slate, 62. 195, 196, 226, 229, 232, 233
Springer, James, 33, 34
Stigler, George, 2, 54, 55, 58, 59, 62, 66,
      67, 73, 80, 92, 112

Turner, Donald, 38, 39, 57

Wiener, Frederick Bernays, 36

Yeats, William Butler, 26–29, 134, 171